Consumption and Identity

Studies in Anthropology and History

Studies in Anthropology and History is a series that will develop new theoretical perspectives, and combine comparative and ethnographic studies with historical research.

Edited by Nicholas Thomas, The Australian National University, Canberra.

This book is part of a series. The publisher will accept continuation orders which may be cancelled at any time and which provide for automatic billing and shipping of each title in the series upon publication. Please write for details.

Jonathan Friedman

Consumption and Identity

h[o]ap harwood academic publishers
Switzerland ♦ Australia ♦ Belgium ♦ France ♦ Germany ♦ Great Britain
India ♦ Japan ♦ Malaysia ♦ Netherlands ♦ Russia ♦ Singapore ♦ USA

COPYRIGHT © 1994 BY Harwood Academic Publishers GmbH

Harwood Academic Publishers
Poststrasse 22
7000 Chur, Switzerland

BRITISH LIBRARY CATALOGUING IN PUBLICATION DATA
Consumption and Identity. – (Studies in Anthropology & History, ISSN 1055–2464; Vol. 15)
  I. Friedman, Jonathan II. Series
  306.3
  ISBN 3-7186-5591-8

DESIGNED BY   Maureen Anne MacKenzie
Em Squared, Main Street, Michelago, NSW 2620, Australia

FRONT COVER   Photograph by Nils Bergendal, 1994

Contents

List of Figures

Introduction

Jonathan Friedman

During the past few years there has been an increasing interest in consumption among anthropologists. This contribution takes as its point of departure, the discussions that have already been underway in this relatively new field. It's focus, however, is not upon consumption as an autonomous social phenomenon, but precisely on the ways in which consumption can and must be understood in a wider context of life strategies, of the constitution of meaningful existences. Thus, as the title suggests, this is a volume about the relation between consumption and broader cultural strategies. The papers are the product of a workshop organized in Denmark under the aegis of the Center for Research in the Humanities which took place in 1989. While the majority of participants were anthropologists, there were also sociologists and historians present and an issue of the journal *Culture and History* (7:1990) was devoted to an early version of some of the papers contained in the present volume.

FROM CLASSICAL ECONOMICS TO ANTHROPOLOGY: THE DISSOLUTION OF A UNITY

CONSUMPTION AS AN ECONOMIC FUNCTION

Consumption has usually been seen as a mere function of a larger economic process rather than as an autonomous social phenomenon. The origin of the problem here is the expansion of the domestic consumer market in the late 17th and 18th centuries, a phenomenon that introduced the question of choice of commodities into the issue of consumption, an area that was previously a rather restricted domain determined by social position and economic necessity. The expansion of the wage sector and the monetization of consumption made it necessary to conceptualize the relation between income and demand in order to understand the economic cycle of the new nation state. As an economic phenomenon it has usually been translated as the question of demand dependent upon the income of the consumer rather than upon the nature of consumer desires and of

1

socially constructed interests. The question of consumption as it appears in the writings of both economists and philosophers in the past is very much a quantitative question, i.e. necessary consumption expressed in terms of standard items and services. In the works of the Physiocrats, the Classical Economists, and Marx, consumption is a function of production in the form of reproduction. It is the cost of reproducing the producers, no more no less. In Marxist philosophy this is further elaborated in a theory of alienation in which it is assumed that the history of world production is the history of the gradual loss of control of producers over their products. Consumption in capitalism is in this way reduced to a question of the way in which those who control production control the producers via the market. The consumption of non-necessities in such a view must be understood as the result of trickery, the psychological manipulation by market researchers and advertisers that lure producers into the project of increasing production and therefore profits via their own demand. Capitalism must create a system of false needs in order to maintain the never ending need to accumulate capital. This is a powerful theme in studies of consumption that can also be found in some of the most recent work, marxist as well as non-marxist. The general sociological conclusion of the economic premises of the simple model of economic reproduction is that all non-productive consumption is simply unnecessary and therefore somehow a product of error, false consciousness, compensatory behavior, ostentation; all in all, a misconstrual of reality. There is an implicit evolutionism in this dualistic construal of economic reality.

a. In the beginning there were only consumers who controlled, by definition, the conditions of their own production, i.e. they produced what they needed which was identical to what they wanted which was equivalent to what they needed to reproduce themselves as domestic units. Here the question of consumption is identical with that of production since the former determines the latter within technological limits.

b. Then came the state, the dominant chiefly elite, the proto-class or whatever organ that separated itself from the direct producers and split the equation of consumption and production. Production was now dictated by the needs of non-consumers, and non-producers created the need for surplus production and drove the production process way beyond the simple needs of the producers. A new level of luxury consumption emerges with the split of society. Luxury is negatively defined here as that which is non-essential and unnecessary for survival.

c. The advent of the integrated wage-labor market further complicates the situation by making increasing production dependent upon the ability and the desire of consumers to acquire that which is produced. Here a new and expanding sphere of needs must be created so that production can continue to expand. Such needs are unnecessary in terms of survival or the simple reproduction of our original producers but necessary for the reproduction of the owners of capital, the dominant class.

The distinction between necessity and luxury is a pervading category in the discussions of consumption in all of the social sciences. Coupled to an evolutionary perspective, it divides the world's populations into primitive and/or traditional subsistence producers, and more complex class based systems of specialized production. In the work of Chayanov on Russian peasants, the entire analytical scheme is based on the relation between necessary labor costs for the reproduction of the food necessary for individual survival and the ratio of producers to non-producers in the household subsistence unit. In this subsistence model it is proposed that a population that is not forced to do so will produce only as much as is needed for its simple reproduction, i.e. for the maintenance of an identical minimal level of production and consumption. Marshall Sahlins made a major mark on anthropology by taking over this model into anthropology where it served to characterize the essence of primitive economies as "domestic" modes of production that were in reality leisure economies since they required very few hours of work in order to reproduce themselves. The tendency to "underproduction" in such societies was based on their productivity in relation to needs which were limited by minimal costs of reproduction. The fact that he only considered the production of food in his arguments was never seen as a flaw. In fact, it was sometimes suggested that the production of prestige goods or ritual objects could best be relegated to the sphere of leisure time, i.e. what people did after their basic needs were fulfilled. The focus on subsistence led to some unfortunate ethnographic conclusions. The Gwembe Tonga of East Africa, for example, were characterized as the ideal type of domestic mode, simply because their considerable activities as cash croppers were left out of consideration. Underproduction, the natural state of society, is overcome only by external leverage, by politics and competitive exchange. In such a view, world history consists of a movement from necessity to surplus as a function of increasing power and hierarchy, a gigantic Engel curve with nature at the bottom and culture at the top.

It might be suggested here that this productionist assumption is not the only possible interpretation of Marxism, even if it is clearly the dominant one. There is a demand based paradigm as well, one that is evident in both the early work of Marx and in Volume 3 of *Das capital* where it is in effect the accumulation of capital that steers the system, an accumulation that is entirely dependent upon the level of demand in the system as a whole. It is the capacity or the lack thereof to generate effective demand which is the dynamic factor permitting investment and accumulation. The turning of money into more money is the driving motivation of the system, and whether this occurs via a circuit of real production or via a circuit of speculation of fictitious capital formation is not determined by the production apparatus itself. The latter is a mere limit that, via liquidity crises characteristic of economic downturns, expresses the contradiction between real and fictive accumulation. The message of this interpretation is that production is an aspect of a larger social process of reproduction that is organized by strategies of accumulation. In this model consumption remains, of course, a quantitative phenomenon, and while it is no longer a mere function of production, it has no sociological properties. The play of credit and debt now disturbs the smooth flow of the economic machine, but the role of specific desires, of the motivational structure of consumption is entirely absent.

Consumption as national income or consumption as utility represent two different facets of a single phenomenon. The former has been dominant in economic and even in anthropological discussions. Among anthropologists consumption in traditional societies has usually been reduced to a mere expression of social structure or culture. As such it has never attracted attention since it could only be understood in purely descriptive terms. Where consumption is predefined it can have no interest other than as an expression of other relations. The only area which has attracted attention is what is thought of as conspicuous consumption, competitive feasting or distributions, but these are treated in the context of exchange. Veblen was very much inspired by Boas' description of the Northwest Coast Indian Potlatch, but within anthropology itself, the phenomenon has been more or less reduced to an aspect of the ranking system. It is surely a stroke of good luck that so much attention was focussed on the act of conspicuous consumption. The very notion contains that which is precisely the break with a purely economic understanding of consumption. Consumption that is conspicuous is consumption whose purpose lies in its social or more precisely symbolic evaluation of the consumer.

CONSUMPTION AS AN AUTONOMOUS FIELD

In the twentieth century, consumption functions were discussed among neo-classical economists in a purely formal way, but much of their discussion dissolved into questions of utility, i.e. that people buy what they want, because they buy what they want. Economists, of course, are primarily interested in the quantitative relations involved in consumption, i.e. the relation between income, savings and consumption, so they cannot be blamed for showing so little interest in what it is that is consumed and the motivations involved. Utility theory replaces the issue of specific preferences with the presumption of a natural motivation to consume that which is available, modified only by marginal utility, i.e. the relation between the value for the consumer of the last unit of a commodity and that which preceded it. Nothing need be assumed about what it is that is needed or wanted.[1] The work of Keynes deserves to be mentioned here. In his doctrine of "the propensity to consume" he proposed that consumption increased as a function of increasing income, but not at the same rate. This would account for the relative increase in savings among the upper classes. A family related principle was "discovered" much earlier by Ernst Engel who postulated that expenditure on food, and by extension, basic necessities, decreased relatively with increasing income. This is often presented as the Engel curve. Engel might be considered as a precursor of all later attempts to introduce social structure into the economic process. Both Veblen's class analysis and more recently, that of Bourdieu, are developed on the basis of a framework that exists in rudimentary form in Engel.

In recent years there has been a vast increase in the literature on consumption. From the realization that economists had somehow ignored the subject there have been numerous attempts to theorize the phenomenon, both within economics itself and recently in anthropology. For some time there has been a growing dissatisfaction with the elegant but empty utility theory of consumer behavior. Attempts to enrich it within economics have become entangled in the problems of formalization. Milton Friedman's theory of permanent income (1957) attempted to account for individual consumption choices in a more developed rational scheme but it did not address the nature of demand, only its quantitative distribution among different kinds of pre-defined commodities (necessary-habitual versus new-luxury). Lancaster (1971) tried to tackle the problem directly by investigating the goods themselves, i.e. by trying to develop a theory of needs based on the concrete properties of commodities, i.e. fast, safe cars, tasty cereals, effective soap powders, calories, proteins, etc., but such an approach was bound to run into problems of tautology since the properties of preference cannot be defined independently of consuming subjects. More recently economists have introduced external variables, such as the life cycle (Modigliani 1986) and household structure (Becker 1976) into the analysis, but still making use of classical rational choice models. The problems of consumption theory in modern economics remain and they are twofold. Utility theories of demand, which have not been replaced, have tended to tautology: people buy what they want, and since producers by and large produce what is demanded, consumption is an asymptotic function of production. At the same time, the source of demand is entirely within the individual subject and is unaffected by the social and cultural context. This im-

---

[1] More recent versions of utility theory, which make use of the principle of "revealed preferences" are simply attempts to avoid the problem of the origins of utility by treating consumer preferences as established facts that cannot be investigated from within economic theory. This may be true, but it might also be said to beg the question. This is suggested in our discussion of recent analyses of consumption in economics that have introduced social variables. On the other hand since economists are primarily interested in the way in which preferences and, especially, changing preferences affect price relations on the market, the actual origin of such preferences plays only a minor role.

plies that curious methodological individualist determinism whereby consumption is reduced to a reflex of supply (or vice versa) all of which is part of the overall rationality of the market economy, at the same time as it is entirely a product of the sum of independent individual demand schedules. Here the invisible hand of the macro-economy works through the micro-economics of individual utility. And the vicious circle is completed by the fact that utility is merely an abstraction from actual demand, i.e. from what people buy. The origin of demand, i.e. an account of what it is that people want and how such needs and/or desires are constituted lies beyond the realm of economics. Only recently have there been attempts to treat consumption in terms of styles of living in which a range of factors, from emotional organization to forms of social identity are explicitly taken into account (Earl 1986). But here there is again the problem that the social and cultural properties of existence cannot, and perhaps should not be properly incorporated into economic theory as it stands.

Sociologists and anthropologists have approached consumption in more concrete, if not less theoretical terms. Before venturing into the substance of some of these approaches, it should be stressed that their common feature is the attempt to supply a motivational structure to consumption, one that is not a function of economic in any sense of the term. The early work of Veblen on conspicuous consumption, perhaps more relevant to the potlatch which apparently inspired it than to the modern world, has influenced a great many social scientists. Bourdieu's theory of consumption as social distinction is the most elaborate form of this approach. Mary Douglas has in more general terms tried to orient the discussion toward grasping the way in which goods are socially defined and marked as a means of defining social relations. Appadurai, et. al have also been concerned to demonstrate the cultural relativity of the definition of goods. Campbell has, in a brilliant analysis of the historical genesis of modern consumerism, argued that we must understand the way in which human desires are constituted in order to account for the formation of demand, and the latter involve a consideration of broad social processes.

The work of Veblen is usually considered by sociologists to be a landmark in the study of consumption . This is primarily because he offers a sociological mechanism to account for the apparent differential nature of consumption in modern societies. Parsons and Smelser, attempting to build on Keynes, offered a social pressure theory of consumption that accounted for increasing consumption by the wealthy in terms of the need to symholize their position and for their increased savings as a need to represent the ideals of social responsibility. This essentially Veblenesque approach was a way of filling economic behavior with specifically social motivations. Douglas and Isherwoood (1980) elaborated upon one aspect of the Veblen theme, the way in which a collection of goods defined a social position. They are more concerned with the cultural properties of social position than with the relation between such positions. Thus they divide the world of goods according to standard economistic categories, primary production (e.g. food), secondary production (consumer capital goods), and tertiary production (information, culture). They argue that the higher the economic class the more time and money must be invested in the tertiary sphere. It is the goods of this sphere that define the distinctiveness of their possessors, their superiority. The poor are restricted to the first sphere and may, as a result, have a surplus of time on their hands. The argument is clearly reminiscent of the Engel curve, applied to the distribution of social classes in modern capitalism. Class is defined in terms of the amount of accumulated cultural capital. It is not clear whether income is the primary differentiating factor or whether the actual cultural strategies of different income groups is equally important. This inflexible classificatory approach is difficult to reconcile with recent trends in lower class cultural consumption, nor even in such consumptionist movements as punks, the tendency to informality during the 1960s that had a strong homogenizing effect on consumption across class boundaries. And even before that, the work of Caplovitz demonstrated a compensatory form of consumption among the poor which directly contradicted the Engel curve model, on the surface at least, since "luxury" consumption by the poor depended upon a particularly vicious credit market.

Sahlins' brief essay on modern capitalism as culture in *Culture and Practical Reason* is a clear example of some of the limitations of this kind of approach. The analysis of consumption in terms of the opposition between work and leisure and the way it classifies different commodities, can never account for changes in the categories themselves. Thus executives who turn up at their plush offices in jeans or other casual attire, can only be understood as breaking the classificatory rules. Yet it is a hallmark of modern capitalism that fashion is always changing, not as a function of other social relations, but as a product of the innovative pressures of the necessity to accumulate capital.[2] The dynamic of distinctions in capitalism does not conform to a static classificatory scheme.

Here it might be profitable to consider briefly both the work of Baudrillard and Bourdieu. Baudrillard's argument regarding modern consumption is concerned to demonstrate the destruction of meaning inherent in increasing commoditization in information society. His model of consumer society is one in which commodities are reduced to mere signs whose referents have disappeared. His general argument against the productivist bias in Marxism, and for a political economy of the sign, is evidently inspired and follows up aspects of the thought

---

[2] It is, of course, true that accumulation is dependent upon demand, so that consumption must be understood by producers if they are to succeed. This is what market research is all about but here again the drive to consume in capitalist societies is more than a reflection of status competition and emulation. Campbell has done much to provide a more interesting argument that links the experience of the modern subject to the desire to purchase the new and different, a strategy of alterity.

of The Frankfurt School, best exemplified in the work of Adorno.[3] But the general source of his kind of discussion harks back to Benjamin's excursions through the Parisian arcades. He is more concerned to understand the social relation between the subject and the world of goods as a whole than between the subject and specific goods or categories of goods. Studies of commodity worlds in general are more or less restricted to the history and social analysis of Western societies. Benjamin suggested that industrial capitalist reality consisted of the creation of artificially produced worlds that offered alternative identities and experiences to the modern individual whose bonds to the World of Nature were permanently severed. Baudrillard argues, more cynically, that in the late modern period the commodity is transformed into a mere sign, a commodity-sign as the outcome of an overproduction of signs via the combination of commodity production with information technology. The result is an emptying of meaning from social life and the disappearance of the latter since it can all happen on or be copied from television. Where the world is a simulacrum with no referent, we are indeed in a self-conscious fantasy. While Baudrillard is consistent in his argument, he grossly oversimplifies and overstates his case. If Disney World is all there is, then there is no Disney World either. If simulacra are the entirety of reality, then there is no way to identify them as such. This is to go much further than the understanding that we live in a reality that is in large part the concrete realization of fantasy. Anthropologists have always insisted on the constructed nature of the social environment; from the symbolic organization of space, to the socially organized meaning of artifacts. If there is a difference, it lies perhaps in the consciousness of artificiality, at least among some intellectuals, and this itself might be argued to be a product of the kind of alterity that is generated by capitalist modernity (see below: also Campbell 1987, Friedman 1989) and not a simply objective condition. The objective correlate of this alterity is the commoditization of large portions of the life-world, thus stripping them of their ability to fix meaning, to anchor identity. But the degree to which this process produces a consciousness of its properties is not established, and completely ignored in the philosophizing of Baudrillard who does not base his propositions upon any research.

Thus, while Baudrillard's work has limited significance from our point of view, his focus on commodity worlds, i.e. the parameters of consumption, rather than the goods themselves, is an important corrective to understanding exchange as value, or even as particular meanings. We need to focus on the way that meaning is attributed and not merely on the products of such attribution. And the

---

[3] His critique of materialism is not, of course, an argument for the kind of cultural determinism witnessed in Sahlins use of his work (Sahlins 1976). For the latter capitalist cultural categories are presented as static classifications elaborated upon divisions of time, gender and class. For the former there are no such stable categories, especially with regard to consumption, and it is the capitalist dynamic itself that revolutionizes the categories and even transforms the way that they are generated, e.g. by turning them into signs.

way that meaning is attributed is an embedded feature of larger social processes that cannot be grasped in acts of exchange and consumption.

The work of Bourdieu in this area is very much more substantial. It can and has been applied to Baudrillard's own production. It might be suggested that his model represents the struggle of an intellectual class to maintain a distinction between high and mass culture which is becoming eroded in the decline of modernism. His work can thus be seen as a cynical statement concerning the mass production of culture and a nostalgia for a more ordered world of meaningful exchange.

Bourdieu's own work is theoretically more developed as well as relying on a great deal of empirical research. His major opus on consumption, *Distinction*, is a study of the relation between class factions and styles of consumption. If Baudrillard is concerned with the most general aspects of consumption as culture, Bourdieu focusses directly on the relation between group identity as life-style and strategies of consumption, expanding significantly on the work of Veblen. Here it is not merely a question of social ranking, but of a more complex differentiation whereby classification of the world is simultaneously classification of the classifier in a situation where there is no absolute rank order, but a more elaborate structure pitting the accumulation of economic capital against the accumulation of cultural capital. Bourdieu does not base his argument on Veblen's emulation theory, but he does assume that competition for cultural capital produces an escalation in distinctions. His approach is vastly more sophisticated than that of Veblen. The model is based on a differential distribution of social conditions, not simply classical class relations, but more refined factions that correspond better to the older notion of occupational group. Each of these groups is engaged in a process of self-identification in competition with other groups. Each of these groups also displays objective tendencies to specific lifestyles, which are, in Bourdieu's theory, the product of class specific habitus. The latter refers to unconscious dispositions to specific forms of practice including taste, consumption and identity. Unlike Baudrillard, Bourdieu focusses upon specific class based forms of consumption, and where the former might see a general change in desire based demand, the latter would assume the existence or emergence of a new class in the process of accumulating novel forms of cultural capital.

The importance of Bourdieu's work in relation to the present volume is his suggestion of the relation between consumption, social context, and habitus, one that attempts to account for the relation between social conditions of existence, the formation of the person, and the practice of consumption as a construction of a life world. The weakness of the work, from my point of view, is its tendency to economic reductionism, a tendency that brings it very close to the uni-causal ap-proach of Veblen. Bourdieu's social actors are driven essentially by two motives, the accumulation of economic and/or cultural capital. The latter refers to the trappings of society associated with education, knowledge of high culture, proficiency in the arts and literatures etc. The two are separate in our world although there are attempts by some to convert the one into the other. It is of course infinitely more difficult to convert cultural into economic capital than the reverse, but certainly not impossible. The essential problem with this approach is precisely that it makes use only of the practice of distinctions to account for differential consumption. Its potential advantage in this respect is that by using the notion of habitus such practices need not be interpreted as conscious goal directed activities, i.e. explicit acts of distinction. The notion of habitus is the essential link between specific conditions of existence and cultural strategies. From this point of view it is not necessary to understand consumption in terms of social distinctions alone, but as a product of particular desires rooted in particular habitii. Nevertheless, Bourdieu restricts his discussion to a model whose motor is the competitive accumulation of cultural distinctiveness and cultural capital, and in this respect it belongs to the same family as that of Veblen.

While the hypothesis that changes in the practice of consumption result from the introduction of new classes, there is no way in such a model to account for the actual cultural content of new tendencies to distinction. Campbell, for example, has implicitly argued against the Veblenesque assumption of Bourdieu, by trying to demonstrate the simultaneous existence of a general shift in the parameters of selfhood and consumption in the eighteenth century. This is, of course, a complex problem, but it must be stressed that acts of distinction cannot account for the content of the distinguished categories, nor for any changes in the larger parameters of consumption.

In our own interpretation of Campbell, Sennett and others who have researched the social changes of the eighteenth and nineteenth centuries in Europe, we have stressed the emergence of the modern individual in the disintegration of older social networks. The emergence of a subject whose existence is experienced as independent of its social form, i.e. personality or character, is a subject for whom alterity is the essential relation to the world. One is what one makes oneself to be. Consumption in such a situation is a grand experiment in life style, the creation of alternative existences. Broad transformations in consumption patterns cannot be explained in terms of the politics of differentiation. In fact, one of the central arguments put forward by Campbell is that the capitalist transformation of Europe led via the process of individualization to a transition from other-directed to self-directed forms of experience. The former, which become peripheralized in the form of the dandy, display the attributes found in Veblen's model, whereas the latter represent the truly romantic tendencies in modernity and which may be said largely to encompass the former; the miserable star who can find no meaning in his fame, the dandy who realizes his own artificiality. Consumption for the presentation of self has the self as a primary audience in modern times. The mirror is our own. In such an approach, distinctions are not just a way of marking a difference in relation to others, they are a way of experiencing their content as a subjective fantasy, a specific identity defined as a world of goods.

THREE ANTHROPOLOGICAL APPROACHES

Any anthropological understanding of consumption is bound to have its origins in the analysis of exchange which is where most previous discussions of consumption are situated. Thus, while the following examples do not represent approaches to consumption as such, they do deal with the essential issues that have and continue to occupy us in this volume. The conflation of consumption and exchange is at least as old as Veblen. Conspicuous consumption in the Pot-latch and other similar ceremonies is not about consumption at all, but about giving, about ostentatious generosity. Those who receive and consume the gifts do not demonstrate their own status, not directly at least, but act as witness to the gift-giver's display of status. On closer analysis, however, many such phenomena turn out to be more complex because of the very nature of the exchange relation itself, of the way in which both the participants and the things transacted are con-stituted. It is primarily in the case of capitalist consumption that the latter appears as an autonomous and well defined phase of a larger process. Where social repro-duction is structured differently consumption may not be easily distinguishable from the exchange process itself. Where the thing appropriated contains some part of the essence of the giver and where the exchange defines the nature of the social relation, then the thing is not a mere object independent of the larger con-text. Similarly, where the object is neutral, replaceable and devoid of any personal characteristics, it is no less socially constituted in a larger context.

Appadurai's theoretical introduction to *The Social Life of Things* is an excel-lent systematic statement of an exchange theory approach to understanding com-modities. His approach begins with Simmel's notion that it is exchange itself that creates value. In Simmel's argument this is related to the very general situation where person A is willing to give up X in order to obtain Y, i.e. to make a sacri-fice in order to gain something that is desired. Value is the result of the politics of exchange in this view, even where, as for Appadurai (3) it is embodied in com-modities. He begins with a lengthy discussion of the commodity form in Marx. For the latter a product becomes an exchange value rather than a mere use value (which all products are — insofar as they are produced by intentional acts) when the labor time spent on its production becomes "expressed as one of the objective qualities of that article" (Marx 1971:67). Appadurai criticizes this approach as all too imprisoned in a productivist perspective. He goes on to state that Marx did admit that "the commodity did not emerge whole-cloth from the product under bourgeois production, it made its appearance at an early date in history, though not in the same predominating and characterisic manner of nowadays". (Marx 1971:86 in Appadurai 9). I would object that what Marx is referring to here is not a primitive commodity form, but the existence of mercantile, market organized production long before capitalism.

Appadurai's own approach defines commodity as beginning with the more general 'production of use value for others' which is more specifically defined as "any thing intended for exchange" which "gets us away from the exclusive preoccupation with the 'product', 'production' and the original or dominant intention of the 'producer'" (**9**). In his further discussion of both barter and gift exchange as forms of commodity exchange it is difficult to see the point of the argument other than that exchange is always in some way calculated whether it is a question of labor costs, use value, or gift value, i.e. exchange is always exchange. It is not difficult to understand in this approach that commodity refers to a phase of the "life of a thing" (Kopytoff) rather than the nature of a thing.[4] This, however does not ring true with respect to the project of Simmel's philosophy of money, where it is the characterization of social relations as things and their representation that is at issue. This is the basis of practically all discussions of what is called consumer culture, of the Simmel-inspired work of Benjamin on the commodification of reality as the production of a lived in yet alienated fantasy world. In this argument commodities are an ever present aspect of those objects that circulate at some stage in a capitalist market. This is marked in the metaphorization of significant domains of everyday life in terms of value-substance — time being a favorite example, i.e. time is money, save your time, don't waste time; or life, or your self, etc. The strategies involved in a commoditized world are not reducible to the transactions of goods and services. Appadurai's focus on the limited aspects of calculation, competition and even accumulation leads him to play down other more structurally relevant differences, i.e. what is calculated, what is competed for, what is accumulated. Differences in these areas are, in my opinion, absolutely critical insofar as they generate very different regimes of social relatedness and social dynamics. One senses a certain surprise on his part in the discovery that non-capitalist strategies of exchange contain many of the same general properties at the level of exchange itself.

One of the problems that arises when defining commodity as a phase in a larger social process is that the logic of the larger system may be overlooked in concentrating on a more limited phenomenon. The discussion of Kula valuables, of monopolized royal or "elder's" valuables and the "coupons" referred to by Douglas are all treated in terms of the act of exchange itself. These are, for

---

[4] Appadurai overstates the universality of the argument presented in Kopytoff, I think, insofar as the latter stresses that commoditization is also an expanding tendency in all systems of exchange and that in modern capitalism it almost annihilates the increasingly privatized sphere of singularization.

example, summed up in the category "restricted systems of commodity flow . . designed to protect status systems"(**25**). In the chapters dealing with central Africa, the logic linking the cosmological nature of such goods as bearers of life-force and well being cannot be dissociated from the way in which they circulate. The goods, prestige-goods, are central constitutive elements of specific forms of hierarchy and cannot be reduced to props "designed" to maintain social relations from "the outside" as is implied. Degree and type of control over the flow of prestige goods is an area to which we have devoted some research which would indicate that the control itself, even in the case of the enshrined Kula, is quite variable over time.

Strategies such as restriction (the formation of monopolies, the removal of goods from the exchange arena) and diversion (the channelling of new objects into the channels of exchange) contain interesting suggestions, but it is my feeling that there is a fundamentally fragmentary view here, due to the fact that no consideration is given to the larger context itself. In this approach, consumption and exchange are different phenomena which is, of course, true at a certain level, that of physical acts, but the logic that connects them is surely where we ought to expect to find the key to understanding the dynamics of demand.

Kopytoff's life history approach does not attempt to justify the use of the word commodity but takes it for granted that it is a concomitant of all exchange, i.e. transfer of objects against one another as discrete transactions. He instead organizes his discussion in terms of two processes: commoditization and singularization. These are tendencies only. Total singularization would imply a total absence of exchange, and total commoditization a situation where everything is exchangeable for everything else. Singularization for Kopytoff is equivalent to Appadurai's restriction. The opposition here is one between culturally fixed order and the disordering effect of exchange, i.e. by equating increasing numbers of things with each other and by breaking down the exclusivity of cultural classes of objects. The tendency to commoditization is limited only by the technology of exchange, i.e. shell money versus abstract money. This has been criticized by Bloch and Parry using numerous empirical examples, the reason being that the way a "technology" is used is not predictable from its mere existence. He does, however, argue that modern complex commercial societies overwhelm processes of cultural classification, at least in the public sphere, so that the only singularization that occurs is in the private sphere. He makes a distinction as well between a broader set of differences, between the construction of persons and the construction of things. This important opening is not, however, developed and instead he concentrates on the ascribed order of the primitive as opposed to the uncertainty and fluidity of the complex. The difference, he says, is one between the conflicts within well defined roles (egoism versus social obligation) or more mythically informed conflicts between different roles in the primitive, and the conflict of identity as such in the modern. The same is true of the biography of things. While our approach is somewhat different, the connection between personhood and goods suggested by Kopytoff is a central theme of the present collection.

Bloch and Parry in a recently edited collection concentrate on the way in which exchange is construed in different societies. In their exceedingly clear and provocative introduction they criticize what we have discussed in another form above, i.e. the opposition between modernity and tradition understood in terms of the series money economy/traditional exchange = gift economy, monetary/non-monetary, secular/ritual. They attack the assumption concerning the historical/evolutionary premisses of this construal and the way it effects ethnographic descriptions. Instead they suggest that the opposition is one that exists in all societies, one that is deducible from Bloch's earlier discussion of the opposition between the short and the long term, between the life cycle of the subject and the permanence of society expressed in the opposition between life and ritual, exchange and the cosmic order. Numerous examples are supplied to argue for the existence of calculated profit oriented exchange as a basic practical aspect of all societies and a larger cosmically defined social hierarchy which lives off the former and which ideologically encompasses it. Somehow, in capitalism, the two cycles become separated and secular exchange becomes the source of social cosmology; individualism, self-development, success.

The arguments dovetail to a large extent with those of Appadurai in their critique of the non-commodity nature of non-Western exchange systems and the suggestion that commodities exist in all societies. Bloch and Parry refer to this in terms of a family resemblance to modern monetary exchange. On the other hand they disagree with Simmelian notions of the disintegrative effect of money and argue instead that money has no social effectivity in itself. They do not, however, indicate what the sources of the disintegration might be, and argue instead for the presence of a strong kinship network together with commodity exchange as proof of the social impotence of money. It is sometimes suggested, on the contrary, that it is the ideology of exchange that determines its social effect. Thus in capitalism,

> "By a remarkable conceptual revolution what has uniquely happened ....
> is that the values of the short-term order have become elaborated into a
> theory of long-term reproduction" (Bloch and Parry 1989:29)

The similarities between this discussion and that of Kopytoff are even more striking: commoditization, singularization, economic exchange as secular, ritual reproduction of structure. For both, the right hand side of the opposition is dependent upon the wealth accumulated by the left hand side, and for both, capitalism tends to obliterate the opposition.

These anthropological approaches represent an effort to reconceptualize the cycle of production-exchange-consumption in terms of more culturally specific characteristics. They are important for our discussion here because of the logical links between the constitution of transactions, the objects of transactions and the structures of consumption.

For example, the way in which goods are experienced by a social group has everything to do with the way in which experience is constituted in such a group. The existence of the capitalist commodity pre-supposes a specific experience of both self and objects/services as individual intrinsic values which can be chosen or ignored by a free individual who is only limited by the amount of income available and by social constraints that are also experienced as either external rules or as internal yet distinctive moral precepts. Simmel's work, as we have indicated, attempts to demonstrate how an entire world is elaborated on the basis of the monetary relation. One might question the proposed historical relations, but, at the same time, the nature of that world establishes a congruence between the modern self, the experience of other people, and the experience of things that is a simultaneity and not a haphazard collection of disparate phenomena. If this is accepted then the universalization of the notion of commodity, or of the monetary relation, while highlighting common aspects of different social orders, also misses essential differences among those orders.

The three approaches share one central feature. They all represent sub-stantial critiques of the opposition between traditional and modern exchange, arguing for a more nuanced view in which features of gift and commodity are combined in various ways in all transactional systems. This is in contradistinc-tion to the recent attempt by Marilyn Strathern to detail the way in which gift exchange represents an entirely different order of phenomenon than commod-ity exchange (see Thomas 1991 for a critique of Strathern 1988). In terms of the present collection, Strathern does offer an important argument concerning the relation between exchange of objects whose content or perhaps value is defined in terms of the persons involved in the transaction in such a way that they cannot be said to be alienable in the sense of modern commodities. On the other hand, all of these approaches maintain an opposition between fixed status and commodity exchange, between stability and accumulation which is testimony to the staying power of the old distinctions.

FROM THE REPRODUCTION OF PRODUCTION TO THE PRODUCTION OF REPRODUCTION

From the perspective of reproduction, consumption is the last phase of the process of appropriation. Appropriation in its turn is the final act of taking or receiving a product or service from another person or persons or directly from one's environment. In terms of the total process of social reproduction consump-tion can be said to have two principle aspects. First it represents a socially organized material act ensuring continued production if carried out within viable parameters, i.e. so that viable conditions of continued reproduction are produced. While in material terms consumption is the passive last stage of the reproductive process, in social terms it is the origin of a specific structure of demand. These two aspects of the reality of consumption are contained in the difference between classical discussions of consumption as a function and the more recent focus on consumption as cultural form. If the classical and classically inspired discussions of consumption envisage consumption in terms of the continuity of the reproductive process, the approach which appears to be emerging is one that focusses on the ways in which reproduction is socially constituted from the vantage point of consumption. By maintaining the general framework of reproduction we are, I think, able to situate consumption properly in a larger social field where it can be said to "make sense" in terms of the social strategies of a particular group.

If consumption is understood to be a distinctive domain in purely material terms, this is certainly not the case in social terms. Degrees of freedom in strategies of consumption reflect degrees of freedom in the constitution of life spaces, the degree to which the subject may possess a conscious strategy of appropriation of the world in the making of his own smaller space of existence, of his own life-style expressive of a given or created identity. Degrees of freedom are also situated in terms of the larger social context. Creativity may be understood as variations on a given theme or as a replacement of one theme by another. The construction of life-styles is not equivalent in terms of social ontology to the construction of ritual variation. It follows from this that consumption does not play the same role in a social field constituted by a strategy of alternate identification as it does in a field constituted by a strategy of elaboration on a single identity. This is perhaps the importance of the tradition dating from Simmel which attempts to understand the general features of a particular world of goods. And it is also in such terms that an understanding of the variable nature of exchange is so important, for it is here that consumption is rooted as a general historical and anthropological phenomenon.

In a very general sense, production is organized to produce the social life space of a population. The demand for worlds of goods is a governing force in social reproduction. The way in which this demand is constructed is the essential variable to be understood. Class or rank demand for hierarchical distinction, for separateness, for primordiality, ethnic specificity, modernity...all are images of potential life forms projected via desire onto a demand schedule. These social projects are the bases for understanding the practice of consumption, and they are, by definition, projects of self-definition, whether they are voluntarily or socially determined; they take the form of projects in which subjects invest themselves and their accumulated wealth.

Bourdieu's notion of *habitus* is clearly relevant here, but particular socially determinate *habitii* need to be situated in that larger context in which they are created and which creates tendencies that cross-cut group differences, as Campbell has suggested. Finally such projects must ultimately be seen in articulation with the reproductive process in which they are materially and socially embedded. West Indian, central African and Swedish consumption are informed and in some cases organized in close affinity to global transactions. Not only the goods but even the identities are part of the relevant social context. The articulation invariably combines local strategies of appropriation and global products and images. The result is a local orchestration of global dependency.

No theory of consumption is feasible because consumption is not a socially autonomous phenomenon. The best we can do is supply a framework of analysis. This framework must connect the macro processes of social reproduction with the formation of social projects of consumption as well as the interaction between the two.

We began our discussion by tracing the emancipation of the notion of consumption from a mere function of a larger production process and its emergence as a sociological domain in its own right. While there may be a tendency in certain anthropological approaches to make a new equation between cultural models or paradigms and structures of consumption, we have argued that a broader perspective reintegrates consumption strategies into the larger framework of social reproduction. This interpretation suggests that the formation of strategies of consumption is deducible from more general social strategies including those of production and the latter are related in the macro structures of a social system, those which form the social context of social practice. This is the message of Simmel, Adorno, Baudrillard and even Bourdieu. It is most explicit in the work of Campbell. All of these authors have stressed that a particular kind of social existence produces a particular kind of personal experience, a particular kind of selfhood, which in turn generates a particular strategy of consumption.

THE CHAPTERS

The first section of the book deals with two aspects of Western modernity. Campbell's chapter is a theoretical discussion of the problem of agency in modern societies, based on his evaluation of contributions by Veblen and Weber. In it he sets out the central theme or issue of the collection as a whole, that of the relation between motivational structures and social practice of which consumption is an aspect. The context of his discussion is limited to modern Western society. In anthropological terms , however, the issue can be relativized to refer to the relation between social process, social experience, personhood and projects of consumption. Löfgren's chapter is a very explicit example of the relation between social identity as a project and the practice of consumption. He traces, over several generations, the way in which changing social identities inform and even organize the way in which Swedes via the market, make their private and public spaces, and furnish their homes and lives with distinctive meanings. In this complex of processes it is necessary to consider both the biography of commodities and the biography of people. He traces the routinization of commodities over time as well as the more important changes in consumption that are related to class, and to national and more general identities such as modernism. The importance of self-identification in acts of consumption vitiates much of the critique of consumer culture as alienating and devoid of meaningful content. Changes in consumption in Sweden in the twentieth century can be understood in terms of the transformation of social projects of consumption, of the life-style goals that become dominant in succeeding periods.

The second section deals explicitly with consumption as a practice of social identity. Miller examines style and fashion in Trinidad. His contribution is meant as a critique of the assumption often encountered in Western cultural studies that a preoccupation with transient self-presentation is somehow an expression of superficiality. In Trinidad, style, as a practice of impermanence, represents a kind of individualization in opposition to the fixed forms of dress and self-presentation characteristic of traditional ceremonial life. Miller associates the former to a strategy in which fixed personal identity is refused and even experienced as dangerous for the individual. The cultivation of display is a consistent and deeply rooted strategy of social survival. The craze, not only for fashion, but for the recombination of elements of fashion into constantly changing and brilliant displays of selfhood is the product of this general strategy. Wilk's chapter deals with the ethnic mosaic of Belize and the way that consumer goods are used to construct conflicting identities. He begins by highlighting the country's dependence on imports and the place they have in defining local prestige. This dependency is opposed to another vision of a strong local culture able to be autonomous from the surrounding world. Belizian discourse on consumption is intimately linked to their visions of the future; a state centered developmentalism with a strong accent on locally controlled development, a cosmopolitan image of a foreign linked upper class who live in an enclave of Western modernity surrounded by traditions worthy of preservation but not emulation, an ethnic or rather indigenous vision emphasizing the maintenance of local identities and forms of traditional life, an urban poor vision based on an opposition between reputation and respectability, one that is moreover applicable to the whole society. He examines this opposition in some detail and connects it to a dichotomous pattern of consumption, related to Miller's distinction between transience and transcendence. In both of these chapters the relation between social conditions, strategies of cultural identity and patterns of consumption is made quite explicit. Orlove's chapter investigates the relation between consumption and social hierarchy in nineteenth century Chile. He insists on the importance of considering the material properties of objects consumed in order to grasp their potential for cultural elaboration, and the latter is a product of the social context itself. Thus, meat consumption involves a hierarchy of distribution that includes dogs as well as humans and integrates meals into the practice of the hacienda hierarchy. The latter are not external to the social order but are its foundation. They quite often serve as symbols, not of nature, but of poverty, in numerous examples proffered by Orlove. Social position could be measured in terms of "how much" and "how often" one received meat. While the first two chapters in this section focus on individual strategies and creativity, this last chapter deals more with what might be called ascribed consumption. But once again it is a question of consumption as self-definition, even if the power of that definition is attributed to external powers. The latter aspect of selfhood is central to the following section.

The third section deals specifically with the role of consumption strategies in the definition and maintenance of status and power. While there is a superficial resemblance, thematically, to the work of Veblen, the actual strategies and identities detailed here provide another logic of status and power. There is a continuity between Miller's discussion and the chapters in this section. His argument against the superficiality of style might be applied in a more general sense to notions of status and power. The latter in the two African examples discussed by Rowlands and Friedman are questions of being rather than appearance. Rowlands discusses how the consumption of western goods in Cameroon is generated by a desire to appropriate the West and to incorporate it into the being of the consumer. Superficially it might appear as emulation, but in this case it is not a question of copying, i.e. of producing an image, but of the production of selfhood, not an image of success, but success itself. Rowlands explores how the strategy of "success" is carried out in numerous domains, from domestic interiors to clothing, from eating arrangements to body care. The conversion of wealth into the material culture of success is shown to be part of a vast social project involving position within the kin group as well the larger social network, a project that is fraught with risk and the dangers of failure since the latter is associated with the diminution of the self, with illness and death. Friedman's chapter deals with the relation between personhood and consumption in the Congo. He argues that the constitution of Congolese selfhood which is powerfully informed by a systemic dependency on the appropriation of life force from external sources, is a historically rooted phenomenon that may take a variety of forms, depending on social conditions. The accumulation of life-force as a strategy is identical to increasing one's social rank and the latter can only be expressed in "other-directed" terms, by its material presentation. The consumption of luxuries is a political-economy of elegance. The analysis of La Sape, a highly organized proletarian movement or perhaps cult whose aim is the accumulation of *haute couture* by whatever means available demonstrates the ultimate limits of this strategy. The establishing of a link to Paris, the source of life force, and the system of age ranks leading to the production of "great men" poses a serious threat to the state-class's monopoly of the expression of power in a system where the expression of power is power. Hirsch's contribution concerns the way in which new objects and institutional arrangements can be substituted for older forms while maintaining the continuity of social strategies. The mission had forbidden the exposure of the dead in funerary ritual. Betel nut had come to play a central role as an income generating product. Betel nut has become a substitute for the dead body of the chief. The latter was associated with "life-force" *tidibe*, a force that maintained the centrality of Fuyuge society, the wealth necessary for its continued reproduction. Betel nut associated with wealth via its popularity as a commodity, replaces the chiefly corpse, taking on the essential functions of the latter. Hirsch links the persistence of Fuyuge culture to the continuity of their cosmology. What appears as, and is in a certain sense, a fundamental change in the local social organization, demonstrates a continuity in cultural strategies at a deeper level, one that engages the motivations and meanings attributed to the world. In all of the examples presented here, there is a striking absence of a distinction between essence and appearance which is so integral to discussions of the relation between selfhood and consumption in the West.[5] The link with Campbell's argument against Veblen lies in the shared interest of attempting to dispel the reductionist assumptions involved in treating consumption as the product of status seeking. The chapter by Kopytoff deals with the effect of the colonial and post-colonial processes on the dismemberment of the traditional dynamics of rural society in Zaire. It analyzes the emergence of a syndrome of boredom as the result of the disarticulation of a former "luxury" consumption complex based on the circulation of prestige goods. Kopytoff discusses the way in which a former division of activities in Suku society predisposed males to specialize in political and exchange activities in which the accumulation of prestige goods via regional trade played a central role. With the breakdown of this system, the focus on such goods remained paramount, but their acquisition now became very difficult. Many sought work in towns or in other regions, but for those who remained there was little to do other than "consume leisure", i.e. boredom. Kopytoff argues that the very organization of Suku, its "lineage mode of consumption" predisposed its resident male population to invest in leisure rather than "development" . As opposed to the first three examples, Kopytoff deals with an elimination of consumables rather than with substitution of new goods for old. As we know nothing of the Suku who move into towns, it is difficult to ascertain whether or not the same strategy of consuming external high status goods is tendentially present. But the situation of the rural Suku, as the obverse of the above

---

[5] In my own article I suggest that it is only in situations of clinical narcissism in the Western context that the distinction between essence and appearance has a tendency to disappear, i.e. insofar as the narcissist experiences his or her self as dependent on the "gaze of the other".

three examples, has the same basic logic in which social value, and indeed the social dynamic, is entirely dependent upon the consumption of external valuables, or, perhaps, life-force.

CONCLUSION

The consistency of this volume, as I have argued, lies in the unanimous focus on the relation between cultural strategies of self-construction and consumption. The examples are ethnographically varied, but the general theme remains the same. All the chapters except Campbell's contain empirical cases. The latter, however, has a significant place in terms of the goals of this collection which deserves comment.

Campbell's essay in this volume is the only one that might to be said to be purely theoretical, insofar as it makes scarcely any reference to any empirical studies, not even his own historical work on the development of European consumerism. As such it might even have appeared difficult to place it in relation to the other chapters. The first section which deals with Western Europe is surely the right geographical location, but alongside of a paper on changing consumption patterns in Sweden, it appears somewhat out of place. It deals, however, with a problem that is clearly of Western origin; the relation between Weberian and Veblenesque inspired analyses of consumption and the connection between motives, motivations and consumer behavior in capitalism.

The importance of the chapter with respect to the overall distribution of themes in the book is its focus on the situating of consumption in a broader context of the construction of meaningful worlds by active subjects. In his critique of Veblen, he stresses the inadequacy of mono-motive theories of conduct and the necessity of understanding both the variability and complexity of motivational structures, their cultural content, and their historical transformations. Included in this discussion is an implicit critique of theories of consumption that do not base themselves upon an understanding of the subjective worlds of consumers. This need not imply that we may not have recourse to more objectivist approaches but, a Freudian inspired account of the formation of motivations is excluded. But it does insist on the necessity of taking account of that substrate of human behavior which is directly implicated in making the choices involved in consumption. In *The Romantic Ethic and the Spirit of Modern Consumerism* he argues that the formation of capitalist production was also the formation of capitalist consumers and that this latter process might best be understood in terms of the transformation of the desire to consume, the structure of a new kind of experience based on the emergence of the "modern" individual, a subject without an ascribed identity, who could create one in the very act of consumption, by furnishing his or her life with a meaningful space. But he goes further in his analysis by suggesting that no consumption can ever be psychologically final because the general state of alterity makes all identities unsatisfactory. Is this a so-ciological version of Says Law whereby consumers are created for the capitalist requirement of infinite accumulation? There is an area here that might well be investigated. More important is the attempt to demonstrate a systematic connec-tion between the structuring of motivations that are the foundation for demand, and the nature of the larger socio-economic field. This is clearly progress with respect to earlier approaches which either assume universal natural propensities to consume whatever is produced, or mono-motivational theories, such as those of Veblen and to a certain extent, Bourdieu, for whom consumption, while not simply being a question of utility, is reduced to a quasi-universal competition for status or distinctiveness. In my interpretation, at least, Campbell's argument ap-pears to be headed toward a characterization of capitalist social forms and certain characteristics of personhood and personal experience that they generate. And in this sense his abstract discussion of sociological classes takes us to the thresh-old of the, perhaps, more self-evident anthropological approaches represented in the ensuing chapters. From the ethnographic point of view, the main problem is to try and make sense out of kinds of consumption that are strikingly different from our own, and the approach stressed in this volume is to resolve the problem by analyzing consumption in terms of the larger cultural strategies in which it is embedded. These strategies consist largely of identity creating or maintaining practices, of which social status may indeed be an aspect. But even here, social status may be constituted in vastly different ways in different societies, as is clearly demonstrated in the central African examples.

In all of these chapters consumption is shown to be, in one way or another, part of a larger socially and culturally constituted project. It is subsumed in this way as a strategy of self-definition within a larger social field. The understanding of consumption cannot be separated from the question of the way in which consumers are constituted. And the latter question is related to the more general way in which social experience is generated in particular social contexts. Here we return to the problem of the congruity between production and consumption which has been battled by economists in terms of where buying power or effective demand comes from and how it is related to supply. But now the question is of a more general nature. How and to what extent does a social system produce a harmonic relation between production and consumption? How is social reproduction possible? Part of the answer to these questions lies in the way in which social identities generate cultural strategies of consumption, the way in which consumption expresses the structures of desire in society, and the way in which life worlds are constructed via the practice of consumption. This volume has, as did the workshop that led to this publication, attempted to come to terms with the fundamental relations involved in the social and cultural production of consumption.

CHAPTER ONE

Capitalism, Consumption and the Problem of Motives

Some Issues in the Understanding of Conduct as Illustrated by an Examination of the Treatment of Motive and Meaning in the Works of Weber and Veblen[*]

Colin Campbell

INTRODUCTION

The necessity of according a central role to typical patterns of motivation in their explanations of the workings of capitalism and the events surrounding the Industrial Revolution was recognized by most of the major social theorists of the late nineteenth and early twentieth centuries whether their focus was on production or consumption. In the case of both Max Weber and Thorstein Veblen, for example, certain distinctive motives (or complexes of motives) are identified as lying at the heart of the conduct which in the one case prompted entrepreneurs and workers to adopt modern attitudes toward work and money making, and in the other prompted the newly affluent to engage in the continuous consumption of luxury goods. They were, of course, not alone in this and other theorists of the time also stressed the necessity of understanding the motives which impelled people to engage in economic activities, although the factors which drove individuals to work received far more attention than the impulses considered to lie behind consumption. Not all these theorists consciously made explicit use of the concept of motive, but even those who did not, like Marx (perhaps the most notable exception), can be seen to have encountered the necessity of drafting in other terms, (in his case 'interests', 'ideology', 'praxis' and 'false consciousness'), to play a similar role in the overall explanatory scheme.[1]

---

[*] This article is based on a paper presented at a conference entitled 'The Culture of the Market', held at the Murphy Institute of Political Economy, Tulane University, from March 9–11, 1990.

[1] For a discussion of the problem of motivation in Marx's thought see John M. Maguire, *Marx's Theory of Politics*. Cambridge: Cambridge University Press, 1978, pp. 117–120.

However, whether they were explicitly stated or merely constituted a taken-for-granted framework for analysis, assumptions about motives can be said to have been an essential part of all theories of capitalism, the market and modern economic life.

What is immediately noticeable, however, is that these various theories do not all emphasize the same motives, even when dealing with identical forms of conduct. Sombart, for example, saw the underlying urge to consume new luxury goods as lying in eroticism,[2] whilst Veblen considered that it stemmed from envy of the rich and an associated desire to engage in emulative behavior.[3] Similarly, in considering the activities of entrepreneurs, Marx tended to stress the importance of material self-interest, whilst Weber focused on the role of religiously-inspired ideas of duty and the associated need for reassurance of election. Whilst these varying accounts are not all irreconcilable (or at least with a little ingenuity it might be possible to render some of them compatible), the fact remains that different theorists have emphasized contrasting motives in their separate accounts of the same phenomenon.

Although the merits of these competing theories of capitalism have been extensively debated, surprisingly little attention has been specifically directed at resolving these differences. Hence what might be called the problem of motives still awaits resolution through a comprehensive programme of research aimed at adjudicating between the rival claims. However, it is also clear that these differences stem, at least in part, from contrasting theoretical and methodological assumptions over the concept of motive and its role in constructing explanations of human conduct, and hence that any serious attempts to resolve this problem requires that these issues should constitute the initial focus of inquiry. Thus, the merits of the claims advanced in favor of one motive rather than another are, in the long run, less important than the manner in which the motivational understanding of conduct is itself conceived. For this will naturally tend to determine both how the nature and content of motives is established, and how these are related to those encompassing systems of subjective meaning which are constituted as values and beliefs. The focus of this discussion will thus be on the contrasting treatment accorded to the concept of motive in the works of two of the major theorists of capitalism, Max Weber and Thorstein Veblen, in the hope that such a discussion will shed some light on how social theorists and historians should best approach capitalism and 'the problem of motives'.

---

[2] Werner Sombart, *Luxury and Capitalism*. Intro. by Philip Seligman. Ann Arbor, Mich.: University of Michigan Press, 1967.

[3] Thorstein Veblen, *The Theory of the Leisure Class: An Economic Study of Institutions*. (New York: Macmillan 1898), London: George Allen and Unwin, 1925.

THE MOTIVATIONAL UNDERSTANDING OF CONDUCT

Before examining the treatment of motives in the works of these theorists it is worth reviewing the grounds for insisting on the importance of motivational forms of explanation of historical events and for rejecting the claim that understanding can be obtained without any reference to subjective meaning. This involves answering some important questions. Is it really the case, for example, as Collingwood has claimed, that to explain actions it is always necessary to 'discern the thoughts' of agents,[4] and hence that the principal task of any investigator (whether historian or social scientist) must be to seek to discover the operative subjective meanings of actors. And that in addition since no historical account can be formulated which does not involve the claim that certain individual human actions took place that this also necessarily includes some presuppositions concerning the nature of the operative motives. A claim which, it has been suggested, applies as much to collectivities such as nations, social classes or organizations, as to individuals.[5] For example, is it really not possible to understand the economic conduct of individuals and hence the processes underlying the Industrial Revolution without recourse to an investigation into those subjective meanings which accompanied behaviour? Cannot the system of capitalism be grasped as a whole and understood in terms of its own inherent logic? Or alternatively, is it not possible, through observation alone, to obtain an adequate grasp of the meaning which is attached to the conduct of individuals?[6]

To begin by tackling the last question first, there is general agreement that some considerable portion of human conduct cannot be understood by reference to subjective meanings. This generally comes under the heading of 'behaviour' and covers obviously unwilled and unintended acts such as reflexes like knee-jerks or sneezing. As Weber observes, this is 'merely reactive behaviour to which no subjective meaning is attached' and is therefore in marked contrast to action which is defined as 'all human behaviour when and in so far as the acting individual attaches a subjective meaning to it'.[7] Obviously it follows from this that

---

[4] Collingwood, *The Idea of History*, pp. 214–215.

[5] W. G. Runciman, *The Methodology of Social Theory: Vol. 1., A Treatise on Social Theory*. Cambridge: Cambridge University Press, 1983, p. 30.

[6] These are, of course, matters of long-standing debate within the philosophy of history and the social sciences as far back as Hume and Kant, and it is not intended to rehearse these complex issues here, merely to summarize the general positions in so far as they impinge directly on the concepts of motive and motivation.

[7] Max Weber *The Theory of Social and Economic Organization*. trans. A. M. Henderson and Talcott Parsons, New York: Free Press, 1964, p. 88. Schutz has qualified this definition pointing out that actors may attach subjective meanings to behaviour. The sneeze, for example, may be seen as indicating the onset of a cold. (Alfred Schutz, *The Phenomenology of the Social World*. trans.. George Walsh and Frederick Lehnert, with an intro. by George Walsh. Chicago: Northwestern University Press, 1967, p. 26f.) What Weber seems to have meant to say is that action is behaviour in which the subjective meaning preceded or accompanied the act in question.

proper interpretive or motivational understanding can only be applied to action, with behaviour of necessity the subject matter of observer-style causal explanations. This, however, still leaves the essentially problematic and difficult task of deciding, in relation to any particular event or item of conduct, how far it would be correct to view it as 'action' or 'behaviour'. For, although there is little dispute over the extremes (rarely is sneezing regarded as 'action' or playing chess treated as 'behaviour',[8] what Weber describes as 'a very considerable part of all sociologically relevant behaviour' is 'marginal between the two'.[9] Significantly however, in the light of the present discussion, economic conduct is one category of human behaviour which most social theorists seem happy to label 'action' in this sense: indeed, for some, including Weber himself, in its inherent rationality it represents the quintessential form of action. Despite this, it is important to recognize that this may not always and everywhere be the case and that some instances of economic conduct might not be informed by much in the way of accompanying subjective meaning but, in the form of habitual or traditional practices, approximate to 'behaviour'. However, even here there is the presumption that such conduct probably originated as action and hence that the process of understanding might require some attempt to recover these initiating meanings.

There is a marked difference, however, between accepting that some portion of human conduct is behaviour and endorsing the claim that all human conduct should be approached as if it fell into this category. This is the central tenet of behaviourism, a movement which was itself a reaction against the excessive reliance upon introspection by earlier generations of psychologists and 'armchair' social theorists. Although this has never been a prominent tradition of thought within history it has been an important strand within social thought and especially so at the turn of the century when biological and evolutionary versions of this perspective prevailed. Veblen, as we shall see, was among those who were influenced by these ideas. Today, behaviourism has little support within the social sciences, whilst even within psychology the cognitive revolution has meant that thought is once more a respectable topic for study.[10]

A much more significant challenge to the interpretivist tradition of inquiry has been mounted in recent decades by Wittgensteinianen inspired perspectives which, whilst accepting that meaning is the principal subject matter of academic inquiry, have sought to locate it within the social context of action rather than

---

[8]   See, for agreement on this if on nothing else, the debate between Rubenstein and Porpora. D Rubenstein, 'The Concept of Action in the Social Sciences', *Journal for the Theory of Social Behaviour* 7 (July 1977) pp. 209–236. Douglas V. Porpora, 'On the Post-Wittgensteinian Critique of the Concept of Action in Sociology'. *Journal for the Theory of Social Behaviour* 13 2 (July 1983), pp. 129–146.

[9]   Weber, *The Theory of Social and Economic Organization*, p. 90.

[10]   See William N. Dember, 'Motivation and the Cognitive Revolution', *American Psychologist* (March 1974), pp. 161–168.

within the individual. Here the central claim is that the meaning of an action can be found in the rules or norms which govern the situation of its occurrence. Hence the 'meaning' to be attached to the motorist's movement of his arm is understood to be a signal of his intention to turn right because 'if a man driving a car extends his arm in the proper manner he has signaled whether he intended to or not', and consequently, 'if the right performance transpires under the right circumstances, the act has occurred'.[11]

Similarly, whether a man's act in putting a ring on the finger of a woman signifies marriage or not depends, not on his subjective motive in performing this act, but on the context in which it takes place. To extrapolate from these examples to the economic system which is capitalism, it could be said that the 'meaning' of such processes as the production, distribution or consumption of goods is not to be found in the minds of industrialists, retailers or consumers but in the institutional settings in which these actions occur. Such an argument clearly has much force and it is obvious that in the processes of learning about an alien or unfamiliar culture any investigator would need to discover precisely just such rules in order to be able to discern 'what is going on'. Yet this form of 'explicating meaning' is also very limited, consisting essentially of little more than a process in which actions are identified or labelled. For whilst it enables the analyst to conclude that this item of behaviour is a signal or that item is a marriage ceremony, there is no accompanying account of the conduct in purposive terms. Thus precisely why the driver wished to turn right or the man in question become a husband remains a mystery. To this extent, the ethnomethodological tradition of inquiry, whilst facilitating a general cultural mapping of conduct, fails to provide an explanation in terms of a personal, goal-directed and motivated model of action. It is in this respect reminiscent of what Weber referred to as the 'direct observational understanding' of action,[12] a process in which the observer draws upon an existing stock of knowledge in order to interpret actions, a stock of knowledge in which familiarity with the rules plays a central part. Thus Weber states 'that we . . . understand by direct observation . . . the meaning of the proposition $2 \times 2 = 4$ when we hear or read it'.[13]

Now there is no particular reason why capitalism should not be 'understood' in a similar fashion. For just as we can comprehend the meaning of mathematical equations once we have mastered the underlying axioms so too may we grasp the internal logic which binds various institutional practices. The relationship between private property, for example, (especially as represented by the joint stock company) and consumer sovereignty, the free market, and the price

---

[11] Rubenstein, p. 215.

[12] Weber, *The Theory of Social and Economic Organization*, p. 94.

[13] Weber, *The Theory Social and of Economic Organization*, pp. 94–95.

mechanism may indeed be understood in this manner. To that extent, capitalism, like any distinct socio-cultural entity, may be described meaningfully without recourse to either motives in particular or subjective meaning in general. Indeed it is precisely because this is true that the nature of the phenomenally operative meanings which did in practice accompany such conduct in eighteenth and nineteenth century Europe and North America has to be regarded as problematic. For the forms of economic conduct essential to the workings of capitalism do not logically require the presence of any one particular set of motives to be present. What is central to the system is conduct which is characterized by certain specific intentions, such as profit-seeking, or utility maximization, rather than any specific motives.[14] But Weber goes on to contrast 'observational understanding' with 'explanatory understanding', a process which does involve comprehending in terms of *motive* the meaning an actor attaches to the propositions twice two equals four, when he states it or writes it down, in that we understand what makes him do this at precisely this moment and in these circumstances' (italics in original). He continues:

> Understanding in this sense is attained if we know that he is engaged in balancing a ledger or in making a scientific demonstration, or is engaged in some other task of which this particular act would be an appropriate part. This is rational understanding of motivation, which consists in placing the act in an intelligible and more inclusive context of meaning[15]

He then provides his famous examples, observing that we understand the chopping of wood or aiming of a gun in terms of motive in addition to direct observation if we know that the woodcutter is working for a wage or is chopping a supply of firewood for his own use, or possibly is doing it for recreation.[16] Now the important feature of Weber's concept does not lie simply in placing the act in an intelligible and more inclusive context of meaning as he states, but rather in the fact that this context is personal and psychological in character. For whilst it is true that perceiving the significance of an act in terms of its position in a means-ends chain is to extend our understanding, unless it is obvious how that chain connects with the actor's pattern of personal gratifications, the character of our comprehension is merely intentionalist and not motivational. Thus, although it

---

[14] It is true as Schutz has observed, (*The Phenomenology of the Social World*, pp. 27–29), that even observational understanding of the kind outlined by Weber actually involves the imputation of meaning to conduct on the part of the observer and hence that mistakes may be made concerning 'what is actually going on'. Considered from the perspective of the individual actor this is certainly true, but as long as the observer focuses upon social patterns of action then what is under discussion is the 'embodied intentionality' which they contain and this can be described independently of the purposes of individuals (as in the case of the car-driver mentioned above.)

[15] Weber, *The Theory of Social and Economic Organization*, p. 94.

[16] Weber, *The Theory of Social and Economic Organization*, p. 94.

is useful to know that the clerk is balancing a ledger or that the woodcutter is an employee this knowledge in itself tells us nothing about motive only about intention. To understand such items of conduct 'motivationally' requires that we relate the actions to the goals and desires of those who undertake them, to outcomes which are desired for their own sake and not simply as means to a further end. Motivational understanding thus involves connecting conduct to psychological states and especially to patterns of gratification. In this sense it goes one step beyond mere intentionalist understanding by dealing with what the action in question 'signifies' for the actor. Hence whilst we may know the 'meaning' of an act we may not know what it signifies personally unless we know how the achievement of a particular result relates to the hopes, fears and wishes of the individual. Thus it is crucial to the process of motivational understanding that one gains insight into what are the critical goals in question. Obviously the clerk is adding up columns of figures in order to balance a ledger, but is that an important goal in his life? Does succeeding in balancing the books provide him with a significant sense of personal achievement? A goal which he looks forward to eagerly? Or is it merely one more tiresome chore to be got out of the way before he finishes work for the day and he can devote his energies to those things which really concern him? That is to say, the crucial question to be asked is what kind of valuation is placed on the different outcomes in a series of acts the intentionality of which is readily apparent. Yet there is a further stage to the process of motivational understanding. In addition to knowing which outcomes are defined as critical goals (what people are really striving towards) and which are merely means, we also need to know why they are striving for them and what general 'meaning' or 'resonance' such goals possess. It is for this reason that motivational understanding leads naturally into a study of people's beliefs, values and attitudes, and why the study of motive cannot really be separated from an associated investigation into more general patterns of 'meaning'.[17]

The above discussion has served to highlight the two dominant and conventionally contrasted perspectives employed in the study of motives. The first, which for convenience can be called the motivation tradition, prevails in psychology and is generally behaviourist in orientation. According to this tradition of inquiry the analyst is primarily interested in the force or energy which it is assumed

---

[17] One reason why this kind of motivational understanding is so crucial to the explanation of conduct is that it provides dynamically constructed accounts, ones which tell us why individuals are prepared to exert their efforts in the ways that they do and in so doing suggests something about the arousal and direction of human energy. Indeed it is precisely this ingredient which provides the explanatory content. Unfortunately it is all too often assumed that explanations which are couched in terms of motivational 'forces' or which make reference to 'energy' are necessarily indicative of a behaviourist mode of analysis and are hence not assimilable to a phenomenological concern with subjective meaning. There is no good reason for such an assumption. Individuals recognize all too well that action requires the expenditure of energy and refer openly to their own 'efforts' to achieve goals. Understanding conduct in terms of the expenditure of energy can thus be approached subjectively as well as objectively.

underlies the behaviour of all living things. As Newcombe summarily expresses this view, 'energy which is mobilized and directed is a motive'.[18] Motives are thus seen as 'temporary energy systems' with a state of apathy posited as the opposite of being motivated. The consequent tendency of those who work in this tradition is to explain conduct in terms of 'drives' or 'instincts' in accord with their predominantly biological and evolutionary outlook. The key questions are taken to be, where does this energy come from and how is it mobilized and directed? The second, or motive tradition, places the emphasis on relating conduct to subjective complexes of meaning which it is assumed are present in the minds of individuals prior to, and while embarking on, action. Motives are therefore identified with goals, intentions or reasons whilst the problem is not seen to be one of 'motive power' but of 'steered conduct', that is, 'how and why human conduct takes a specific direction'.[19] This perspective tends to predominate in social-psychology and sociology. The treatment accorded to the concept of motive (or motivation) by the major social theorists of capitalism can be seen to stem from the degree to which they subscribe to one or other of these two traditions, or, more interestingly, attempt to integrate them into one overall theory of social conduct.[20]

THE TREATMENT OF MOTIVES IN HISTORICAL EXPLANATIONS

It is useful to begin an examination of the way that historians (drawing, of course, on social theory) typically invoke motives in the course of explaining events by considering the topic of the revolution in consumption which occurred in eighteenth century England. Here a standard explanation has emerged to account for that surge in demand for luxury goods on the part of the middle classes which proved such a vital factor in facilitating the concomitant revolution in production. This explanation, whilst noting the role of other factors, draws heavily on Veblen's theory of conspicuous consumption to support the claim that 'emu-

---

[18] Theodore M. Newcombe, *Social Psychology*. London: Tavistock Publications, 1952, p. 115.

[19] Hans Gerth and C. Wright Mills, *Character and Social Structure: The Psychology of Social Institutions*, London: Routledge & Kegan Paul, 1986, p. 113.

[20] There is a third tradition in which the concepts of motive and motivation are replaced by that of 'interests'. It is not possible to include a full discussion of this body of thought and its connection with the analysis of motive in this paper but generally speaking the concept of interest, in so far as it is clearly defined, is taken to refer to a particularly stable variety of goals or ends. As Hindess observes, 'interests define some of the objectives that actors set themselves, or would set themselves if only they were in a position to do so. Interests belong to that broad class of entities that have been supposed . . . to provide actors with ends, and therefore with reasons for action.' (Barry Hindess, 'Interests in Political Analysis', pp. 112–131 in John Law (ed.) *Power, Action and Belief: A New Sociology of Knowledge?*, Sociological Review Monograph 32, London: Routledge & Kegan Paul, 1986, p. 11; see also Katherine Betts, 'The Conditions of action, power and the problem of interests', *Sociological Review* 34 1 (1986), pp. 39–64.). This suggests that an interest-type analysis is essentially an intentionalist one, and not a fully 'motivational' one as outlined above.

lation' is the 'key to consumer demand'[21], and hence that the subjective meaning to be attached to the readiness of farmers' wives and fashionable young ladies to purchase the latest clothes, furnishings, china, prints and novels is that they saw such conduct as a means of improving their social position.[22] Now there are several pertinent features to note about the character of this widely accepted motive-style explanation of a specific historical event. Firstly, the nature of the activity to be explained — what it is that the individuals concerned could be said to be doing — is decided by the observer through a process of labelling which appears to make no concessions at all to the actors' subjective viewpoint. To this extent it would seem to be an example of observational understanding in which little attempt has been made to discover the system of beliefs and attitudes which give this conduct meaning. Hence such activities as selecting a bonnet, borrowing a book from a circulating library, buying a print, going to a dance or furnishing a house, are lumped together unproblematically to constitute a single category, that of 'consumption'. Next what might be called a 'category theory' is invoked; that is to say, one like Veblen's which claims to be able to identify a single motive as underlying a single 'species' of conduct.[23] In effect, a simple argument which asserts that consumption must stem from emulation. From this it is then concluded that 'what is going on' as far as the conduct of the eighteenth century English middle classes is concerned, is that they are consuming goods out of a desire to emulate their social superiors. A conclusion which, it can be noted, is arrived at without reference to any material concerning the actual ideas, thoughts, intentions, feelings or motives of eighteenth century people. All that is offered by way of evidence are the statements of those contemporary observers whose views happen to coincide with modern-day historians in attributing emulative motives to these 'new consumers'. In other words, the crucial issue of the nature of the operative motives is not settled through any attempt to establish what might be called first-order 'confessional' evidence, but through a process of assertion and imputation.

---

[21] Harold Perkin, *The Origins of Modern English Society*. London: Routledge & Kegan Paul, 1968, pp. 96–97.

[22] See, for example, the argument developed in Neil McKendrick, John Brewer and J. H. Plumb, *The Birth of a Consumer Society: The Commercialization of Eighteenth-Century England*. London: Europa Publications, 1982.

[23] A close examination of Veblen's discussion actually reveals more than one possible 'motive' for emulative conduct. The first of these is the protection or enhancement of esteem. One of Veblen's clearest arguments about the psychological mechanisms involved in conspicuous consumption is as follows. Wealth confers honour whilst individuals are esteemed to the degree that they possess wealth: an individual's self-esteem is dependent on the esteem accorded by others. It follows from this that fluctuations in an individual's perceived wealth will lead to changes in self-esteem. Hence, in order to protect or enhance his self-esteem an individual will find it necessary to display greater 'pecuniary strength'. But Veblen also suggests other and rather different motives for such conduct. He refers, for example, to the 'satisfaction' which comes from having 'widened the pecuniary interval' between oneself and those with whom one is in the habit of classing oneself (*The Theory of the Leisure Class*, p. 31), and of the 'gratification' which comes from 'possessing something more than others' p. 31.

This form of motive-style historical explanation, although very common, is clearly based on some contentious assumptions. If, for the moment, the first and highly significant practice of identifying categories of conduct without reference to the actor's subjective meaning is set aside, the unquestioned application of category theories is clearly problematic. The central assumption here is that a given activity always stems from a given motive, a presumption which, in turn, is often derived from more general 'monomotive' theories of human conduct as a whole. This is only partly true in Veblen's case, for in addition to the desire to emulate, he postulates an 'instinct of workmanship' underlying the behaviour of all humans.[24] Despite this complication, Veblen is still clearly classifiable as a member of the 'instinct school' of social theorists because of his tendency to seek explanations of human conduct in terms of single and simple 'drives' or innate tendencies which are assumed to be common to the species. Thus, he says of the emulative motive that it is 'of ancient growth and . . . a pervading trait of human nature', judging it to be, after the 'instinct of self-preservation . . . probably the strongest and most alert and persistent of the economic motives proper'.[25] It is clear from this that Veblen identified with the motivation rather than the motive tradition of analysis. However, what is also clear is that this position involves some obvious difficulties.

In the first place, if the motive underlying human conduct is assumed to be always and everywhere the same, then motive itself ceases to be an important explanatory variable. The problem of explaining how changes occur in the dominant pattern of activities in a society has to be resolved by reference to some other factors (usually material or structural). This tendency can be seen in discussions of the eighteenth century consumer revolution, where resort to Veblen's theory fails to explain why any significant change in consumer conduct should have occurred at this time.

Recognizing this, historians have turned to such variables as an increase in disposable income, developments in marketing and sales techniques, or the rise of modern fashion, naming these as the key facilitating factors responsible for the revolution in demand.[26] Secondly, assuming the reality of universal motives in this way involves accepting an overly specific conception of what constitutes a common 'human nature'. This, in turn, stems from a failure to recognize that whilst all human beings may experience common needs and emotions, these are moulded into the specific complexes of meaningful effort which constitute motives through processes which embody the particularities of culture.

---

[24] Thorstein Veblen, *The Instinct of Workmanship and the State of the Industrial Arts*, New York: Macmillan, 1914.

[25] Thorstein Veblen, *The Theory of the Leisure Class*, p. 110.

[26] McKendrick et al.: see also Colin Campbell, *The Romantic Ethic and the Spirit of Modern Consumerism*. Oxford: Basil Blackwell, 1987, chp. 2.

Thus motives are as much subject to historical and cultural variation as are material or institutional constraints on conduct.

However it is not necessary to assume a constant human nature or to postulate predominant and universal motives to make the error of presuming a one-to-one link between action and motive, as many historians who would no doubt repudiate the former assumptions seem ready to accept the latter. Yet it must be forcibly stated that there is no good reason whatsoever for presuming that a particular activity must always stem from a given motive. It is not just that there are grounds for doubting whether consumption arises out of emulative desires or production from greed or self-interest, but that there are grounds for doubting whether any general transcultural correspondence exists between particular activities and motives. On the contrary, the evidence suggests that any one activity may stem from any one or more motives, just as any one motive may give rise to various activities. In addition, an activity initiated for one motive may be continued for another, whilst one over-riding motive may lead to a sequence of different acts.

WEBER AND THE MOTIVES OF CAPITALISM

It is to Weber's great credit that he perceived these truths with some clarity, firmly repudiating the view that capitalism was to be understood as the outcome of acquisitiveness. The reason for scepticism, as he makes clear, is that 'an uncontrolled impulse to make money' seems to be present in many people in many different societies. It is an impulse which 'exists and has existed among waiters, physicians, coachmen, artists, prostitutes, dishonest officials, soldiers, nobles, crusaders, gamblers and beggars' having been 'common to sorts and conditions of men at all times and in all countries of the earth'.[27] Indeed, he goes on to claim that not only is 'the greed for gold' 'no less powerful outside of bourgeois capitalism' than within it,[28] but that an 'absolute unscrupulousness in the pursuit of selfish interests by the making of money' is even more common in traditional than in modern societies.[29] From this he deduces that the 'impulse to acquisition' can have nothing whatsoever to do with capitalism or its spirit.[30] A conclusion which might perhaps be more accurately expressed by saying that such a motive has no special or distinctive relationship to capitalist activity and

---

[27] Weber, *The Protestant Ethic and the Spirit of Capitalism,* trans. Talcott Parsons, London: Unwin Books, 1930, p. 17.

[28] Weber, *The Protestant Ethic,* p. 56.

[29] Weber, *The Protestant Ethic,* p. 60.

[30] Weber, *The Protestant Ethic,* p. 17. One reason for this conclusion is that no 'instinct' can have anything to do with capitalism since capitalist activity requires systematic, organized rational conduct — conduct controlled by an 'ethic' — and this is incompatible with any form of 'impulsive behaviour.' Indeed an 'impulse' could not possibly be a 'motive' in Weber's terms.

hence cannot be invoked as its cause. But Weber also appreciated how the relationship between conduct and motives could change over time with a given activity being initiated for one motive only to be continued for another, and it is essentially for this reason that he treated the problem of the origins of modern capitalism as separate from that of its continuation.

One of the principal reasons for assuming that the originating motives were different from the perpetuating ones is that they lay behind conduct which challenged the established order. In other words, the first capitalists need to be regarded as acting out of 'revolutionary motives'.[31] This was necessary if the inertial force of tradition was to be overcome and what is most interesting in this context is Weber's observation that this cannot be achieved by a rational, calculating attitude; because, as he observes in his discussion of traditional economic attitudes, the pre-capitalist attitude is rational in its own terms. It involves the calculation of exactly how much work is needed in order to meet basic needs, whilst beyond that point leisure is preferred to additional work. This attitude has to be displaced so that the worker 'at least during working hours, is freed from continual calculations of how the customary wage may be earned with a maximum of comfort and a minimum of exertion. Labour must, on the contrary, be performed as if it were an absolute end in itself, a calling'.[32] In other words, modern bourgeois capitalism, which is characterized by a rational calculating attitude on the part of its economic agents, requires the suspension of just such an attitude with regard to work in order to emerge. The meaning attached to work must be a 'transcendent' and not an instrumental one; one must be motivated to work by the 'desire to show virtue and proficiency in a calling'[33] and not by the simple need to earn enough to maintain a standard of living. This is a good illustration of the earlier point about how the activities of individuals cannot be understood in terms of their intentions alone, but only by relating those intentions to outcomes or goals which have profound personal significance. In this case the crucial difference between understanding the work engaged in by traditional and modern 'capitalist' workers is that for the former it is seen as merely a means to the further goal of satisfying needs or enjoying leisure, whilst for the latter it is a goal in itself. In addition, as Weber demonstrates, it is only possible to understand this particular 'motive' by comprehending the larger system of beliefs and attitudes which causes work to be accorded this special significance. The common activity of 'work' can thus be seen to have contrasting meanings and to be undertaken out

---

[31]   At the same time, as Weber makes clear, all innovators are typically met with mistrust, hatred and moral indignation and hence need to act with intense self-confidence and conviction (*The Protestant Ethic*, p. 69). This is most likely to stem from some belief or beliefs which involves a 'transcendent' reference.

[32]   Weber, *The Protestant Ethic*, p. 61.

[33]   Weber, *The Protestant Ethic*, p. 54.

of different motives in a 'traditional' and 'modern bourgeois' society. But Weber also carried this analysis forward, recognizing that the 'originating motives' might fade away and be replaced by other 'perpetuating motives'. Thus, in the course of his discussion of the characteristic attitudes of modern capitalists, he notes that 'the desire to eat well may be a correct though incomplete characterization of the motives of many nominal Protestants in Germany at the present time. But things were very different in the past'.[34] Then the operative motives were the glory of God and a concern with one's own salvation, but over time these religious motives first 'gradually passed over into sober economic virtues',[35] and then finally became stripped of even this ethical meaning as the pursuit of wealth became little more than a 'sport'.[36] At the same time capitalism came to rest on 'purely mechanical foundations' with the result that there is no longer a 'conscious acceptance of (the) ethical maxims' which constituted the spirit of capitalism,[37] with the result that anyone, whether manufacturer or worker, who does not adhere to the iron rules of capitalism will be 'thrown into the streets without a job'.[38]

Now this description of the way in which the meaning attached to an activity may decay and eventually disappear is central to Weber's pessimistic view of the nature of human existence in a world which he foresaw as increasingly dominated by the processes of disenchantment and rationalization. Considered in a more mundane and restricted context, however, it may be regarded as no more than part of a normal process through which the meanings attached to motives may atrophy when routinization sets in. Robert Merton, for example, has drawn attention to the widespread nature of the process which he calls 'the displacement of goals' through which 'that which was originally an instrumental value becomes a terminal value'.[39] His example, drawn from a study of bureaucracies, concerns the manner in which upholding the rules of an organization, although originally conceived as no more than a means of achieving its ends, becomes for many bureaucrats the aim and object of their endeavours. Weber's analysis of attitudes toward work and money-making in capitalism employs a similar argument. An activity, the making of money, which originally had enormous significance to the individual because it was a means of indicating virtue and proficiency in a calling, gradually becomes merely an end in itself as the system of religious and ethical ideas which provided that meaning disappeared. In both cases individuals end up engaged in tasks which they have difficulty in justifying or rendering fully

---

[34] Weber, *The Protestant Ethic*, p. 41.

[35] Weber, *The Protestant Ethic*, p. 176.

[36] Weber, *The Protestant Ethic*, p. 182.

[37] Weber, *The Protestant Ethic*, p. 54.

[38] Weber, *The Protestant Ethic*, p. 55.

[39] Robert K. Merton, *Social Theory and Social Structure*, rev. and enlarged edn., Glencoe, Illinois: Free Press, 1968, p. 199.

meaningful, either to themselves or others. In this respect, their conduct becomes characterized as 'habit' and may begin to resemble 'behaviour'. Weber makes this point repeatedly, observing that modern capitalists are hard put to account for their continuing accumulation of wealth.

> If you ask them what is the meaning of their restless activity, why they are never satisfied with what they have, thus appearing so senseless to any purely worldly view of life, they would perhaps give the answer, if they know any at all: 'to provide for my children and grandchildren. But more often and, since that motive is not peculiar to them, but was just as effective for the traditionalist, more correctly, simply: that business with its continuous work has become a necessary part of their lives. That is in fact the only possible motivation, but it at the same time expresses what is, seen from the view-point of personal happiness, so irrational about this sort of life, where a man exists for the sake of his business, instead of the reverse.[40]

Such a person, Weber says, engages in business 'because he must' getting nothing out of his wealth except 'the irrational sense of having done his job well'.[41] What in effect Weber is saying is that such conduct does not have a 'motive' as such (even though it is clearly motivated) having become a habitual form of conduct.[42]

This last example raises an important issue concerning the status of an individual's understanding of his or her own conduct, for whilst earlier it was argued that the interpretive method demanded that explanations of conduct should accord a central role to the subjective meanings of actors, the conclusion reached here is that some conduct may not be accompanied by any such meaning. In claiming that modern capitalists work 'because they must' and that accumulating wealth provides them with an 'irrational' sense of satisfaction, Weber clearly implies that these individuals don't really know why they are doing what they are, and that their conduct is effectively 'meaningless'. Obviously if this is really the case then what they are doing is not 'action' according to his own definition and hence not capable of an interpretive understanding. Although, as we have seen, this does not exclude the possibility of discovering, through historical investigation, the original meanings which accompanied the introduction of such a pattern of conduct, it does cast doubt on the value of attempting to solicit subjective meanings from those currently engaged in them.[43] Unfortunately, as Weber himself

---

[40] Weber, *The Protestant Ethic*, p. 70.

[41] Weber, *The Protestant Ethic*, p. 71.

[42] Charles Camic has drawn attention to the virtual neglect of the concept of habit by contemporary social scientists and also demonstrated its central role in Weber's work. See Charles Camic, 'The Matter of Habit', *American Journal of Sociology* 91 5 (March 1986) pp. 1039–1087.

[43] It is not suggested that individuals don't know what they are doing in the sense of what they intend, merely in the sense of what their motives are. There is a separate issue in psychology

recognizes, individuals may in such situations attempt to respond to the bewildered inquirer by producing what they hope will be seen as acceptable reasons for their conduct rather than admit that their actions are in some way 'meaningless'. He suggests, for example, that businessmen might be prompted to declare that their activity stems from a desire to provide for their children or grandchildren when, in practice, this plays little part in motivating their conduct.[44] This forces the investigator to consider the possibility that under some circumstances what individuals report about their own conduct may not be the key to its interpretation.

THE PROBLEM OF 'REAL MOTIVES'

There are some traditions of thought which have routinely claimed that investigators should discount what actors have to say about their actions in favour of observer-based interpretations and which consequently frequently contrast nominal or expressed motives with what are claimed to be the 'underlying' or 'real' ones. Psychoanalysis is obviously one such tradition, whilst Marxist social thought also tends to endorse the discounting of expressed or avowed motives in favour of the 'real forces' revealed through 'objective analysis'. In fact, the universal, mono-motive theories mentioned above can only be made to appear plausible if the very apparent variation in expressed motives is explained away in such a fashion. There are two main strategies favoured here. Firstly, individuals are assumed to be well aware of their 'real' motives but to be covering them up or dissembling by advancing spurious reasons for their conduct. In other words, their expressed motives are mere rationalizations or justifications for conduct and should be understood as such. Secondly, individuals can be assumed to be quite unaware of the 'real motives' which are actually determining their conduct, sincerely believing that they are indeed acting for the reasons they give. It is merely that the experienced and informed observer of their conduct is in a position to see that this is not the case.

To deal with the second argument first. The essence of this is the claim that what might appear to be action (in Weber's sense) is actually behaviour and that although individuals think they are acting voluntarily in pursuit of their chosen goals and in full consciousness of their motives, their conduct is actually being determined by forces of which they are unaware. Thus this argument actually

---

concerning how far individuals can be said to have a correct understanding of either their own cognitive activity or the causes of their behaviour. See as important contributions to this debate, Richard E. Nisbett and Timothy DeCamp Wilson, 'Telling More Than We Can Know: Verbal Reports on Mental Processes' *Psychological Reports* 84 3 (May 1977), and John McClure, 'Telling More than They can Know: The Positivist Account of Verbal Reports and Mental Processes', *Journal for the Theory of Social Behaviour* 13 2 (1983) pp. 111–127.

[44] Weber, *The Protestant Ethic*, p. 70.

turns out to relate to the central issue, noted earlier, of distinguishing action from behaviour. The point here being that whilst the subject believes it to be the former, the observer knows it to be the latter. But of course the presumption that whole areas of conduct which individuals believe to be willed on their part are, in reality, 'determined' by forces they don't recognize, has to be shown to be valid in each case. It cannot simply be posited as a self-evident axiom.[45] Even then, of course, some explanation of the nature and form of the consciously, avowed purposes is still required. However, the basic argument has already been accepted. If what is under discussion is 'behaviour' then indeed it would be inappropriate to base one's explanation upon actors' subjective meanings. It should be clear, however, that the term 'motive' is not really applicable to such conduct. From an interpretative and phenomenological perspective there cannot be 'unconscious' or 'subconscious' motives, only drives, instincts or responses, for 'motive' refers specifically to 'a complex of subjective meaning which seems . . . an adequate ground for the conduct in question'.[46]

The first argument is more interesting, recognizing as it does that human beings are capable of deceit and therefore that the motives which are avowed and expressed may not be those which accompanied the conduct in question. Such a view is understandable, although it naturally requires that some grounds be given to justify such a suspicion, as it would seem unreasonable to claim that lying constitutes a standard and universal human response. The difficulties with this position can be illustrated by turning once again to Veblen's theory of conspicuous consumption. This is a pertinent example because those who make use of this theory frequently observe that consumers seem reluctant to admit that their purchases are governed by considerations of status, let alone prompted by emulative desires. Although Veblen himself is somewhat ambiguous on this point, at times apparently content to assume that individuals will readily confess to such motives and at others suggesting that consumers might be inclined to dissemble,[47] other commentators have been more forthright. Thus Mason states that the conspicuous consumer 'anxious to display wealth and gain in prestige, will rarely if ever explicitly admit to any such intentions'.[48] Such a claim immediately raises

---

[45] See Jon Elster, *Sour Grapes: Studies in the subversion of rationality*. Cambridge: Cambridge University Press, 1983, chp. IV, for a cogent critique of this argument.

[46] Weber, *The Theory of Social and Economic Organization*, pp. 98–99.

[47] Whilst Veblen makes several comments which strongly suggest that he considers individuals to be consciously seeking to 'excel in pecuniary standing and so gain the esteem and envy of (their) fellow-men' (*The Theory of the Leisure Class*, p. 32) thereby deliberately emulating their social superiors, he also observes that most wasteful consumption 'does not stem from a conscious effort to excel in the expensiveness of . . . visible consumption' but that 'the law of conspicuous waste guides consumption . . . chiefly at the second remove.' (*The Theory of the Leisure Class*, p. 102).

[48] Roger S. Mason, *Conspicuous Consumption: A Study of Exceptional Consumer Behaviour*. Farnborough, Hants.: Gower Publishing, 1981, p. 42.

the question of why individuals should find it necessary to lie about their intentions. To which the usual answer given is that they do so because they know only too well that social climbers are regarded with disapproval. But then this answer only raises further questions. In particular it is difficult to understand why such behaviour should be subject to negative sanctions, if, as Veblen claims, it is the universal basis of consumer conduct. It certainly seems odd that whilst all consumers know only too well that their own behaviour and that of others is guided by this one over-riding consideration, they nevertheless conspire with each other to pretend that this is not the case and combine in condemning anyone who admits the truth. However could societies have become characterized by such a conspiracy? But then reflection suggests that this is a unconvincing account, implying as it does that not only all social and ethnic groups within one society, but even across all societies, are marked by such double standards of behaviour. A more realistic assumption would be that efforts to improve one's social position would be subject to differential evaluation by diverse social groups, as it has been in different civilizations and epochs, and although condemned in some, in others it would be either condoned or encouraged. Such an assumption would lead to the conclusion that the degree of openness in admitting to emulative intentions would correlate with the extent to which the conduct is itself endorsed. However, it would be unjustified to assume from this that consumers in those societies in which such conduct is condemned could therefore be presumed to be lying about their motives. For to do so would not only involve endorsing a universal monomotive theory of conduct but also constitute a failure to recognize that the prevailing value system of a society is as much a constituent ingredient in the construction of motives as it is in the creation of moral attitudes. There is therefore no good reason to accept the presumption that dissembling or lying is a standard feature of people's talk about their motives.

JUSTIFICATORY ACCOUNTS

There is, however, a rather more sophisticated version of this argument which, whilst also leading to the conclusion that actors' self-reports of their conduct should be treated with scepticism, emphasizes the fact that accounts are frequently justifications rather than merely lies. That is to say, the nature of the account should be understood as determined more by the accountant's need to represent conduct in a favourable light to those who may constitute a critical or hostile audience than by any desire to provide an accurate account of subjective experience. This claim goes beyond the simple suggestion that individuals may lie or dissemble to the further and more specific claim that what is said is presented in order to fulfil the function of justifying the conduct in question. According to this perspective, accounts should not be understood in relation to the events which they supposedly describe but rather in terms of the social situation of 'account-ability' in which they are presented. In sociology this perspective is most closely associated with the name of C. Wright Mills, and has come to be known (some-what misleadingly) as the 'vocabulary of motives' approach.[49] Mills rejected the traditional view of motives as constituting 'springs of action' located 'within' indi-viduals, arguing that 'motives are words' which stand for 'anticipated situational consequences of questioned conduct'.[50] This leads on to his definition of a motive as 'a word which is to the actor and to the other members of a situation an un-questioned answer to questions concerning social and lingual conduct'.[51] In other words, 'motives are accepted justifications for present, future or past programs or acts'.[52]

This is a perspective which tends to present the imputation and avowal of motives by actors as the phenomenon to be explained (rather than that tradition which favours turning to the concept of motive in order to explain the conduct of individuals), and attempts to do so by proposing two linked hypotheses. Firstly, there is the claim that individuals learn vocabularies of motive, along with rules and norms of action for various situations, through the common processes of so-cialization. Hence just as we learn the appropriate language, values and attitudes for each social situation which we occupy so too do we learn what form of motives to ascribe to our own conduct. This view leads to the assumption that operative motives are compartmentalized in individuals, being manifested according to sit-uation, and that motives should thus be studied as correlates of occupation or social class.[53] Mills illustrates this by referring to the businessman who articulates the motives of self-interest and money-making whilst acting in the marketplace but promptly proclaims a public spirited vocabulary when speaking as a mem-ber of the Rotary Club,[54] and by referring to people who change their declared motives when moving from one class to another. This position has also been en-dorsed by Talcott Parsons, who similarly emphasized the view that the true lo-cation of motives was to be found in institutions rather than in individuals. He too rejects the simple notion that individuals might possess a 'drive' to acquisi-

---

[49] C. Wright Mills, 'Situated Actions and Vocabularies of Motive', *American Sociological Review* 5 (1940), 904–913. For a review of the work in this tradition see G. R. Semin and A. S. R. Manstead, *The Accountability of Conduct: A Social Psychological Analysis*. London: Academic Press, 1983. The phrase has become a misleading designation because the focus has actually shifted from a concern with the vocabulary of motive terms to an analysis of motive talk.

[50] C. Wright Mills, p. 905.

[51] C. Wright Mills, p. 907.

[52] C. Wright Mills, p. 907.

[53] Karl Mannheim makes some interesting observations on how motives vary with social class, claiming that whilst the proletariat work in order to earn a living and the middle classes for the sake of power and prestige, the intelligentsia seek the intrinsic satisfaction which only a vocation can supply. (*Man and Society in an Age of Reconstruction: Studies in Modern Social Structure*. London: Routledge & Kegan Paul.), 1935. Rev. and enlarged 1940, p. 315f.

[54] C. Wright Mills, p. 908.

tion, stressing that the 'profit motive' is a 'situationally generalized goal which is learned in the course of what has been called the secondary socialization process', and that 'it is not general to human beings, but is very specifically culture-bound to certain types of roles in specific social systems'.[55] Secondly there is the claim that the nature and content of the public avowals of motives can be understood 'functionally' in terms of the individual's need to justify his conduct in that particular situation.

However, the fact that motives can be seen — like other cultural material — to have a social and institutional location does not mean that one cannot engage in motivational-style explanations of conduct. People may indeed change their motives when moving from one social location to another but this does not mean that the expressed motives are not real and effective all the same. If the processes of socialization proceeded correctly and the appropriate values and norms were internalized then the motives articulated in any one situation should indeed be regarded as the individual's real motives. A more difficult problem is presented by the issue of justification.

The crux of this argument is the claim that accounts are linked less to the actions which they supposedly describe than to the context in which they are presented, and it is a claim which assumes, not only that the need to justify actions is universal, but that this is likely to lead to a discrepancy between 'truthful' and actual reports. However, it cannot automatically be assumed either that the need to justify conduct is universal or that it necessarily leads to a discrepancy of this kind. The fact that some individuals are, in some situations, called upon to justify their actions to a suspicious or critical audience does not mean that all are (or will consider themselves to be) under all circumstances. Much conduct is routine or habitual in character and as such frequently passes without comment and hence without the need for overt justification. On the other hand, however, this form of 'behaviour' rarely features in self-reports whilst 'action' is indeed typically accompanied by justifications.[56] More to the point is the fact that because an actor perceives a need to justify or excuse an action this does not mean that what is said is thereby merely a justification or an excuse, for the truth may fulfil these functions perfectly well. It follows that establishing that an account fulfils a justificatory function is not thereby to prove that it is untrue. At the most it could be considered grounds for inquiring further into its validity.

The significant mistake which is made in relation to the concept of justification, therefore, is to assume that it provides support for the view that accounts

---

[55] Talcott Parsons, 'The Motivation of Economic Activities' in *Essays in Sociological Theory*, rev. edn. Glencoe: Illinois.: The Free Press. 1954, p. 243.

[56] At least one analyst has actually chosen this as the defining feature of meaningful conduct claiming that 'social behaviour can therefore be defined quite simply as justified action.' See Richard Totman, *Social and Biological Roles of Language: The Psychology of Justification*. London: Academic Press, 1985, p. 74.

cannot be relied on as sources of valid information about the actions to which they refer, when all it actually indicates is that accounts may be 'dynamically' related to the contexts of their 'production'. Whether this dynamic relationship is such as to obscure or reveal the truth remains an open question. In other words, the fact that the form and content of an account may be 'functionally' related to its context of 'production' does not automatically mean that it is therefore inaccurate or unreliable. The need to satisfy the expectations of one's listeners, or to meet the normative requirements of the role one occupies, may, under some circumstances, cause the 'accountant' to dissemble, distort or qualify actions in a manner thought to render them acceptable. But, on other occasions, it may work in the opposite direction, causing the individual to abandon such dissembling, and recognizing an obligation to be truthful, strive to 'tell it like it was'. Such one might say, are the normative expectations surrounding the role of confessant, or indeed that of a witness in a court of law.

However, despite these grounds for scepticism concerning the extent to which the need for justification might be viewed as a serious obstacle to the use of self-initiated reports as a guide to conduct, there is a sense in which justifications can be considered to be fundamentally implicated in all action. The nature of this relationship is hinted at by C. Wright Mills when he observes that individuals often imagine the possible outcomes of their conduct before embarking on a course of action. He writes: 'Often anticipations of acceptable justifications will control conduct. "If I did this, what could I say? What would they say?" Decisions may be, wholly, or in part, delimited by answers to such queries'.[57] Now this is an interesting observation. Firstly because it makes the actor's imaginative activity in anticipating a future possibility the crucial factor which brings the justification into being (rather than the directly experienced need to justify actions arising from the 'context of justification') and, secondly, it suggests that the construction of what the actor takes to be acceptable justifications might be a prerequisite for embarking on a course of conduct in the first place.

This second point has been taken up by Quentin Skinner in his study of the functions of political thought. Here he stresses that although it is usual for people to believe that a political agent first decides upon a course of action and then subsequently 'professes just those principles which best serve to describe what he is doing in morally acceptable terms', thereby relating the selection of these principles to his conduct in a purely *ex post facto* manner, this is to 'misunderstand the role of the normative vocabulary which any society employs for the description and appraisal of its political life'.[58] He continues by illustrating his point:

---

[57] C. Wright Mills, p. 907.

[58] Quentin Skinner, *The Foundations of Modern Political Thought, Vol. 1. The Renaissance*, Cambridge: Cambridge University Press, 1978, p. XII.

Consider, for example, the position of an agent who wishes to say of an action he has performed that it was honorable. To offer this description is certainly to commend as well as to describe what has been done. And as Machiavelli shows, the range of actions which can plausibly be brought under this heading may turn out — with the exercise of a little ingenuity — to be unexpectedly wide. But the term obviously cannot be applied with propriety to describe *any* Machiavellian course of action, but only those which can be claimed with some show of plausibility to meet the pre-existing criteria for the application of the term. It follows that anyone who is anxious to have his behaviour recognized as that of a man of honour will find himself restricted to the performance of only a certain range of actions. Thus the problem facing an agent who wishes to legitimate what he is doing at the same time as gaining what he wants cannot simply be the instrumental problem of tailoring his normative language in order to fit his projects. It must be in part be the problem of tailoring his projects in order to fit the available normative language.[59]

The importance of this observation lies in the way in which it suggests that the processes of motivation and justification should be seen as inextricably inter-twined. There are not two processes, separated in time, with conduct first moti-vated and then subsequently justified; but one process in which individuals for-mulate plans to engage in 'justifiable actions'. However, even this reformulation is inadequate in so far as it still carries the implication that individuals experience the 'available normative language' as a constraint and that their principal concern in devising their projects is to tailor them to the expectations of others. This is not so, for actors have an equally powerful need to 'justify' their actions to them-selves: or, more accurately, to engage in what they themselves see as 'legitimate conduct'.

Again it was Weber more than any other theorist who perceived the inti-mate connection between motivation and legitimation and whose discussion of the rise of capitalism focuses on the issue of how it was that individuals came to believe that they were *right* to see the making of money as their dominant pur-pose in life. The problem of understanding the motivation of the early capitalists and the way in which the value system of society itself changed to accommodate capitalism is one and the same; it is the question, as Weber puts it, of how 'an ac-tivity, which was at best ethically tolerated', could 'turn into a calling in the sense of Benjamin Franklin?'.[60] Whilst one can, for the sake of convenience, treat the is-sues of motivation and legitimation separately, Weber's theory of action presents them as intimately connected, arguing that the individual's overwhelming pre-disposition is to engage in 'moral conduct'. This means that an exploration of the

---

[59] Quentin Skinner, *The Foundations of Modern Political Thought*, p. XII.

[60] Weber, *The Protestant Ethic*, p. 74.

motives of capitalism is less an investigation into those terms 'which appear to the actor himself and/or to the observer to be an adequate reason for his conduct'[61] — which was Weber's shorthand version of his definition of this crucial concept — but rather 'those terms which appear to the actor to be adequate and legitimate grounds for his conduct.'

If this understanding of conduct is now applied to the problem of the eighteenth century revolution in consumption and the presentation of Thorstein Veblen's theory of conspicuous consumption as the standard 'solution', then its central weakness becomes very obvious. For if it is indeed the case that individuals commonly experience the need to engage in legitimate conduct how can a revolution in consumption have been accomplished by large groups of people engaging in activities which were universally condemned? At the very least, one would have expected some countervailing moral claims which could have served to provide some legitimacy to the activity of social climbing.[62] It is for this reason that this writer has elsewhere suggested an alternative explanation, one which attempts to embody some of the principal conclusions reached in this discussion.[63] It is an approach which attempts to start, not with some arbitrarily imposed category of conduct such as 'consumption' but with the actor's own world view and, in particular, its moral and ethical dimensions. Once these have been established it becomes possible to perceive what forms of conduct eighteenth century members of the 'middling classes' might have considered it 'right' and 'proper' to undertake and what, by contrast, they may have viewed as 'reprehensible'. This is not a simple matter of learning what moral code was publicly endorsed, but rather, as Weber demonstrated, a matter of discovering what might be the predominant and practical moral concerns of individuals. It is then, in the light of this knowledge, that their conduct is motivationally understood.

CONCLUSION

Although considerable emphasis has been given to the claim that the identification of subjective complexes of motive and meaning is essential to the explanation of human behaviour this should not be taken as implying that this is *all* that is needed to explain human conduct. Rather, following Weber, the assumption is that the investigator's aim is to 'attempt the interpretive understanding of social

---

[61] Weber, *The Theory of Social and Economic Organization*, p. 116.

[62] This problem is partly acknowledged by McKendrick et al. (See *The Birth of a Consumer Society*, pp. 14–16.) but they seem to think that it is the consumption of luxury goods which needs justifying when really the motive and not just the activity requires legitimation.

[63] See Colin Campbell, *The Romantic Ethic and the Spirit of Modern Consumerism*, esp. Part 2.

action in order thereby to arrive at a causal explanation of its effects'.[64] A process which accords what people think that they are doing a crucial place in any such explanation without presupposing that individuals always know what they are doing. Indeed, as has been stressed earlier, human conduct is a mixture of action — which can only be understood via the actor's subjective meanings — and behaviour, for which such an approach would be entirely inappropriate. What is critical, however, is that once one has set aside the relatively small number of trivial responses which the observer can unequivocally identify as behaviour (such as sneezing, blinking, etc.), it is not possible for the external observer to judge in relation to any given sequence of conduct how far what is being witnessed falls into one or other of these two categories. A difficulty rendered more intransient because of the marked tendency for action to become routinized over time into those special behavioural-type categories called habit and ritual whilst, under special circumstances, these can in their turn become transformed back into action. It is therefore necessary for this reason alone that any analysis must begin with an attempt to comprehend the viewpoint of the actors and thereby establish what actions they consider themselves to be undertaking. This will not only provide a basis for distinguishing between the two categories of conduct in this instance but will serve to establish what constitutes the unit of action which is open to meaningful understanding. Once this has been done it is open to the investigator to link the action in question both to the actor's personal world of psychic gratification and to the cultural world of beliefs, values and attitudes with which it is inextricably intertwined. Only in this way is the conduct in question open to motivational understanding and therefore to any form of satisfactory explanation.

If the individual's subjective understanding of what he or she is doing is not taken as the starting point for investigation but the analyst relies instead upon direct observational understanding of the conduct in question then certain difficulties will be encountered. In the first place, unless the conduct in question can be clearly identified as behaviour, any such externally based comprehension can only really amount to a description of action in intentionalist form and cannot provide an explanation. Even here, however, there is grave danger of misattributing intentions. If, however, the analyst is tempted to frame accounts in an explanatory form then they will usually involve invoking universal monomotive theories and hence lack the capacity to explain why the particular conduct in question has occurred when and where it did.

Since any given pattern of conduct — as identified by an external observer — may actually be consistent with a variety of motives and meanings there is an ever-present danger that the analyst, having found an explanation in terms of motive and meaning which seems to fit the data, will not then seek to confirm the

---

[64] Weber, *Theory of Social and Economic Organization*, p. 88.

correctness of this diagnosis. This problem is exemplified in many treatments of consumption behaviour, where, because the social emulation hypothesis appears applicable, it is unquestionably accepted as correct with no attempt made to investigate alternative interpretations. Clearly the important first stage of any analysis should be to recognize the possible existence of alternative hypotheses, whilst the crucial and difficult second stage is to try and determine which is congruent with the operative subjective meanings. However, the more fundamental problem, as indicated earlier, is the initial arbitrary judgement concerning the item of conduct to be studied. This, as we saw, was an observer-invented category called 'consumption'. But as Schutz has noted, the unity of action cannot be determined by an observer, for 'what use is it to talk about the intended meaning of an action if one ignores that phase of the action which is relevant to the actor and substitute for it as the interpretation an arbitrarily chosen segment of the observed performance . . .?'[65] In other words, the analyst cannot proceed by first choosing an item of conduct and then seeking its 'subjective meaning' but must instead start with the actor's world of subjective meaning and discover how it is divided into units.[66]

Such an interpretive approach naturally presents the researcher with considerable methodological problems, ones which appear especially intractable for the historian who lacks the option, open to the sociologist, of directly interrogating subjects. However, this may not be such an overwhelming obstacle, nor indeed constitute a such marked difference in method between the two disciplines. This is because the focus of attention is less on the conduct of individual persons than on types or categories of actions performed by distinct classes of peoples and it is the complexes of meaning collectively adhered to by these groups and manifest in beliefs, values and attitudes, which form the starting point for any investigation. Since these are embodied in the historical record in manifold forms such meanings are, in principle, easily recoverable. What is more difficult to reconstitute and yet, as the above discussion has attempted to show, is in effect the essence of any successful explanation of conduct whether past or present, is the distinct motivational form of such complexes as they are experienced by individuals engaged in the practical day-to-day business of realizing their goals, satisfying their desires or achieving their ambitions through legitimate actions.

---

[65] Schutz, *The Phenomenology of the Social World*, p. 62.

[66] This stress on the understanding of motives and associated meanings should not be understood as implying that all explanations in either the social sciences or the humanities are necessarily psychological in form. Rather what is being claimed is that any successful explanation must make reference to the concept of motive. This can be done without endorsing an extreme methodological individualism if these assumptions are embodied in ideal-type accounts or associated with structural and cultural variations. In addition, there will always be a need to examine those aspects of human conduct, such as unintended consequences, which have no relationship to motives.

CHAPTER TWO

Consuming Interests

Orvar Löfgren

It's Daria's thirtieth birthday party. There are fifteen or twenty people in the room; I don't know most of them. Stash and I sit on the couch and watch her open her presents; the gift from us of a Godzilla lighter (flames shoot out of Godzilla's mouth); a record of Maria Callas singing Norma; a silk survival map of the Arctic Circle; a glue gun; a casette tape of Teenage Jesus and the Jerks; a a large black plastic object with a pink pyramid-shaped cover (possibly made by the Memphis Design Collective) which might be a bread box or an ice bucket; a ten-pound bag of Eukanuba health food for dogs; a book about wrestling; and a Statue of Liberty hat - a spiky helmet of flexible foam. Daria puts it on.

I know that this assortment of gifts means something specific and symbolic about people my age who live in New York and are involved in the arts. A list of gifts received by a flapper in the Jazz Age could tell you things about the period, and this stuff has significance as well. But what the gifts actually represent, I have no idea. (Janowitz 1986:154)

$\mathbf{D}$eep down in the jungles of Lower Manhattan there lived in the 1980s an exotic tribe, sometimes called "the slaves of New York". Further north along Park Avenue one entered the territory of "yuppiedom", depicted by Tom Wolfe in his *The Bonfire of the Vanities* from 1987. These Manhattan subcultures have often been used to symbolize a truly postmodern way of life: a world of free-floating signs, fragments and fads, a shallow and superficial lifestyle. Here is a commodified world where things may signify anything, everything or nothing.

The rise of a new interest in the cultural analysis of consumption in the eighties has often been linked to a postmodern cosmology with strong evolution-ary or devolutionary overtones. Contemporary culture was described in terms of the birth of new kind of consumerism, a hyper-consumption. The evolutionary element is conjured up in concepts like "postmodern consumption", "late con-sumer capitalism" or "advanced consumer culture", to borrow a few phrases from an ethnography of a Pennsylvania suburb (Dorst 1989). The other side of the coin has to do with a devolutionary premise: the assumption that contemporary history is the history of a gradual but irreversible erosion of stable social identities and ways of life. Traditional forms of continuity and integration give way to a new kind of social being, who is a master of the new art of lifestyling.

I am not, however, quite convinced that everyday life in the eighties was postmodernized to the same extent as some of the culture theory of that decade. It may well be that we live in a period where the consumption profiles of individuals are more fragmented and fluid than before. If this is the case, it may be interesting to ask how we in our everyday lives succeed in dealing with such fragmentation and fluidity, and what role consumption actually plays in this adaptation. The danger lies in equating the quickened turnover of commodities with postulates of changes in personality structure.

Another problem of the postmodern debate is that arguments like the ones above have a familiar ring to them - they belong to a specific and fairly old tradition: the critique of consumer society. To what extent are we dealing with a recurring genre or with profound changes in social life?

I will start with a discussion of these questions and then move on to a more empirical presentation of an ongoing research project on consumption as Utopia, ideological battlefield and everyday practice in twentieth century Sweden.

THE RETURN OF THE YUPPIE

Facing the choice between plague and cholera they have opted for expensive things. They are facing the problem, not of living but of living in a grand manner. They wear neckties which stand in geometrical proportion to their lapels and wear well-mannered and quiet shoes. They prefer Porsches and American Gold Express Cards... They usually have a grand piano in their expensive flats or hasten to acquire one, in order to give their party guests something to lean on, champagne glasses in hand.

This is a 1980s newspaper version of a traditional argument: the birth of a new breed of overconsumers, whether they are called nouveaux riches, parvenus or "goulash barons", a breed usually characterized by having too much economic and too little cultural capital. There are many classic elements in this genre, for example the piano. For some reason it has been especially infuriating to witness upstarts investing in this particular piece of furniture. Already in eighteenth century England the old elite made sarcastic comments about new capitalists who bought pianos for their daughters. In late nineteenth century Sweden a stock joke about well-to-do farmers was that they bought pianos not for putting champagne glasses on but rather in order to have somewhere to put their hats. In the 1930s a popular type of social classification talked about four Swedish strata: those without both piano and education, those with education but no piano, people with piano but without education and the happy category who possessed both.

The piano has been a key symbol of civilized manners, but also a social marker guarding the boundary between the two rival camps of economic and cultural elites in the Bourdieuan sense. (There is even some empirical evidence for this: an ongoing study of the Swedish middle class shows that the ownership of a piano is the safest way of identifying the cultural wing.)

The importance of the piano illustrates one theme in the yuppie discourse and its many earlier forerunners. It is a genre often used by intellectuals or traditional elites for waging a cultural battle on several fronts, both against the vulgarities of mass consumption in the lower classes and against the tasteless over-consumption of the newly rich.

Another theme in this genre has to do with the disintegration of social identity and the emergence of a *homo consumens*, whose fragmented identity is constantly rearranged by the winds of fashions. Behind such arguments we often find a (conscious or unconscious) comparison: in the good old days there existed *authentic* ways of life, *real* personalities, stable and well-integrated identities. This kind of discourse can be traced back in history, as the historian Jean-Christophe Agnew (1987) has shown in his study of the emergence of the Theatrical Man in seventeenth century England and America, a type of inauthentic role player linked to ideas about a market-directed personality.

Most of the present-day arguments, however, have their roots in the critique of consumer society developed among members of the Frankfurt School. From Adorno's and Horkheimer's attacks on mass culture in the thirties and forties to Erich Fromm's version of the new market personality who transforms everything (including himself) into a commodity; from personal values to his smile.

There is a basic structure behind the historical variants of such descriptions of "the new personality" or Modern Man. One corner-stone is the previously quoted idea of over-consumption or *commodification* — these new people lack a true self but carry themselves through life with the help of commodities: consumption gives their life structure, meaning and direction. The second has to do with a basic notion of *shallowness* (or emptiness) — there is no real depth in the personalities, beliefs and activities of such persons (i.e. they have attitudes rather than values, they lack authenticity, being performers rather than moral beings). Thirdly there is the idea of *fragmentation*: a lack of integration and coherence.

A semantic analysis of this kind of argumentation is important, because the recurrent use of metaphors like deep/shallow, whole/ fragmented, real/faked can be both powerful and seductive. A metaphor like shallowness may, for example, colonize other arguments. The advent of television, which was described as a one-dimensional media with its flickering, fast-changing images, tempted some observers to project the same qualities on to the viewers: a shallow medium produced shallow personalities.

It would, however, be a gross simplification to reduce the critique of consumer society to the constant rebirth of a traditional genre. What is interesting are the changing ways in which this kind of argumentation is given cultural form and direction during different historical periods. In that sense the yuppie of the 1980s is not a simple clone of the dandy of the 1780s or the railway baron of the 1880s. We need to ask at what points in history this kind of argumentation is carried out, by whom and against whom? Which groups are singled out as the victims of consumerism and market manipulation? Who is accused of crossing the boundary between necessary, reasonable consumption and the world of over-consumption? (In the twentieth century debate it is not only the social upstarts but the working class, the teenagers, the housewives and also the affluent American tourists or, more recently, inhabitants of what used to be called Eastern Europe, who are often described as extremely materialistic.) The reason I am stressing this is that when the critique of consumerism turns from an analysis of market forces and tactics to a discussion of the consumer it may slip into a problematic moralizing and often fall back on ideas about the false consciousness of those consuming "others": the passive victims, the easy prey.

Debates on over-consumption may often be linked to another problematic issue in consumer theory: that of a watershed idea, the attempt to locate a consumer revolution in space and history. The candidates are numerous: Late Middle Ages (Lipovetsky 1987), eighteenth century England (McKendrick *et al.* 1985), mid nineteenth century France (Williams 1982) or three different periods in the USA: the late nineteenth century (Fox and Lears 1983), the years between the two World Wars (Marchand 1985) and the postwar "Affluent Society" (Galbraith 1958), to name a few.

Rather than trying to choose between these contestants it seems more fruitful to look at what kind of arguments and what kind of processes are emphasized in the different interpretations. The disagreement is at least partly the result of a vagueness in the conceptual apparatus. What is actually meant by consumer society or mass consumption? What is it we compare when measuring a before and after, is it quantative or qualitative changes? The very use of concepts such as "mass consumption" and "modern consumption", moreover, often implicitly presupposes a polarity: a "traditional consumption", which is seldom defined.

The consumer society has been defined as a system where wants are satisfied through a market or as a society with mass production and mass marketing of goods; it can be based upon the role consumption plays in identity formation or as a pervasive element in the society studied. There will probably never develop a consensus around definitions like these, but that is not necessary as long as the concept is contextualized.[1]

The watershed approach often gets trapped in an evolutionary argument about more or less. But if we look at the examples mentioned above they not only talk about periods of increased consumption of certain material goods, but also about times when the cultural phenomenon of consumption is very much on the public agenda. It thus seems reasonable to distinguish between situations of intensified consumption or of intensified *debate* about consumption (or periods which are characterized by both).

THE LIFE CYCLES OF COMMODITIES

A comparative historical analysis of consumption may help us to problematize the role of consumption as action, utopia or moral dilemma in different settings over time, but the historical perspective may also help us to understand certain processes of change. In developing their case for a consumer revolution in late eighteenth century England the historians McKendrick, Brewer and Plumb stress the ways in which consumer goods were made available to new groups in society but also how patterns of consumption were redefined as the market broadened and the turnover of goods speeded up:

> "As a result 'luxuries' came to be seen as mere 'decencies', and 'decencies' came to be seen as 'necessities'. Even 'necessities' underwent a dramatic metamorphosis in style, variety and availability.
> Where once material possessions were prized for their durability, they were now increasingly prized for their fashionability. Where once a fashion might last a lifetime, now it might barely last a year." (McKendrick *et al.* 1985:1)

Without worrying too much about whether this really should be called *The* Consumer Revolution, it seems fruitful to develop this discussion about the ways in which the boundaries between necessary consumption or overconsumption have been moved around. How are yesterday's consumption dreams transformed into new possibilities and later turned into trivialities? How does the exclusive become commonplace? How are traditional necessities changed into luxuries? Processes like these remind us of the ways in which the verbs of consumption have elusive definitions. The boundaries between wanting, desiring, needing, requiring, obtaining, controlling, using and owning are constantly changing.

Sidney Mintz has explored some of these processes in his study of the marketing and consumption of sugar. He discusses the expansion and incorporation

---

[1] (Cf. the discussion in Campbell 1987; Miller 1987 and Williams 1982.)

of new commodities, mentioning two types of "ritualization" (Mintz 1985:122 ff.). The first is *extensification*, the ways in which sugar is brought into new situations, becoming a more "homey" part of everyday habits, the second is *intensification*, "the attachment of sugar uses to ceremonial occasions harking back to older usage but freed of much of the social and political content they formerly carried", a process of ritual elaboration and emulation.

His tentative discussion could be developed into a more systematic analysis of the ways in which commodities or patterns of consumption are introduced, institutionalized, expanded and elaborated. Such a perspective also calls for a look at the other side of the coin, the ways in which traditional forms of consumption are dislocated or go out of fashion.

Igor Kopytoff (1986) has discussed similar processes in his appeal for a "biography of things". In our Swedish research project we have been looking at the history of the car, the radio and the television in this perspective, asking people to write a kind of consumption life history: my life as a car owner, radio listener and television viewer. In this material certain patterns emerge, for example in media use.

Both the introduction of radio and television at first meant a period of happy experimentation and a multitude of utopian schemes. As the new commodities reached the homes they were surrounded by a sacred and formal aura, which was also evident in the marketing. People remember the solemn atmosphere and the intense concentration in early radio listening, or the ways in which you dressed up for television evenings, hushing both grandma and the kids. Both the radio and the television set were given a prominent position in the best room, rather like home altars. Gradually the media became routine, people learned how to listen with half an ear or having the television on as background screen for conversation. The radio moved into the kitchen and the bedroom (see the discussion in Löfgren 1990).

Commodities like these may pass through a life cycle of sacralization to routinization or trivialization and then on to a process of cultural ageing which is often more rapid than the actual physical wear and tear. As they are redefined as anachronistic they are degraded or discarded, but some of them will undergo a recycling through which they may gradually be transformed into kitsch, nostalgia and finally antiques.

The material on car ownership tells a similar story. Here we can follow the ways in which the car has turned from sensation to routine during the twentieth century. In the pioneer days people could bring picnic baskets to the local main road in the hope of seeing a motorist and they vividly remember their first car ride: a very solemn moment or a festive event.

But cars are also a good example of what Igor Kopytoff calls the process of singularization, through which a commodity is personalized. The minute we drive away from the car dealer with a new vehicle two things happen: the market value falls drastically as the status of the car is transformed into a used one, and at the same time it becomes an extension of the owner, whose personal imprint makes itself felt in many ways.

In his book *The Crying of Lot 49* the American author Thomas Pynchon lets the secondhand car dealer Mucho Maas read such biographical messages - doing a personal archaeology of the car:

> [He was] seeing people poorer than himself come in, Negro, Mexican, cracker, a parade seven days a week, bringing in the most godawful of trade-ins: motorised, metal extensions of themselves, of their families and what their whole lives must be like, out there so naked for anybody, a stranger like himself, to look at, frame cockeyed, rusty underneath, fender repainted in a shade just off enough to depress the value, if not Mucho himself, inside smelling hopelessly of children, supermarket booze, two, sometimes three generations of cigarette smokers, or only of dust - and when the cars were swept out you had to look at the actual residue of these lives, and there was no way of telling what things had been truly refused (when so little he supposed came by that out of fear most of it had to to be taken and kept) and what had simply (perhaps tragically) been lost: clipped coupons, promising savings of 5 or 10c, trading stamps, pink flyers advertising specials at the markets, butts, tooth-shy combs, help-wanted ads, Yellow pages torn from the phone book, rags of old underwear or dresses that already were period costumes, for wiping your own breath off the inside of a windshield with so you could see whatever it was, a movie, a woman or a car you coveted, a cop who might pull you over for a drill, all the bits and pieces coated uniformly, like a salad of despair...

In the written representations of "my life with the car", people let their different cars materialize stations in life. A woman talks lovingly of her first teenage acquisition:

> The car I remember best was my first. She became a part of my teenage self. I called her "Olga". She was painted as loud as my teenage protests. She was very noisy when changing gears, but the sound level was supposed to be high during my teenage years.

She also recalls how proud the family felt every time Dad returned home with a new car, and this pattern is found in other answers. In retrospect life can become a drive along an upwardly mobile freeway, where the buying of better or bigger cars marks a family on the move, going somewhere.

LEARNING TO CONSUME

In a life history perspective of individuals rather than commodities there is a possibility of looking at the ways in which people learn consumer skills. This is the focus in the interviews on "my life as consumer" which we are carrying out as another part of the project. The aim is here to compare male and female consumers from different class backgrounds and age groups.

The interviews deal with the acquisition of consumer skills, starting with the early memories of learning how to construct a list of Christmas wishes or becoming a collector of tin soldiers or Smurf figures. These early memories often have a certain freshness: they are memories of the first confrontations with novel styles and scenes of consumption, such as the first visits to the department store or the eager reading of the new mail order catalogue at the kitchen table. They also stress the role of childhood consumption as a process of experimentation. A middle-aged woman with a working class background recalls:

> In my generation we had paper dolls. We never used the ready made cut out dresses but made our own. None of us girls came from homes where there was money for a lot of clothes. We got our ideas from the fashion pages of a more middle class ladies' journal, which we tried out as clothes for our paper dolls. In a way all these fantasies about clothes, creating some kind of image for those paper dolls, helped us to create an image of ourselves as girls or women.

There are other memories of the endless hours spent in front of the mirror, trying out styles, clothes and poses in order to find forms of self-expression. Another dominating theme in teenage consumer life has to do with learning the fine social distinctions. A middle-class woman in her fifties remembers the importance of moderation:

> You never dressed in too provocative a manner, or else you were classified as belonging to the rockers. You used make-up, but always very discreet — never too shiny...

Another woman describes the teenage battles with the parents over clothes and make-up, which ended in the lipstick being applied in the stairs outside the flat.

A special category of memories are found among those class travellers who where resocialized into new patterns of consumption, as they were introduced into middle-class circles. Memories of this transition can be crystallized into a situation or an object. A working class boy who, unlike his friends took the step up to grammar school in the sixties brought his moped to the new school only to find out that this cherished symbol of teenage affluence was not the thing to have in the new middle-class setting. "After a few days at school I sold it. You were supposed to have a plain, quality bike, nothing else."

There is often an organizing principle of "now" and "then" when people narrate their life as consumers. For some it becomes important to stress how one learnt how to make do with little and this often is meant as an (indirect) critique of the youngsters of today "who get everything for nothing" and who never learn to forsake desires or think twice about consumption. Such moral lessons can also be condensed into situations or objects.

A good example of this is the memory of the improvised football (which interestingly enough turns up in several life histories); a memory of how one made do with a football made out of rags or crumpled paper, while the rich kids could afford a real ball — or more often: "Nowadays, the kids demand all sorts of fancy equipment for their play — they are never content as we were — and probably not as happy as us."

Another common perspective deals with the feeling of having developed into a much more skilful and critical consumer: "Back in those early days I was so confused. Now I know what I want, I have found my personal style and taste." In the same way there might be a need to distance oneself from earlier ideals. A woman born in 1960 recalls how she longed for a room in pink with laces and frills, just like her working-class playmate had. At home a middle-class aesthetic of restraint and rationality ruled. Everything was to be simple, practical and of good quality. Slowly her admiration for the neighbour's pattern of consumption was turned into dissociation. It was the ideal of the parents that triumphed in the long run.

The need to distance oneself from earlier patterns of consumption often involves an element of irony, which illustrates the ways in which earlier habits and styles are "tackified". What was once most desirable, natural or elegant has been redefined into something hopelessly old-fashioned or comical: "How could I ever dress like that!"

There are striking class differences in the material. For example the life histories of intellectuals are characterized by an obsession with questions of distinction and taste. There is a recurrent need to distance oneself from other consumers, to stress one's role as a critical observer of the consumption habits of "the others". Individuality is a central virtue in this as in other aspects of middle-class cosmology.

DOMESTIC CONSUMPTION AS A MORAL PROJECT

The processes of learning and un-learning consumer skills are obvious in one specific field we are studying more closely: that of home furnishing. There are several reasons for choosing this arena of consumption. Outside observers often stress the strong emphasis Swedes put on the project of home-making and, statistically, Swedes spend more money on home furnishing than other Europeans. Since the 1930s a specific Swedish (and Scandinavian) tradition of "modern living" has evolved with a stress on light furniture, natural materials, mild colours and rational lay-outs.

Our study looks at the emergence of this Swedish passion on several levels: the ways in which the home and, its props are marketed, the important role of the welfare state in the planning and development of housing as well as domestic consumption, and the ways in which people actually design and use their dwellings.

At the beginning of this century home-making was an important topic both in public debate and among those groups who could afford to invest time and money in interior decoration. Elsewhere I have discussed the middle-class obsession with order and functional divisions in the home: the motto of "there is a time and place for everything" expressed a need to separate activities and people through the arrangement of rooms and passages. The extent to which a conscious effort was made to create different atmospheres for different rooms is mirrored both in contemporary advice from the growing body of professional interior decorators and the childhood memories from this period of bourgeois life. Boundaries of class, age and gender as well as between public and private were modelled through this stage-setting. Separate colours, fabrics and furniture were used for boys' and girls' rooms. Father's study (often forbidden territory) was preferably characterized by a masculine austerity and a disciplined order, echoing its role as a domestic incorporation of the sphere of production. The drawing-room was decorated in a way which emphasized its role as a main stage for greeting visitors, whereas a more relaxed and cosy atmosphere could be created in rooms mainly intended for family togetherness, etc. (cf. the discussion in Frykman and Löfgren 1987:125 ff).

The home was also a frequent topic in public debate. The Victorian cult of domesticity was part of a campaign for the moral rearmament of the lower classes. To become a home-builder was an important element in the sacred project of civilization and this tone also found its way into advertisements for home furnishings.

During the twenties and thirties the tone changed, the new cult of modernism and functionalism slowly entered the marketing world as well as the blueprints for the making of the new welfare state. The great Stockholm exhibition of 1930 became a major manifestation of the new functionalist ideas of modern living:

> A whole new city of steel, glass and concrete had been erected on the plain. Houses, restaurants and music grandstands looked like birds rising with stiff wings. In the crowd people spoke about the new architecture which would give birth to a new spirit of life. A door handle, a picture window, a matter-of-fact piece of furniture would in a short time influence the family living in the house so that their feelings and thoughts became open and transparent.

Thus the author Ivar Lo-Johansson (1957:5) recalls the appeals for modern living, a programme for reschooling Swedes into modern consumers by letting things teach them the lessons of modernity. But he also noted that many of the visitors flinched from the modern steel furniture and instead flocked around the old rocking chair, which had been placed in the corner of the model home as a bad example. In the new functionalist ideology such a piece of furniture symbolized a backward way of living. In the modern chrome chair your body was kept alert and upright, it was a piece of furniture for people on the move forward, not for those who thought that spare time should be frittered away by dozing in a rocking-chair or taking a nap on the kitchen sofa.

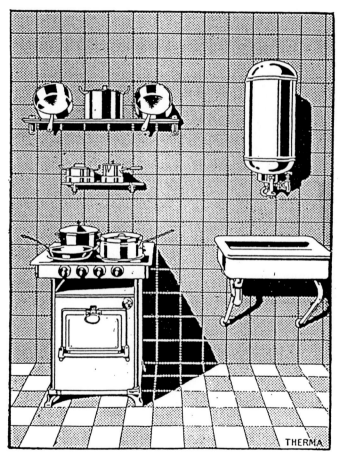

Figure 1   *The 1920s introduced the idea of the kitchen as a domestic laboratory in Scandinavia, a utopian dream that did not become common until the fifties: "the time when everybody who could affford it modernized their kitchen with shining white paint on hardboard and tried to make the kitchen look like a surgery with a white operating light on the ceiling", as the Norwegian author Odd Børretsen has put it (Swedish advertisement for kitchenware from the 1920s).*

Swedish intellectuals continued their reform battle, and at the New York World Fair in 1939 the functionalist formula of Swedish Grace was presented:

> We know that good homes can only be created by healthy people in hygienic dwellings through education and knowledge, with furnishings that are in harmony with the times. We know that beauty and comfort should be for everyone. . . This is, briefly, the idea of the Swedish Modern movement.

In this nationalization of modernity there was a heavy focus on home-improvement. A public and rather normative discourse on the art of good living emerged. Architects, planners, interior decorators and teachers of home economies were united in a crusade against "the unnecessary ugliness" of bad taste and old traditions. The battle was carried out during the 1940s and 1950s in many arenas and with different means: evening classes, home exhibitions, school books, furniture catalogues and interior decoration hints in magazines. School children were trained to furnish model flats, while their fathers took part in photo competitions on the theme of hominess, and housewives went to evening classes to learn modern living. Here questions of taste in consumption and above all in interior decoration were discussed in great detail. The aesthetics of modernity could be expressed in the pedagogical task of making the right choice between two glass bowls. In these normative examples the beautiful was always the same as the utilitarian, the simple, the practical, the restrained.

The focus on the aesthetics of everyday life was strongly linked to ideas about mentality and morality. The peaceful and light, the restrained and low-key, the orderly and practical home should create a setting for light-hearted, open-minded, harmonious and rational minds.

The reformers of the 1930s and 1940s, however, tended to talk to deaf ears. Their middle-class discourse on good taste and rational living was largely ignored in working-class homes; it was quite out of tune with everyday realities and ambitions. Most Swedes lacked space and resources for this kind of home-making. Housing conditions in the 1930s were still among the worst in Europe. Furthermore the functionalist utopia was based upon middle-class values stressing the need for functional differentiation, which had little relevance for working-class culture (cf. Löfgren 1984:52 ff.).

Consumer surveys from the thirties and forties showed that middle-class families spent a proportionately greater part of their income on housing, cutting back on other items. The representative role of the home was much more marked than in working class settings, but during the 1950s and 1960s a growing working-class affluence also made the home a priority. An intensive programme of housing development drastically changed the standard of housing and Sweden moved from the bottom to the top in the European housing standard league.

MATERIALIZING MODERNITY

It was thus not until the 1950s and 1960s that modern living really caught on, and then in forms of which the intellectual avant-garde did not always approve. With increased spending power and shorter working hours, the working class acquired new opportunities to attain a modern life with the aid of the growing range of commodities on offer. By this time the international style of chrome chairs and naked walls had been confronted with Swedish traditions and emerged in new forms which were more acceptable to ordinary consumers. Already at the world exhibition in New York 1939, Swedish avant-garde modernism had been nationalized. In *House and Garden* a reviewer stated that Swedish Modern was "a simple unaffected style, developed in natural wood" and the chairs in tubular steel had quickly dropped out of the furniture catalogues during the 1930s. Swedish modernity was "peasantized" in interesting ways.

The optimistic faith in development was reflected in the postwar design: everyday life and consumption were to be imbued with speed, flair, and verve. During these years the importance of being modern became a standard argument in the marketing of everything from kitchen pans to ashtrays. In the advertisements the two most frequent adjectives used during the fifties and sixties were "new" and "modern".

There was an optimistic atmosphere of really going somewhere. The winds of change and rejuvenation would blow through the home, and the housewife was defined as the vanguard of modernity. In 1960 the Swedish marketing journal called her "Sweden's no. 1 consumer" and added: "compared with other European housewives, her habits are undoubtedly less conservative and she responds more quickly to new products and methods than most."

This enthusiasm cannot be reduced to the persuasive power of home economic teachers or the seductive techniques of marketing. A new space for creativity had emerged in the framework of life forms, a possibility to develop talents and interests among people who had lacked both time, money and energy to invest in their own home settings. During the 1950s and 1960s a new kind of aesthetification of everyday life developed. As never before people got busy fixing, improving and decorating their homes. The first generation of Do-It-Yourselfers was born.

This is the era of when the American design experiments of streamlining from the thirties entered the home, an era of objects with a sense of urgency, objects with the promise of the future. Toasters, refrigerators and radios were rounded in such a way that you almost wanted to hurl them through the air. The Norwegian author Odd Børretsen has captured this longing for modernity in his childhood memories of shopping trips to Swedish department stores after the Second World War:

We longed for elegance, modern and special things from the world out
there, glossy, shining beauty - America!

We bought illuminated globes, nickel-plated hat racks, coffee cups with
gold stripes, toy cars in white enamel for the kids, nickel-plated umbrella
stands, exotic fruits in shiny tin cans.

Looking back one may ask why we bought umbrella stands, when we
didn't use umbrellas? It was stupid, and so on... But: This had nothing to
do with being sensible or reasonable. This had to do with with A Love for
Shiny Things. It was about feelings. (Børretsen 1985:50)

The marketing history of the refrigerator is a good example of the ways in
which the message of modernity could be concentrated into a single commodity.
Roland Marchand (1985) has pointed to the ways in which the fridge was introduced almost as an altar of modernity in the United States of the twenties and
thirties. Advertisements depict a family solemnly gathered around the new acquisition, a scene framed and glorified by the bright light oozing out of the open door
or flooding down from above. In the US of the fifties the fridge had been transformed into a piece of kitchen fashion. Advertising not only talked about the new
model of the year, but also of the new colours of the season ("Bermuda pink, fern
green, sand beige, dawn grey, buttercup yellow, lagoon blue..."), colours which
made the old white fridge look hopelessly out of date (Hine 1986:22).

In the Sweden of the fifties the fridge came to symbolize the modern
American way of life, as in this advertisement from 1955 (when a majority of
Swedish homes still lacked both fridge and bathroom):

Haven't you, as a Swedish housewife, been focusing on the American way
of life for quite a long time, a way of life characterized by comfort, hygiene,
time-saving and a both practical and charming way of tackling everyday
tasks? Now KITCHEN COMFORT brings to Sweden all that you have
admired and envied in the American kitchen. Soon you will be able to take
care of household tasks as easily and elegantly as the American wife – just
as fresh-looking and attractive as her you will greet your husband at dinner
– served in your new, lean and cosy kitchen.

At that time Sweden was often portrayed as the most Americanized of
the European nations, but America represented both an utopia of modernity,
informality and efficiency, as well as Hollywood vulgarity and low taste. The
contemporary discussion about Americanization mirrored this ambivalence and
a middle-class fear of losing the position as a clearing-house for the import of
international fashions as well as the role of unquestioned arbitrator of good taste.
Through the new popular press American ideas and ideals were now made
available to everybody and anybody.

This fear of the wrong kinds of imports was very evident in the debates of
the new phenomenon of teenage culture. When people describe their careers as

teenage consumers in the fifties there is one piece of Americana which stands out in the memory of many: the butterfly chair.

This import came to symbolize modernity both through its daring design, bright colours and novel materials (steel and galon), but also because the chair often was the first piece of furniture a teenager chose on his or her own. In a way it became "a chair of defiance", because it modelled the new loose teenage body – in it you sat in a way which the older generation often found provocative.

INFORMAL LIVING

Despite the new marketing winds home furnishing in the fifties followed rather well-established routines. Consumer surveys showed that people still bought most of their furniture as "sets" when they married and followed fairly strict routines. A living-room set consisted of a sofa, two easy chairs and a small coffee table, while the dining set was made up of four or six chairs, a table and a sideboard. Styles were rather conservative and furniture supposed to last a life-time.

In the middle of the sixties a new tone crept into marketing messages, which only can be understood against the striking informalization of Swedish life, in all arenas from forms of address and deference to the development of causal manners in dressing, socializing and interior decoration. The trend is international, but for various reasons the informalization of Sweden was in some ways faster and more far-reaching than in many other European settings (see the discussion in Löfgren 1988).

A book on modern design from 1970 mirrors this transformation. Here the rigid routines of older generations of home-builders are contrasted to the flexibility of the new generation. A young middle-class family is chosen as an example of the new mentality:

> Here, status is *not* owning things, there are no sets of furniture in the conventional sense. There is no cleaning mania... They are content with open shelves, often from floor to ceiling, where everything is visible, a big table and cheap folding chairs. Roomy tables for work and play are needed, as are good beds. What is missing? The lounge suite, the easy chairs and the soft, expensive materials! No paintings, but rather easily changeable prints and posters. People are as open for novelties if they are good, that is; practical. (Larsson 1970:121)

This was avant-garde living among students and academics in the early seventies. Similar interiors are described in interviews with home-makers of that period, when bedroom doors were left open and guests entertained in the kitchen. People remember the intensive experimentation with new combinations. This was an era when secondhand buying and swapping became part of young middle-class life, along with a critique of unnecessary and wasteful consumption. (For older generations there was still a social stigma attached to secondhand buying.) One woman recalls how her mother-in-law fought hard to keep a stiff upper lip when confronted with all the the young couple's improvised furniture made out of boxes. Another woman remembers the symbolic significance of the sofa: "it was the symbol of bourgeois rigidity and drabness and we would never buy one".

But the heavy media-exposed lifestyle of the generation of 1968 may over-shadow the fact that the informalization of home life and home-making was a much broader social movement. The enormously successful furniture chain store IKEA owed much of its success to this transformation of consumer habits. Maga-zines were filled with advice for a simpler and more flexible way of living, replac-ing doors with draperies and fixing new beds out of chipboard. The sale of eti-quette books dropped drastically, while the consumption of candles rose sharply. Cosiness, improvisation and practicality were strongly emphasized and the in-formal style of the home also invaded workplaces. Offices, for example, become more home-like during this period.

Later during the seventies this message of informality became strongly linked to ideas about natural living, with an interest in simple and rural lifestyles, demonstrated for example in a marked rise in the use of pine furniture and textiles like linen and cotton. Swedish modern living was peasantized - the use of peasant iconography and styles expanded much further, in an interesting blend of nostalgia and modern "natural" living.

In the eighties the language of marketing home furnishings changed again. There was often an implicit or explicit reference to the drab, unexciting and puritanical seventies. Now the message began to focus much more on the need to *indulge yourself*, to treat yourself to some luxuries or new pleasures. Leather sofas and silk curtains, dark and strong colours became more popular. America returned as an ideal in the advertisements, although in quite different forms than during the fifties.

These shifting market messages describe a development from home-making as a moral and sacred activity, to one of science and modernity, and then to one stressing the *fun* of consumption as a form of creative art. Parallel to this there is also a heightened tempo of consumption. In the forties the advertisements could tell you that it was about time you bought a new set of china, in the fifties a pop-ular slogan was "repaint the kitchen on Saturday!" In the sixties it was time to get rid of old furniture, in the seventies you had to redecorate the whole living room and in the eighties the argument could be: "when did you last change your lifestyle?"

Thus fashion colonizes new territories in the home, often using the classic rhetoric of Parisian haute couture. (During the postwar era producers of refrigerators, sofas and kitchen wares learned to announce with pride the advent of this year's new colours, styles and models.)

The postwar patterns of consumption turned out not only to open doors for international influences but also had a nationalizing effect: people could dream out an American refrigerator, a subscription to *Reader's Digest*, a glass of ice-cold Coca-Cola or an encounter with the Cartwright Brothers, but the end result was rather an increased homogenization of Swedish lifestyles. It was during the fifties and sixties that a Swedish style of living became not only an export commodity but also a shared aspiration in many social settings. Outsiders marveled at the homogeneous ways in which factory workers, office clerks, and academics decorated their homes and organized their family lives. It was not only the tone of family life which became sober and moderated, it was also the colours of the wallpaper and the cover of the sofa. Swedish living meant a special taste for colours and materials as well as an emphasis on the practical,

Mai 68, on a refait le monde.
Mai 86, on refait la cuisine.

Figure 2   *During the 1970s and 1980s the Swedish furniture chain store IKEA expanded over the world, marketing an image of Swedish modern living and informality. Here a French advertisement from 1986 urges the generation of 1968 to redo their kitchen instead of the world.*

but also a certain set of attitudes towards family life, sex roles, and child rearing as outside observers noted. There was no way a Swedish living room or a Swedish day-care center could be mistaken for a German or American one. The point is that, although Swedes became more international in their consumption pattern, modern living at the same time took on a distinct national flavour; a more marked national habitus of shared dispositions, understandings, routines and practices emerged.

CHANGING BUT REMAINING THE SAME

The marketing perspective on consumption tends to emphasize change, discontinuity and flexibility in the life of consumers. A lot of attention has been devoted to the cultural and economic production of fashions, but far less to the de-routinization or de-stabilizing of earlier habits of consumption. The introduction of modern living first of all called for the deconstruction of established routines: "There is a time and place for everything" had to be changed into "let's find new places and times for everything, from breakfast habits to leisure plans".

When we look at the informalization of Swedish living in the sixties and seventies, and above all at the avant-garde of the progressive, young professionals it is paradoxical that the critique of consumerism and the call for a simpler and more natural living opened up new spaces for marketing and consumption. Doing away with traditional forms of living and experimenting with new forms of cooking, interior decoration and socializing actually meant shedding some earlier restraints. An older generation had been brought up with the idea that furniture should be bought as sets and last for a life-time. Clothes should be bought in the autumn and spring. Buying a new hat and new pair of shoes in time for the First of May was still a common ritual in the fifties. In the same way a weekly rhythm of eating persisted; Sundays meant roast and Thursdays pea soup in many households. Consumption was on the whole rather ritualized and much of the shopping fixed to certain occasions. This changed in the sixties and seventies, but new routines gradually emerged, just as the "traditionalism" of the fifties once upon a time was the result of earlier innovations.

The focus on the role of fashion may also lead us to overemphasize elements of change in consumer life. We may mistake "the fireflies of fashion" for more profound changes in everyday life and world view. It is for example striking that the group that has been most innovative, flexible and fashion-minded in the field of interior decoration, the middle-class, is also a group which shows a very marked degree of continuity in their way of life. As Jonas Frykman has pointed out, in an ongoing study of Swedish intellectuals, they can afford to experiment with fashion because it in no way threatens their identity and basic values.

Expressive and fluid lifestyles may thus hide a marked cultural stability on a more fundamental level.

It was also the intellectuals who started to complain about the conservative taste of working-class homes, in which traditional boundaries, categories and patterns were upheld, in everything from the sexual division of labour to the arrangement of the lounge suite. In the seventies the bohemian flexibility and lust for improvisation certainly wasn't a working class virtue. The many Swedes who changed class during the boom years of the sixties and seventies often faced a tough process of un-learning and re-learning as they were socialized into new middle-class habits and tastes. The Swedish author Gunder Andersson has described this confrontation in his (rather autobiographical) novel *Komma ifatt* ("Catching up") from 1980. Here is the hero's reaction when he is bringing his new university friend to see his old working-class parents:

> He felt tense, nervous, all of a sudden a stranger in his own home. The greeting ceremonies were over, they were standing in the living room and Tomas wondered if they saw the same things as himself: the lack of planning in the way the furniture was arranged, the lack of any aesthetic feeling or overall vision. The colours fighting each other. The furniture randomly combined. The chaos of lottery prizes and commonplace porcelain figures, which for some reason had been permitted to populate cupboards, shelves and tables. The lack of style, the want of any personal taste.

Another arena where class differences in consumption emerged was the division of labour between the sexes. A study of working class households in the small town of "Asketorp" (Rosengren 1991) shows the same focus of the home as a family project, where love, solidarity and care are materialized in the continuous ambitions of home improvements, but in comparison with middle-class families gender and domestic life are organized differently. Women are very much in control of home and consumption:

> ...the entire home is usually her creation, from the choice of wallpaper and furniture, to curtains, table-cloths and flowers. But also the external appearances of the members of the family are marked by her. She chooses and buys clothes, not only for herself and her children, but also for her husband... When the couple goes to a party on a Saturday evening or he goes to ice-hockey on a Tuesday evening, his outward looks are very much a creation of her ideas of how a man should look. If you visit him at home you will find him sitting and talking to you in clothes chosen by her, and in a surrounding created mostly with his money, but mainly through her ability, ideas and wishes. (Rosengren 1985:84)

CONCLUSION

This look at changes in home-making during the twentieth century must not be read as an evolutionary text; as a market colonizing new territories, dislocating traditional stability and routines. Rather we may view it as a continual process of de-routinization and re-routinization, transformations which could be found in any historical period.

But this arena of consumer activity also illustrates the problem of viewing consumption as either liberation or seduction. The history of home-making in the twentieth century can be written (and has been written) as the story of a gradual but irreversible privatization of modern life, where home becomes a sheltered corner of compensatory freedom for alienated individuals who have only slight chances of changing society or experiencing personal satisfaction in their nine to five jobs. In this kind of narrative market forces move in and successfully exploit people's needs and anxieties, as in this statement of a British sociologist:

> Undeniably, the home has become a primary site for an unprecedentedly privatized and atomized leisure and consumer lifestyle... The Puritan notion of the home saw it as a 'little kingdom', the Victorian concept stressed 'Home as Haven'. The Late Modern Elizabethan concept constructs the 'Home as Personalised Marketplace'. It is where most of us express our consumer power, our cultural tastes...
> ...Thrown back upon the reserves of those few close to us in 'an intimate society', we stumble traumatized towards 'the end of public culture'... (Tomlinson 1990: 67, 70)

Such a description is far too one-dimensional. It does not take into account that the most important influence in twentieth century home-making has to do with the emergence of the home as a family project, uniting wife, husband and children in a manner which was unthinkable in 1900 or 1930.

Market manipulation does not explain why people have chosen to invest so much of their time, money and creativity in this specific field of consumption. Home-making has become very closely related to identity formation: home is a place where you very actively try out different sides of the self, it is an important arena of cultural production rather than a site of anxious cocooning.

This family project called the home is never finished. People are busy redecorating, fixing, planning, day-dreaming, producing new sofa cushions, putting in new floors, ripping out old ones, changing wallpaper, driving to the hardware store, leafing through furniture catalogues, taking the whole family to IKEA, moving things around and moving the family on. In a way the family is constantly being repaired and renovated. The home builds the family together, creates a common ground of interests as well as conflicts between spouses and generations.

The home has become an arena for creativity and artistic ambitions. People who never (or rarely) would consider visiting an art gallery or drawing a picture do not hesitate a second about designing a new living room, matching colours, fabrics and objects. As Marianne Gullestad (1989:58 ff.) has pointed out in a discussion of Norwegian home-makers, interior decoration may become a labour of love for married couples but also an arena of playfulness, hidden under the legitimation of home improvement.

The life histories of consumers give many examples of these creative processes with a constant dialogue between day-dreaming and fantasies about "the ideal home" and the attempts to turn at least parts of utopia into reality. The skills of home-making are acquired early on, in play with dolls' houses or in the use of one's first teenage room as a laboratory for experiments with styles of decoration (choosing provocative colours and furniture combinations in order to distance oneself from the hopelessly old-fashioned taste of the parents). As a home-builder one then progresses to the proud and solemn moment of moving into home of one's own and from there one continues a career of dreaming, planning and re-decorating.

There are great generational differences here, of course. Growing up in the poor housing conditions of the thirties meant more day-dreaming about a future home than an actual scope for creative ambitions, in the fifties the first do-it-yourself crazes swept over the country, in the sixties even working-class families could realize the utopia of a surburban home.

Producers and marketers have of course exploited these interests, by developing different strategies to increase consumption, for example by trying to shorten both the physical and the cultural durability of home furnishings. On the other hand, changes in twentieth century home-making also stress the ways in which consumer expertise has developed over time. It is, for example, evident that, contrary to some ideas about "the mindless consumer", consumers have become more critical and sophisticated over the last decades. Marketing strategies or advertisement tricks which may have worked in the 1940s were unthinkable in the 1960s.

My aim is not to replace a devolutionary argument ("modern Man is becoming more and more commodified and market-directed") with an evolutionary one ("consumption is becoming more and more creative"). It is rather that we need to look at the siting and constant relocation of cultural creativity and everyday aesthetics over time, with respect to gender, class and generations. Different historical conditions open up different arenas of self-expression and symbolic production: during the twentieth century the home has developed into one such arena.

There is a balance to be struck here between the Scylla and Charybdis of consumption studies. Scylla is represented by the famous Standard Oil advertisement from the 1940s: "Freedom is the freedom of choice", the idea that the market provides a happy consumer life as the ultimate freedom of choice, self-expression, and egalitarian democracy. Charybdis stands for the view of consumers as mindless, passive objects of manipulation.

If we look at the development in consumption studies there may be a slight pendulum effect here. At times the focus has been very much on the seduction of consumers: locked up in the iron cage held together by market forces. At other times, and often as a reaction against this perspective, the focus has been on consumption as a liberating force, an arena of personal creativity, self-realization or counter-hegemonic strategies.

The argument for striking a balance focuses on the need for seeing consumption as cultural production and consumers as actors rather than objects, but at the same time remembering that not all actors are created equal. We need to continue to look at the ways in which "the freedom of choice" is staged or shaped by market interests, but also how ambitions to monitor and predict consumer choices often prove to be as utopian as some of our consumer day-dreams.

References

Agnew, J-C.

1987   *Worlds Apart: The Market and the Theatre in Anglo-American Thought, 1550–1750.* Cambridge: Cambridge UP.

Børretsen, O.

1985   Sverige, svenskerne og jeg. *Samtiden,* **94**:2: pp. 49–57.

Campbell, C.

1987   *The Romantic Ethic and the Spirit of Modern Consumerism.* Oxford: Basil Blackwell.

Dorst, J. D.

1989   *The Written Suburb. An American Site, An Ethnographic Dilemma.* Philadelphia: Pennsylvania UP.

Frykman, J. and Löfgren, O.

1987   *Culture Builders: A Historical Anthropology of Middle Class Life.* Brunswick: Rutgers UP.

Galbraith, J.K.

1958   *The Affluent Society.* Boston: Houghton Mifflin.

Gullestad, M.

1989   *Kultur og hverdagsliv. På sporet av det moderne Norge.* Oslo: Universitetsforlaget.

Hine, T.

1986   *Populuxe. The Look and Life of America in the 50s and 60s, from Tailfins and TV dinners to Barbie Dolls and Fallout Shelters.* New York: Alfred A.Knopf.

Janowitz, T.

1986   *Slaves of New York.* London: Picador.

Kopytoff, I.

1986   The Cultural Biography of Things: Commodization as Process. In: Arjun Appadurai (ed.) *The Social Life of Things. Commodities in Cultural Perspective.* Cambridge: Cambridge UP.

Larsson, L.

1970   *Vill våra barn ärva våra Ijusstakar?* Stockholm.

Lipovetsky, G.

1987   *L'empire de l'ephémère. La mode et son destin dans le sociétés modernes.* Paris: Gallimard.

Lo-Johnsson, I.

1957   *Författaren.* Stockholm.

Löfgren, O.

1984   The Sweetness of Home. Class, Culture and Family Life in Sweden. *Ethnologia Europea,* **XIV**: pp. 44–64.

Löfgren, O. (ed.)

1988   *Hej, det är från försäkringskassan! Informaliseringen av Sverige.* Stocholm: Natur och kultur.

Löfgren, O.

1990   Medierna i nationsbygget. Hur press, radio och TV gjort Sverige svenskt. In: Ulf Hannerz (ed.) *Medier och kulturell,* Stockholm: Carlssons, pp. 85–120.

Marchand, R.

1985   *Advertising the American Dream. Making Way for Modernity 1920–1940.* Berkeley: Univ of California Press.

McKendrick, N., Brewer, J. and Plumb, J.H.

1985   *The Birth of a Consumer Society. The Commercialization of Eighteenth-Century England.* Bloomington: Indiana Univ Press.

Miller, D.

1987   *Material Culture and Mass Consumption.* Oxford: Basil Blackwell.

Mintz, S.

1985   *Sweetness and Power. The Place of Sugar in Modern History.* New York: Penguin.

Rosengren, A.

1985   Contemporary Swedish Family Life Through the Eyes of an Ethnologist. In: *The Nordic Family: Perspectives on Family Research,* J. Rogers and H. Norman. (eds) Uppsala: Essays in social demographic history 4, Department of History, Univ of Uppsala, pp. 80–93.

Rosengren, A.

1991   *Två barn och eget hus. Om kvinnors och mäns världar i småsamhäl-let.* Stockholm: Carlssons.

Tomlinson, A.

1990   Home fixtures: Doing-it-yourself in a privatized world. In: ibid (ed.) *Consumption, Identity and Style: Marketing, meanings and the packaging of pleasure.* London: Routledge.

Wightman F., Richard and Jackson Leers, T.J. (eds)

1983   *The Culture of Consumption: Critical Essays in American History 1880–1980.* New York: Pantheon.

Williams, R. H.

1982   *Dream Worlds: Mass Consumption in Late Nineteenth-Century France.* California: Univ of California Press.

CHAPTER THREE

Style and Ontology

David Miller

INTRODUCTION

The title of this paper is intended to offer a challenge to one of the most pervasive assumptions in contemporary cultural studies; that which is embedded in the term 'superficial' and which implies that there is a relationship between surface and lack of importance. At the heart of Western philosophy lie a series of interrelated assumptions, embedded in metaphor, which greatly constrain our ability to comprehend major transformations in the modern world. The culprit is the pervasive ideology of what may be called 'depth ontology' whereby we tend to assume that everything that is important for our sense of being lies in some deep interior and must be long-lasting and solid, as against the dangers of things we regard as ephemeral, shallow or lacking in content. These become highly problematic metaphors when we encounter a cosmology which may not share these assumptions, and rests upon a very different sense of ontology.

The importance of these metaphors lies not only in the narrow and some-times parochial pursuit of philosophy but in the tendency of these ideas to be infused in more general, often moral, judgements on the world at large. Most re-cently we have seen a spate of criticisms of modern society as increasingly super-ficial, ephemeral and lacking in depth. Writers on post-modernism, in particular, talk of a loss of authenticity under the conditions of late-capitalism (e.g. Harvey 1989; Jameson 1991), which they identify with a new superficiality. Fashion is held up as a mechanism which accentuates all those elements of the modern condition, its fragmented, transient and superficial nature, which seem to result in almost a quantitative loss of being.

For the purposes of this paper, however, it is the particular application of these ideas to the world of clothing which is of concern. Fashion and style refer to a relatively ephemeral relationship with one's sartorial presentation and thereby invite the accusation that this relationship is also a trivial one. People who appear to devote considerable resources of time and money to this pursuit thereby demonstrate the triviality of their nature. This example of depth ontology is clearly bound up in ideologies of gender, since it is women, in particular, who are associated with such activities, and there are several well-known newspaper cartoon strips (e.g. Blondie, the Gambols) which have for decades used the image of the fashion conscious female to 'illustrate' the superficiality of women more generally. In this paper I will, however, concentrate on an equally insidious form of prejudice which is directed again black people where an emphasis on style is again seen as a sign of lack of capacity for depth or seriousness.

It is not easy to confront assumptions which manage to unite abstract philosophy and mass circulation cartoon strips. An attempt to reverse both the assumptions and implications will be attempted in three stages. Firstly, a description will be given of the actual operation of style through ethnographic observations on the social relations of clothing in contemporary Trinidad. Secondly, I will discuss some recent writings on the possible existence of a particular 'black trope' which has been argued for in recent studies of language and literature, but which here is then re-applied to the case of clothing. Thirdly, it will be argued that underlying this perspective on style and the process of Signifyin(g) (Gates 1988), may lie an alternative approach to ontology which reverses the typical assumptions of the Western depth metaphor.

STYLE AND FASHION IN CLOTHING

It is surprisingly hard to find discussions of fashion which investigate in any detail its implications for the more profound consequences of modernity. Even Simmel, who is often seen as the original sociologist of both, in an article which specifically addresses fashion (1957), emphasizes the more general question of the relationship between individuality and sociality, rather than what might have seemed a more promising extension of his studies of the tragic contradictions of modern life whereby we attempt to appropriate a material culture that has grown to such an extent that we can no longer assimilate it (1978). Most other accounts can be divided into three classes. Those (e.g. Bell 1976; Veblen 1970) which emphasize the use of sartorial forms as status symbols; those (e.g. Barthes 1967) which examine the internal structure of fashion as code and those (e.g. Ewen and Ewen 1982) which critique fashion as the vehicle of capitalist control over consumption behaviours. Rather different from any of these are anthropological works which examine the social relations of clothing in comparative contexts (Weiner and Schneider, 1989).

Wilson (1985) provides the best summary of British work on the subject, and in her final chapter addresses the more general question of authenticity through an examination of the extremely interesting relationship between fashion and feminism. In her work fashion is allowed a major role as an expressivist medium potentially both exemplifying but also confronting the key problems of alienation and identity in the modern world. She identified a wide range of sartorial attributes which have been given social and expressive consequence. This paper will address the implications for individualism, competition and order, but the attribute which above all provides the specific articulation between clothing and fashion is the ability of clothing to express a sense of time or change. It is therefore, this feature which will be emphasized in the ethnographic enquiry.

TRINIDAD

The choice of Trinidad for a case-study in style is hardly fortuitous, since this area stands high in many peoples projection of stylishness upon particular regions and peoples, thanks largely to Trinidad's association with Carnival and Steelband. It also stands within a more general relationship between the black diasporan population and ideas of contemporary style. This association is hardly new. Early accounts of slave society in the area focus upon the particular relationship of slaves to clothing. A.C. Carmichael stated in 1833 (1969:75) 'Generally speaking, the coloured women have an insatiable passion for showy dresses and jewels... The highest class of females dress more showily and far more expensively than European ladies'. As in later accounts the idea that some servants would only wear silk stockings in preference to cotton ones clearly offends the writer not only in relation to her idea of the 'proper' distance between white and black peoples, but in her sense of the proportion of expenditure going on such items.

The same feature of conspicuous expenditure upon clothing, jewellery and hairstyles remains prominent within the contemporary ethnographic setting. My research, which took place in 1988-89, was in the context of a recession, following upon a decade long oil boom which had had dramatic effects upon Trinidad. The phenomenal rise in incomes during this period appears to have been relatively wide-spread in its effects compared to other oil boom countries, so that for a short period one is able to view the consumption patterns not only of the wealthy and nouveau riche but also of what may be called the habitual poor, people who are brought up in poverty and now with recession have returned to poverty, but who for a short period were able to obtain resources to construct consumption forms which allowed them to realize cultural projects that would normally not be visible under the constraints of scarcity. Both seamstresses and their clients talked of the extreme demands of the oil boom period where clients were expected to have a new outfit made for every event to which they were invited. Two new outfits a week was often quoted as common for women in work. This degree of expenditure was clearly a product of the oil boom, but Freilich, carrying out ethnographic research in an impoverished village in 1957-58 reports 'the wife of one of the peasants said "every new function needs new clothes. I would not wear the same dress to two functions in the same district"' (1960:73). It seems, at least for the ex-African segment of Trinidad's population, that the use of mass consumption during the oil boom is more fulfilment of a previous imperative than a demand created by the mere existence of wealth.

There exists no approach to clothing which would valorize such behaviour. Whether clothing is judged as conspicuous consumption, status competition, or the effect of capitalist pressures, the implication is that people of low incomes who put this much expenditure into clothing are making some kind of mistake. They do not fully understand what ought to be their proper priorities. Implicit also is this underlying critique of women as inveterate shoppers who are here afflicted by some kind of addiction or obsessive behaviour which is morally offensive. An attempt to understand such an activity is here inevitably then also an attempt to justify it. Anthropologists are adept at this kind of thing, providing they reposition the ethnographic as 'traditional' society. After all no one condemns Trobriand Islanders who cultivate absurdly long yams and then mount them up into heaps as an example of 'conspicuous consumption'. The problem is to retain this comparative empathy within a context in which the behaviour is seen as commensurate with 'Western' norms rather than mere exotica. The first stage in this exercise has to be an elaboration of the context.

The study was based on four communities within the small town of Chaguanas (the birth-place of the novelist V.S. Naipaul). In general Chaguanas has been a centre for the ex-East Indian population, but is now home to a large number of ex-African and mixed groups so that the ethnicity of the field study area reflects that of the nation as a whole (approx. 40% ex-East Indian, 40% ex-African, 20% mixed with a dozen other points of origin). The four communities comprised Newtown – a government housing scheme populated mainly by public service workers imported from the capital and elsewhere; St Pauls – a village incorporated into the town; Ford – a large squatting area including immigrants from the smaller Caribbean islands, and the Meadows – a middle-class residential area, the wealthiest in the district.

In Trinidad it is useful to distinguish between what might be called 'style' and 'fashion'. One of the differences between these two is that style appears as a highly personalized and self-controlled expression of particular aesthetic ability, as opposed to fashion which is the dissolution of individual identity through appearance in a strictly conventional, if internally diverse, category of appearance. With style, however, there is the search for the particular combination of otherwise unassociated parts which can be combined to create the maximum effect. Here originality is a major criteria of success as is the fit to the wearer. Thus the bearing of the person, the way they move, walk, turn and act as though in natural unity with their clothes is vital to the success of the presentation. This distinction seems to be established in colloquial use, for example the fashion column of the *Trinidad and Tobago Review* (February 1991) states 'Fashion is sameness. To be in fashion is to be wearing the similar designs, fabrics, colours, etc. that everyone is wearing. Style is an individual matter, it is one of personal choice, it is wearing what you look best in'.

The distinctions are easier to view in men's clothing. In general men are much more resistant to the development of separate conventional clothing forms for major functions. At a wedding, the best man and closest relatives may appear in a suit though often with some flamboyant element such an extravagant bow tie which distinguishes this from the merely conventional suit. Other men, however, wear clothing which is only slightly more formal than daily wear, appearing in well-creased, belted trousers and sports shirts (termed jerseys) and buttoned shirts. In general these would be similar to clothes worn for work. Some of these same men will however embrace a highly competitive sartorial display for occasions such as fêtes and house parties. Here the key elements are shoes such as designer trainers, jeans and a wide variety of hats. Out of this group a certain portion attempt to carry through such conspicuous dressing into their everyday appearance. Twenty years ago such males were termed *saga* boys, today there is no clear term but the word dude borrowed from the United States is perhaps the most common label. These males combine sartorial originality with ways of walking and talking that create a style which is generally regarded as never letting up from conspicuous display. The local term for such behaviour is 'gallerying'.

The notion of style as a personalized context for fashion items emerges more clearly through an examination of fashion shows. These shows are an ubiquitous feature of modern Trinidadian life, and are found at all income levels. The people of the Meadows might go to the show of a well known Port of Spain designer hosted by the Lions or Rotary club, or at a major hotel in the capital, but they also might meet people from St Pauls or Newtown at a fashion show hosted at one of the shopping malls, while fashion shows are also held for small fund raising ventures in Ford, and at many school or church bazaars. For wealthier audiences the models may perform as rather cold or austere mannequins, as such they are essentially vehicles for demonstrating expensive items for sale. This is however, the less common form of modelling and is reserved for the more exclusive designer shows. In most fashion shows and in all those held by low income groups, the clothes are displayed in a very different mode which emphasizes a unity between the form of dress and the physicality of the body which displays them. Movements are based on an exaggerated self-confidence and a strong eroticism, with striding, bouncy, or dance-like displays. In local parlance there should be something 'hot' about the clothing and something 'hot' about the performance. For fashion shows at bazaars, schools and in Ford or similar communities, the models are not professional but local people and the clothes are either purchases of, or made by, the wearer. At these local events there is no attempt to sell the clothing and the whole ethos of the show is outside the commercial arena. The origin of the clothing is often of no concern to the audience and nor is any intrinsic quality or monetary value. The clothing is really an adjunct to the performance itself, to the way the persons move on the stage, and the frame for the performance is established by the models being friends, relatives or schoolmates of the audience.

The concept of style which emerges from such shows comprises two main components; individualism and transience. The individualism emerges through a necessary fit between the clothes and the wearer. The person attempts to develop a sequence of sartorial forms which are seen as expressive of themselves and their character. The clothing is complemented here by a selection of belts, costume jewelery, shoes, a wide variety of hair forms and styles and skin tone. The aim is to construct a style which can be judged in the performance. Although they may refer to current general trends such as 'ragamuffin' style or tie-dye, they are also idiosyncratic juxtapositions of elements in ways that make this wearer conspicuous and able as against the competition. The sartorial achievement is easily incorporated into a general sense of easy accomplishment at a variety of arts, ranging from music to witty speech.

The second element of style is its transience; the stylist may take from the major fashion shifts in Trinidad but only as the vanguard. Hand painted shirts are fine when they have yet to be acknowledged as the dominant fashion, but at that point the forms are given over to be incorporated into more conventional forms such as young teenage fashion while the stylist moves onto something new. Apart from the fête the key arena for such display is the workplace, especially for the female working in an office environment. Although the office party in particular is the occasion for tight fitting dresses with sequins and frills at the bottom and bare back and shoulders, the daily work-place is also an arena of intensive sartorial display and competition. Where there is a standard uniform as at a bank, small variations and alterations are still discernible that allow room for this element of transient display.

The link between clothing and transience is most forcefully expressed through Carnival for which, traditionally, individuals constructed elaborate and time consuming costumes which, even if identical forms were worn each year, had to be discarded and re-made annually. Seasonally relevant clothing may also be purchased for other events such as Christmas or commonly a new swimsuit for going to the beach during the long Easter weekend.

The source of the originality in a sense is irrelevant, it may be copied from the soap operas or the fashion shows which come on television, it may be sent from relatives abroad or purchased while abroad. The oil boom encouraged imported elements when 'everybody and their tantie went to the big apple and returned with designer or imitation designer things', it may be simply re-combinations of locally produced elements but it is, if possible, always new and vanguard and destined for a particular occasion. In practice only certain persons can achieve these ideals but others will attempt to follow as soon as possible and at any rate before their own peers.

The desire for unique style encourages a reliance on the seamstress and tailor (or self-production) but even ready-made clothes may be altered through hand painting or additional accessories. Alternatively imported clothes can be both ready-made and unique. Local production also meant that ideas from soap operas or other influential television shows such as *Miami Vice* can be appropri-ated that much more quickly. The seamstress is a common figure in every part of Chaguanas. It is one of the ideal forms of work for the still often severely re-stricted East Indian woman, since it can be carried out at home and since nearly all women were brought up with some knowledge of the sewing machine. It is also a possible profession in areas such as the Meadows and Newtown where the house deeds do not permit more conspicuous commercial activities. In 1988 there were however far more people who desired work as seamstresses than those actually working as such, owing to the collapse of demand with the recession.

The oil boom also saw a speeding up of change in other areas, for example, items such as drive-in movies, amusement arcades, snooker, microwaves and food processors came and went generally leaving little trace. The continuous demand for newness, a refusal to replace with the same as last year's form was also noted by retailers in goods such as paints and curtains. In some cases newness was closely related to increasing status and expenditure, as, for example, the oil boom transformation in pet retailing, where mongrels were replaced by fashions for miniature pedigree dogs for women, and Alsatians and later Rottweilers for homes, all expensive breeds requiring considerable maintenance costs. Similarly local tropical fish were replaced by goldfish and other exotica; only the older tradition of training birds for whistling competitions seems to have retained its traditional forms and affectionados.

The above description was becoming increasingly invalid during the year's fieldwork as the recession acted as a constraint on such strategies. This was not however observed as a simple correlation with wealth. People from the Meadows often reined back on their clothing purchases long before those of lesser incomes. One group of largely unemployed males in St Pauls managed to keep a tailor busy simply because new pants remained of extreme importance even in a period of highly insecure and plunging incomes. Nevertheless, taken more generally, wealth was reasserting itself as the key criteria for determining the levels of purchases.

The demand for new clothes is often linked to the presence of a current relationship (or marriage), since the money that males are expected to provide to the females they are with may be the source of any new clothing. But the demand for new outfits is equally strong for the single working woman, so that it is the existence of the resource rather than the relationship itself that seems to be the key to the level of purchase (though not necessarily its interpretation). The workplace is itself a key arena for sartorial competition closely followed by the fête or house party. By contrast, for most females, dress codes at home are extremely relaxed and women will meet visitors in very informal attire, including night clothes, without any suggestion of impropriety.

Not every Trinidadian is stylish. Style exists simultaneously with a quite different orientation to clothing which expresses another side to Trinidadian life, one devoted to religion, to the family as a descent group and to the celebration of the home and the interior. Such clothing is closely associated with life-cycle events such as weddings or christenings and also religious events such as attendance at church or temple. Clothing for such occasions is marked by shiny surfaces (as opposed to the matt of informal attire); preferences may be for silver, gold, metallic greens, blues and reds, and shiny or slinky black, pearl and white. The covering-up aesthetic is continued into this arena with the considerable use of layering and ruching (gathering up in layered crescents) in dress and skirt patterns, always complemented by stockings and high-heeled shoes. Stockings appear to be one of the key emblems of a more formal dress, which carries over to work situations. Shoes also must be appropriate, the tendency being to wear closed-in forms for church and open toes for leisure. There are variants to this, for example, the dress code for elderly females and for young girls of East-Indian descent is based around white and pastel dresses with an abundance of frills, flounces, bows and lace effects. These forms are not shiny but equally are quite distinctive from the matt informal wear of most other groups. Young women would also vary the basic code by using similar fabrics but creating slinky low-cut or body-hugging dresses or striking combinations of, for example, black blouses and silver skirts complemented by highly conspicuous displays of elaborate costume jewellery.

Attendance at a few such life-cycle events reveals a striking degree of conventionality and repetition. It is as though nearly all the clothing is made from a few agreed elements of material and design. The use of shiny surfaces of ruching, slits and straps are simply recombined so that one works merely with the permutations of this highly restricted set. Indeed often the dresses themselves appear as patchworks of elements with a silver lozenge set within a pearly white layered bodice for example. Amongst the older generation, in particular, these are associated with wide-brimmed hats of similar shiny materials. The result may be new but not novel and is therefore still conventional. The players act competitively but within constrained and agreed parameters of display, such that again it seems reasonable to talk of a normative form.

The desire for new outfits may have very different consequences within the opposed frame of their appearance. Although the wedding epitomizes a normative sartorial style it is more accurate to broaden this into sections of the population who even at other events tend to wear clothes within the permutations of the selected range of elements, thus the newness of the event based item is countered by the ever-sameness of the collective apparel. The clothes do represent the individual wearer in competition, but only within highly restricted forms where to go beyond the convention would be to fail within the terms of the event. For the stylist, however, the appeal is precisely to the unprecedented (at least for them) nature of the event and the appearance. Fashions may be used but they are not sufficient for the purpose which must then be supplemented by the creative ability of the wearers. This should not be exaggerated, since most individuals also have particular items such as dresses which are especially comfortable for dancing or a hat by which they have become known and which establishes a more stable personalized repertoire.

For fashion, as opposed to style, the idea of newness is accepted as an expression of individual competition but in a manner which does not encourage genuine innovation. This is also reflected in the response to another kind of fashion, the new ideas for women's clothing which break like waves over the island's shores during the course of the year. Examples were exceptionally wide belts or belts with butterfly clasps, treated denim such as acid wash or individually painted T-shirts and dresses. Those who emphasize the normative are not vanguard in their acceptance of such fashions, but it seems that if the style reaches a kind of critical mass then virtually the entire community acknowledge it through purchasing at least one representative item, as indicated through a survey questionnaire. In a sense, by doing so, they suppress the threat of disconformity through the ubiquity of acceptance. They have turned the new into the conventional.

This is reflected in a dichotomy noticed by workers in market research. In their analysis of regional difference the central area and the south are seen by the major companies as areas of high brand loyalty, such that the name of a brand was usually synonymous with a product range, all toothpaste is.. etc. This was associated with general stability compared to the capital but when change came it came quickly and massively. The previous dominant brand was drastically reduced and a new brand emerges so that beer which was always brand A is now brand B, etc. The pattern seems closer to the cusp image of catastrophe theory than the more familiar lenticular curve of product diffusion.

There is a clear opposition between the stylist and the merely fashionable. As a means of characterizing traditional clothing norms in order to transcend them the two most common derogatory terms were moksi (pronounced mooksi) and *cosquel*. *Moksi* is a general term for things which look old fashioned and has related connotations of country based as against town or poverty based as against middle class. *Moksi* then is the unsophisticated backwoods look which has yet even to acknowledge its own demise or indicates the inability of the person to enter into competitive display. There is not surprisingly a resistance to such depreciation. Householders with a dominant maroon will affirm that maroon is bright in contrast to red. Bright, which is the term for modern, here refers back to the period when maroon did indeed replace red as the more up to date version of this color category.

The other pejorative term, *cosquel*, is a term for something overdone or juxtapositions which fail, it is a vulgarity that indicates an attempt to style but a failure of taste. The wrong colors have been placed against each other, or an effect has been overdone and thus its possibilities lost. There are also some more general taste parameters, for example, too exclusive a concern with matching colours shows wealth, in that this can be an expensive project but also a certain lack of taste, since as a retailers put it 'some who would know better, will contrast'. Terms of approval often use reverse slang, as the well dressed are flattered by being told that they are looking 'sick', 'bad' or 'cork'.

The advent of recession is a useful indicator as to the place of fashion and style in the kinds of new prioritization of basic needs imposed by constraints on available resources. A survey conducted in all four communities suggested that within families which appeared to be hard hit by recession, and had very little in the way of material items in their houses, there might still be individuals with a dozen or twenty pairs of shoes. Shoes are indicative of style since the notion of the shoe matching the outfit is central to the taste criteria applied to style, such that many shoppers would feel incumbent to purchase new shoes for every new display outfit. An example has already been noted of the continuing demand for new pants amongst the unemployed male. For teenage males the equivalent would be demand for designer trainers.

To conclude this description, the ethnography of clothing use suggests a clear tension or dualism, on one side of which lies that relationship with dress which we term style. Style is a transient aesthetic which favours individual originality in new combinations. It is orientated to the exterior and to display and is based around particular events. There is a considerable stress, not only on individualism but also competition and the refusal of normative order. There co-exists in Trinidad a relationship to clothing which by international and local canons tends to be denigrated as dowdy, vulgar and unappealing. Style is closely related to new forms of the arts and design, to Carnival and to steelband. Here, Trinidad is usually accredited with a highly developed aesthetic positively appraised by visitors and linked to the general articulation today between black diasporan populations and the sense of style, which is the larger context I now wish to address.

STYLE AS SIGNIFYIN(G)

The ethnographic evidence suggests that there is indeed a strong association between some Trinidadians and the sense of style, one which is as much accredited by those who practice style as by those outsiders who attest it. There are a number of ways we could attempt to account for this. One perspective would follow Fanon (1986) who was perhaps the most successful theorist in accounting for a wide range of attributes which were seen as essential qualities of 'black' peoples during colonialism. Fanon tended to concentrate on the projection of attributes by whites which were then introjected by the black population as an expression of their relationship to the hegemonic group. For example, the attribute of sexuality as raw 'nature' was objectified in this personification of otherness, but also introjected into an appropriated sexuality by black West-Indians, particularly in their sexual relationships with whites. It might be argued in an analogous fashion that style as superficiality was introduced as the 'other' to the Western self-construction of itself as true Civilisation with roots in deep classical history. Thus black people could be seen as expressing something as immediate and close to the surface as style, because they lacked the historical and ontological depth, which made whites inept at style but profound. Fanon would probably have then argued that over time this situation would be transcended dialectically by a new self-conscious black identity which constructs style as critique.

A number of more recent studies have adopted an alternative view of the attributes ascribed to the black diasporan population and its subversive potential vis à vis colonial powers. In some cases the attribute is also credited with origins prior to slavery in West African traditions which were then refined or tempered by experiences in the diaspora. The most relevant version, in as much as it focuses on the question of a particular black style, is found in the book *The Signifying Monkey* by Gates (1988). Gates is mainly concerned with language, and the second half of his book is entirely devoted to black fiction in the United States. His concepts were, however, much influenced by a series of studies on the particular nature of black speech or black 'talk', including the work of Labov and the ethnographic studies of Abrahams on black vernacular styles.

The core of Gates' argument is contained in chapters 2 and 3. Here he focuses on the concept of 'to signify'. In conventional semiotics this implies a symbolic relationship between a signifier and a signified, i.e. we signify about something. But for Gates there is a particular form, which he calls 'Signifyin(g)', where it is more appropriate to think of Signifyin(g) upon something. Gates suggests that: 'Signifyin(g) is a rhetorical practice that is not engaged in the game of information-giving, as Wittgenstein said of poetry. Signifyin(g) turns on the play and chain of signifiers, and not on some supposedly transcendent signified' (ibid: 52) Gates argues that the relationship is an interpretive one which refers back to previous interpretations, rather than to any original signified. One of the best images comes from jazz. Music is an especially interesting media in as much as Langer (1942) pointed out that it does not usually symbolize in the conventional discursive sense, i.e. it does not generally signify something (although it can be made to do so). In jazz, music more clearly signifies upon, that is the musician not only takes up themes and develops them fugue-like but very often returns to pastiche or development of well known rhythms and tunes from previous compositions. In ordinary speech both musicians and others will refer to Signifyin(g) upon someone or something.

The primary concern is, however, with language. Here Gates follows the work of Abrahams on the ethnography of speaking 'When a black person speaks of Signifyin(g), he or she means a style-focused message...styling which is foregrounded by the devices of making a point by indirection and wit'...Signifyin(g), in other words, turns on the sheer play of the signifier. It does not refer primarily to the signified; rather it refers to the style of language, to that which transforms ordinary discourse into literature. Again, one does not 'Signify something; one Signifies in some way' (Gates l988: 78, quoting Abrahams 1976: 52). The implication is quite similar to the observation overheard by the anthropologist Manning (1973: 62–63) during research in Bermuda, where the bartender at a club says 'no conversation around here is boring until you stop and listen to it.'

From chapter 3 onwards Gates concentrates on rhetorical forms such as parody and pastiche as used in literature in particular. The implication of this is to link the black trope with the advent of postmodernism since forms such as pastiche have been argued to be the key attributes of this era. For Gates, as in some accounts of postmodernism, there is a celebration of these forms as embodying resistance against hegemonic cultural dominance. Gates gives various examples of pastiche employed by black diasporan populations for subversive purposes. There is, however, a tension in this book between the more politicized aspects which tend to implicate a relationship between a manifest content and a hidden polemic, and the main argument which is directed precisely against any such relationship of depth and surface in order to develop the idea of Signifyin(g) working along a single plane.

During the 1970s there were countless attempts to utilize models derived from the study of language and apply them to non-linguistic forms, in particular, influenced by the success of structuralist and semiotic studies. These transpositions were often of limited success and any analogy between clothing and language should be attempted with caution. I will, however, provide two examples which may help construct just such a bridge. In an article called "Black hair/style politics", Mercer (1987) tackles the dynamic and complex use of hair by black diasporan populations, mainly in Britain and the United States. The argument starts with an attempt to excavate the possibility of hair as symbolic material and particularly the attempts to analyze it as a relatively simple political symbol. Clearly there have been moments, as with the original construction of 'Afro' hairstyles or 'Dreadlocks', when a semiotics of hair as politically symbolic has been pertinent. But as the article develops its historical materials with evidence for complex cross-overs between black and white communities, which often take quite paradoxical turns, the interpretation becomes necessarily correspondingly complex. Mercer turns increasingly to the struggle to forge versions of a black identity and a black aesthetic, as a self-conscious exercise in 'modernist' intervention to create a 'look'. In a sense the role of hair comes to appear as the more profound the more its superficiality as aesthetic is granted. Mercer notes that it no longer becomes possible to ask who is imitating whom and he goes on to quote Oscar Wilde's judgement that 'Only a fool does not judge by appearances' (ibid: 52). As with Gates there seems to be an increasing tendency to focus on black style as part of what might be called the black contribution to the project of modernity, but here applied to the appearance of the body rather than language.

This may be taken a stage further and linked directly with clothing styles with an instance which seems remarkably effective as an illustration of Signifyin(g). *Paris is Burning*, a recent documentary, noted for its ethnographic qualities, examines the emergence of a dance form called 'Vogueing' amongst transvestite male black gays in New York. Vogueing is shown as an intricate combination of clothing, walking and dance. The term comes from the magazine *Vogue* and the characteristic poses in which fashion models are photographed. In vogueing the individual dresses to a specific role, such as 'the streetwise kid', 'the executive' or 'the homely girl next door'. Having achieved 'realness' the dance is used to display, often aggressively, in competition against others from the community. Since the period documented in the film, vogueing has become well-established, mainly through its appropriation by Madonna, who used vogueing as a back-up to her singing and also made it the subject of one of her most popular hits.

Vogueing as documented in *Paris is Burning* seems to work extremely well as an application of Gates' thesis to the domain of clothing. The origins of the style are in *Vogue* and other fashion magazines. The genre of photography employed in these magazines is rarely realist. They do not utilize typical forms of walking and sitting, but generally exaggerated displays of the languorous or provocative in body position. Vogueing then extends this genre into a deliberate self-cultivation of the 'over the top' element, as has often been the case with transvestite dress codes. Thus vogueing exemplifies Gates' sense of a genre which takes up and comments upon previous interpretive genres. All those qualities of brilliant wit, pastiche and parody which are found in 'talk' are here found in the creative appropriation of clothing. Finally vogueing in its original manifestation seems to possess that same combination of aesthetic and politically subversive connotations which Gates grants to Signifying.

Vogueing is however exceptional, and although it demonstrates the possibilities of style, it should not be used to imply that this is necessarily the implication of style. In turning back to the ethnographic account the differences between clothing and language become as important as their similarities. In Trinidad clothing is rarely used for humour and parody outside of the specific context of Carnival. There is much more concentration on the construction of images than on forms such as innuendo or elision. There is evidence, however, for at least equal quantities of cultivation and care devoted to looking good as to sounding good. The focus on language as Signifyin(g) brings language as practice much closer to the world of clothing in so far as we generally see sartorial forms as commenting upon each other as genre rather than as directly symbolic of some transcendent signified.

The work of Gates is clearly an aid in the development of a model of style which directs attention to identity as constructed on the surface. But the problem with which this discussion commenced was the attitude which remains condemnatory of this cultivation of the surface, rather than spending time and money on what are usually regarded as proper values and deep concerns. To relate these two aspects of the problem we need not only to document the form of style but also to address the question as to why a particular population might be identified with it.

As a first step we can go back to Gates and the various arguments over the origins of this tendency. Gates provides one of the clearest arguments for a black diasporan trope with specific origins in West Africa. His first chapter is titled 'A myth of Origins: Esu-Elegbara and the Signifying Monkey'. The origins of Signifyin(g) are traced to the position of certain Yoruba trickster figures within West African cosmological systems. I am unable to comment on the validity of this argument, but in so far as it is used to ground contemporary tendencies in postmodernism, in particular ethnic origins, there are clearly difficulties. Not the least of these would be the availability of alternative origin myths. For example, one would guess that twenty years ago when hermeneutics was more prominent in cultural studies, an argument could have been put forward that the Judaic tradition of textual interpretation and Talmudic discourse which was acknowledged as an influence in the emergence of the hermeneutic tradition was thereby the precursor to that element of circularity, that is the interpretations of interpretations, which are now used to link Signifyin(g) to post modernism. Furthermore other interpretations of West African e.g. Yoruba art would stress quite different elements of 'transmission' (e.g. Thompson 1983).

Gates does not, however, rely merely on the documentation of origins. There are, after all, many aspects of West African culture which clearly do not figure in the world of diasporan black populations. The second stage in any attempt to construct a linkage between these two would need to apply itself to the historical developments which took place during and after slavery. The most powerful argument of this form rests of the notion of surface as a defensive strategy against the condition of extreme degradation. Toni Morrison in her novel *Beloved* has a number of sections where she seems to implicate such a response: 'so you protected yourself and loved small. Picked the tiniest stars out of the sky to own...Anything bigger wouldn't do. A woman, a child, a brother, a big love that would split you wide open in Alfred, Georgia' (1987: 162). The precarious existence given by the condition of slavery precluded any internalization of love, since there was no knowing when this love-object might be wrested from one. The result being a kind of adaptive tendency to keep things on the surface, to refuse any internalization and thus to minimize one's sense of loss.

Again I do not want to attempt to assess such an 'explanation', but it may be useful to note again the limitations of too close an identification between ethnicity and any phenomena as general as style. Firstly the wider ethnography of Trinidad (Miller, 1994) reveals that style is only an attribute of a section of even the ex-African element in the population. There are equally powerful and authentic expressions of the black community which eschew any such concerns and are devoted to quite different values orientated towards the project of internalization, creating a sense of stability, property, descent and religiosity. It would be quite wrong to, as it were, disenfranchise half the black community because they do not conform to an image of radical form which happens to appeal to a certain intellectual fraction. Their cultural orientation may be quite as authentic an expression of their historical experiences as style.

It may therefore be preferable to contextualize the arguments made about black style within the more general contention that within modernity is a struggle for the objectification of freedom within which this sense of transience and surface has a particular attraction. The contemporary relevance of style emerges then out of a continued relevance. It may be that there are precursors in particular regions, and it is certainly the case that the condition of slavery would have fostered an ex-treme concern with the expression of freedom, but it is the continued imperative to objectify forms of freedom which make this historical trajectory complete itself, as it were, within contemporary forms. For this reason, the authenticity of style derives not from whether one can claim descent from some particular origin, such as slavery (though for writers on postmodernism it is increasingly often 'creolized' descent which is romanticized), but rather whether as consumers we appropriate the possibilities given by these histories for strategies of identity construction to-day. Certainly in contemporary Trinidad the sense of West Indian style may be as fully expressed by those of Chinese or East Indian origin as those of African origin.

ONTOLOGY

To account for the continued significance of style we can turn instead to the argument with which this paper started. I want to suggest that the metaphors used in colloquial discussions of 'being', a reflection, in part, on philosophical discussions of ontology, are the context within which we formulate attitudes to style. It is not merely that ideas of depth and surface are applied in both cases but that they have consequences for each other. Indeed it is the taken for granted aspects of our language of being which makes it so difficult for style to be properly appraised. We lack a relativist perspective on ontology, which would allow us to consider properly that construction of being which is radically different from the assumptions of Western philosophy and its associated colloquial discourses.

The concept of superficiality may well be responsible for the extreme difficulty in writing about clothing as fashion with any profundity and overcoming the resistances established by our immediate sense of the trivial nature of this subject. Probably the most successful attempt to pronounce on some 'core' to fashion was Simmel's (1957) essay on the subject which rests on the tension between individualism and sociality. In my ethnographic account of Trinidad this tension is clearly present but in a very different form. In Europe Simmel implies a simultaneity to these two imperatives, fashion operates to relate and reconcile them as well as to express this contradiction. In Trinidad, by contrast, the relationship to clothing splits into two. We have a highly normative form of fashion in which individuals are subsumed into convention, and we have opposed to that a highly individualistic and competitive sense of style.

Style, as a particular and separate mode, has its context in a wide range of other aspects of culture which again seem to take a feature identifiable as a tendency within Europe and extend it or clarify its logic as a form in Trinidad. If individualism is taken as an example of this difference, then its consequences in Trinidad may be explored. The form of individualism found in the Trinidadian stylist results in a cautious approach to the construction of relationships, avoiding the sense that they are maintained merely in order to fulfil normative obligations. Many of the features of 'West Indian Kinship' (e.g. Smith 1988) may be understood as a desire to keep social relations within a voluntaristic framework, such that one chooses to have a close relationship with a sibling or cousin because one wants to and not merely because one is expected to do so by reason of birth. This provides much more fluidity and flexibility as to who actually performs the role of 'mother', or 'close' relative. This family is of tremendous consequence and just as 'viable' as that form of bounded and constant family which local churches and educationalists have insisted Trinidadians ought to have adopted, but it is distinctly different.

Similarly the stylist may resist being defined by their type or place of work, or any similar institutionalised source of identity (Yelvington, forthcoming). Work is often relegated to a minor aspect of life, such that it is leisure which is considered to be the true and proper arena where real life takes place, while work is a mere interlude. This attitude does not prevent complex organizations being built up and sustained by people committed to these values. A steelband can form and persons put in many weeks of practice in order to give a performance of Bach, Wagner or calypso, but with a feeling that this is within their own control. It is a voluntary organization in competition with others and highly sensitive to any attempt to impose control or threaten the self-conscious voluntarism of the participants (see Mandle and Mandle 1988 for the comparable case of basketball in Trinidad).

Individualism then becomes part of the more general objectification of freedom, and the transience of style and its opposition to interiorization is found to be echoed in attitudes to social relations. One of the most common expressions heard in response to any misfortune, from a passing insult to the break up of a relationship, is 'doh (don't) take it on'. Littlewood (1985: 277–278) provides a clear instance of this in his analysis of a depressive condition known as 'tabanca'. This is a kind of moping sickness, leading to solitary contemplation and even suicide, but as Littlewood notes it is also something of a standard joke. The reason for this is that tabanca represents a failing in the maintenance of those values which espouse transience. A man in his relationship with women is expected to retain his phlegmatic cool, relationships are something he can take or leave. If, however, he starts to become more deeply involved, if he allows this relationship to become internalized as something in which he has invested himself, then he stands in danger of considerable loss if the relationship should fail. When this woman leaves him or when she commits adultery his failure to keep the relationship on the surface becomes evident, and *tabanca* follows.

Austin, in her work on Kingston, Jamaica has a similar point to make with the emphasis on the implications of property. She notes that it is after a man has bought the furniture in the house that his partner's infidelity would make a complete fool out of him (1983: 231). The weekly press in Trinidad contains many stories which exploit this theme, the hard 'Bad-John' who has fallen in love. Women, by contrast, use this as evidence for their toughness and resilience in not taking things 'on'. Such examples suggest that a general sense of ontology is found which colloquially has its own spatial metaphors. But in this case the idea of not taking things 'on' is closely related to the refusal to take things 'in'. That is, the proper place of being, appears to be the surface and there is a commitment to an avoidance of interiorization. The larger ethnography provides considerable additional evidence for the importance of this spatial metaphor. There is a constant opposition between the process of interiorization, such as the furnishing of the interior, which is celebrated in Christmas and the exteriorizing project of the stylist which is celebrated in Carnival (Miller, 1994).

Perhaps the most popular leisure activity in Trinidad is the 'lime' in which a group of people either hang around a street corner or travel in a group, for example, into the countryside to 'make a cook'. A feature of the lime is the genre of verbal insult which is known as 'picong' or giving 'fatigue'. One of the attributes of fatigue is to ensure full group participation in events. For example, on a river lime, the individual who did not strip down and bathe would leave themselves open to becoming the major recipient of the developing rounds of insults. The individual characteristics of the limer would then be picked upon, an older male might be asked 'when you alive yet you could cook?' or about whether any remaining hair is really his. An inappropriate piece of clothing, an accident or mistake might be thrown back at the 'guilty' party many times in a variety of forms with appellations such as 'mother-cunt'. Such picong almost always remains good-humoured, because the recipient knows that they are being judged by their ability not to take this on.

This often witty and always barbed invective between friends makes the lime a kind of training ground in which one is steeled against taking in the abuse which can be received in life. Most Trinidadians would certainly assert humour and wit as central to their self-definition and would see it as contributing to their sense of cool, and their ability not to take things on, as well as to their sense of style. The person without a sense of humour would be in danger of being seen as 'ignorant' and prone to violence. Humour helps to keep things on the surface, it keeps conversations focused upon delivery and style rather than content and message, and in this sense is a good complement to clothing.

This context to style also effects the wider relations of consumption. These may be summarized by reference one of the most popular contemporary novels in Trinidad at *The Dragon Can't Dance* by Earl Lovelace (1981). This book focuses upon an impoverished community, but one closely associated with style and the creativity of steelband and Carnival. For the protagonists there are clear views as to the proper nature of consumption, and the value of transience over accumulation: 'but nobody here look at things as if things is everything. If you had more money, you buy more food; and if is a holiday, you buy drinks for your friends, and everybody sit down and drink it out, and if tomorrow you ain't have none, you know everybody done had a good time' (ibid: 103).

It is consumption, and most especially the purchase of clothing as reciprocity, which establishes relationships, especially across gender. Clothing is central to the project of externality but the novel stresses the complex relationship between person and surface evident in the metaphors of masking and masquerade. Clothing may become problematic as when the calypsonian Philo embarrassed by success: 'decorated himself in gaudy shirts and broad-brimmed hats with long colourful feathers stuck in them, as if he wanted to hide himself, to make himself appear so *cosquel* that any fool would know that he had to be found elsewhere, apart from the costume, within it' (ibid: 155).

This concern with the relationship between the surface of the person and the mask is evoked by the title of the book (the Dragon is a form of masquerade) and by Carnival itself. This self is created by its displays 'he wanted nothing but to live, to be, to be somebody for people to recognise, so when they see him they would say: "that is Fisheye !" and give him his space' (ibid: 59). The book ends in the tragic consequences of style as a medium for radical action, as the protagonist's political protest becomes a gesture of defiance but with no clear idea of how this should be followed up. Their failure implicates the contradictions of style as the construction of being: 'So many things we coulda do, and all we wanted was to attract attention! How come everything we do we have to be appealing to somebody else? Always somebody to tell us if this right or wrong, if it good or bad.... Is like we ain't have no self. I mean, we have a self but the self we have is for somebody else. Is like even when we acting we ain't the actor' (ibid: 188). Under such conditions the novel seems to argue a political revolt could be no more than playing masquerade as in Carnival. Indeed the history of radical politics in Trinidad from the 1970 Black Power revolts to the attempted coup by Black Muslims in 1990 seems to bear this out, in as much as both movements were closely articulated with the sense of style and both seemed to begin and end as political gestures.

This wider context to style provides for the bridge to questions of ontology. There is a consistency between this cultivation of the surface and the transient with the consistent refusal of interiorization or sedimentation or fixity derived from institutional or role given forms. This must have implication for identity and in turn for the sense of being. At first the concept of identity appear to be rendered quite empty. There is not social status or agreed position to give placement, or substance which is constant within. Instead being is created through a strategy of display and response. In going to a party or forming a relationship, the individual usually aims high, attempting the best style, the wittiest verbal agility and, if possible, the most prestigious partner. But one only finds out if this is the case from the response of the day, how people react to you and appraise you. It is each particular and assumed transient activity that tells one who one is. It is the event itself that gives judgement, that acts as a kind of reverse omen-taking which establishes also who one has been. However, this is only a specific event or relationship, there is no accretative value. Its implications hardly carry beyond the event itself, so that the position has to be recovered again on the next occasion. It is in this manner that an identity is constructed which is free, that is minimally subject to control. In this strategy style plays a vital role, since it is the ability to change which renders one specific to the event.

The concept of superficial is entirely inappropriate here. Certainly things are kept on the surface, and it is style rather than content which counts. This is because the surface is precisely where 'being' is located. It is the European philosophical tradition and, in particular, the conservative philosophers such as Heidegger, for whom being and rootedness are effectively synonymous, that make it difficult to understand how the very possibilities of modernist speed and ephemera can become the vehicle for both viable and authentic existence.

The consistency of this strategy often shocked me as an outsider. For example, one of the main cultural expressions of contemporary Trinidad associated with, Carnival is the calypso or in its current form soca. The best known living master of the genre is The Mighty Sparrow, although there are new soca stars such as David Rudder. Calypsos are seasonal, they come out soon after Christmas and reach their climax in the competitions at Carnival. In the first Carnival period which I observed, Sparrow's calypsos were simply never played on radio, his tent attracted small audiences and to all intents and purposes he seemed finished. The star of that year on the media and the streets was David Rudder, but in the following year the position was reversed; Sparrow's calypso 'Congo Man' was the most widely played and Rudder could barely raise applause from the audience. Although there are some expectations based on the past, people cannot expect careers with clear trajectories. Each year is a new event in which one starts almost from scratch and one is only regarded highly in as much as that year's songs and performance appears to warrant it. This systematic wiping clean of the slate is symbolized in the attitude to Carnival costume. Even if one plays the same figure every year, and spends a prodigious amount of time on the costume, it is incumbent upon the performer to dispose of their costume after Carnival and create it anew each year.

A parallel may be drawn with recent work in Melanesia. The idea of the event as a kind of omen taking in reverse which establishes who one is, seems similar to Strathern's representation of the relationship between event and causality in that region (Strathern 1988: 268–305). There are clearly differences in as much as in Melanesia the event draws out the implications of the social relations which have led up to it, while in Trinidadian style there is a more extreme presentness and the past has fewer consequences. Where, however, Melanesians are engaged with aspects of modernity the examples may come closer together. Recent work by Carrier and Carrier (1991) on the island of Ponam has shown that under the pressure of its articulation with the wider economy and, in particular, the increasing dependence on remittances sent back by islanders working elsewhere in New Guinea, the forms of exchange have taken on a new dynamic. On this island the particular view one has of social relations are literally laid out in the form of exchange gifts on a regular basis, such that it is local peoples, and not just anthropologists, who construct maps of kindred. Since the islanders are related to each other by many complex routes, the exchanges select particular relationships to express. This practice seems to have intensified to the degree that contemporary islanders are engaged in plotting their relative positions through elaborate exchanges during one in every four days. In effect, they are devoting an ever increasing amount of time to establishing who they are in relation to each other.

The parallel between these two areas would seem to rest in a long observed aspect of many Melanesian societies, that is the relative importance of achieved as opposed to ascribed status. The relative absence of institutionalization of social position is associated with an emphasis on the externalization of selfhood, turning oneself into an object for the gaze of others, in order to know who one is, a variant of objectification which Strathern calls personification (1988: 176–182). The form of individualism found in Trinidad is, however, very different from Melanesia since it is perceived as the result of one's self-cultivation of style, while in Melanesia it is a particular outcome of the effect of those social relations though which one is created, such that from the Trinidadian perspective, Melanesia can scarcely be said to have individuals. Both are, in turn, extremely different from the American form of the individual as a project or autobiography in process, with constant concern to rebuild the past and project the future of individuals (Bellah 1985; Giddens 1991). Again these relationships between individualism and sociality as expressed as interiors and exteriors have quite specific historical meanings in the emergence of German modernity (Dumont 1986). Each regional study demonstrates the problem in asserting a generic modern form of individualism, and in privileging the assumptions drawn from any one regional tradition.

A comparative approach does not extinguish differences by insisting upon commensurability; on the contrary, it prevents the universalism of the usual discussion of modernity which allows for only one homogenizing and global approach to identity. The specific comparison with Melanesia serves two purposes. Firstly, when in the Melanesian case the anthropologist documents an extreme concern which body and self-decoration for display purposes, in a contemporary, but neither capitalist nor modernist context, this turning oneself into an object for display has no connotations of superficiality. Instead it is used to express the authentic 'other' to the postmodern West. Melanesia therefore provides a model of the non-superficial surface.

Secondly, this comparison helps us to analyze another feature of Trinidadian life which is often misunderstood. Clothing, as well as expressing individualism, is also perceived as central to cross-gender relationships. A woman with style expressed in the transience of clothing is assumed to be acting within a relationship in which she receives the money for clothing from the man with whom she has sexual relations. The expectation that money will be received with some constancy during such a relationship is derided by those Trinidadians with opposed values as evidence that such relationships are merely a variant of prostitution.

For the women involved the implication is quite the opposite. The money received is viewed as a sign that the relationship is sincere and that the man cares for her, indeed the amount of money may be explicitly viewed as indicating the degree of care. She reciprocates with a sexuality which is most overtly expressed in her clothing. Within a comparative context this can be viewed as a kind of brideprice without marriage. The relationship is objectified in exchange as is often the case in Melanesia, but unlike Melanesia, these relationships remain 'common-law'. In lacking the institutionalization of marriage, the partners retain the sense of voluntarism, such that the relationship has to be constantly recreated in the constancy of the exchange.

Clothing as fashion, and money as commodification are here not opposed to clothing as gifts in the Maussian sense but represent an articulation between the imperatives of modernity and the imperatives of gift based sociality. This observation indicates the importance of a factor rarely mentioned in the voluminous literature on gift exchange, that is its frequency. If it is exchange which constitutes the relationship, then for social groups which value transience as an avoidance of stable obligations which would constrain their sense of freedom, there remains the option of transient exchange. It is this new temporality, this frequency of engagement in acts by which being is reconstituted which evokes the sense and spirit of modernity.

Money and transient clothing, as used by the Trinidadian stylist, are neither demeaning nor do they express some loss of humanity. If the Trinidadian stylist were viewed as constructing exchange systems which extend elements found in Melanesia instead of being viewed as some degeneration of 'Western' capitalist culture then it would be much easier to appreciate the necessity for a relativistic ontology in order to appreciate the implications of style. The problem is that Melanesia is granted historical 'roots' which allow us to regard the articulation with capitalism as some kind of 'taming' or 'localizing' of a global process. By contrast, Trinidad born as a periphery to the world-economy, and constructing its cultural norms, a posteriori, out of a long engagement with capitalism and colonialism, is not credited with this capacity.

The situation in Trinidad is complicated by the sheer force of those authorities within the island who would wish to retain the denigration of superficiality. The demands of style, the desire to keep things on the surface, and a preference for constant change may very easily become elided with a sense of the trivial and of mistaken prioritization in consumption. It should be noted that this critique comes not only from institutions of the establishment, such as the church and the education system, but is equally shared by the radical political movements who despair at the lack of commitment they associate with an orientation to style, an ambivalence evident in Lovelace's novel. There is then no single 'Trinidadian', let alone 'black diasporan', cultural form. I have attempted to abstract and normativize that approach associated with 'style' but this is constantly opposed even within the communities associated with particular abilities or affinities with style.

The implications of this relativist anthropology of consumption are rather different from that usually found in cultural studies or in the work of Gates. These latter works stress the politicization of style and its implications for 'resistance'. My argument is that the consequences of style may be found to act in favour (as pastiche) or equally against (as transience) the desires of radical politics, but they are not born out of the imperative to radicalism. Rather they arise out of the articulation between modernity and the desire to objectify a sense of voluntaristic freedom. This is quite compatible with the sense of historical sources given above by Gates (and Morrison in *Beloved*) which help us to understand why freedom, for example, should have such presence. History helps us understand the significance of a desire which attempts to deal with the state of abuse, of de-humanization, by providing an alternative construction of being which externalizes and refuses any fixity or institutionalization in which the person would inevitably be placed at the bottom or the exploited fraction of society. But I would follow Mercer in arguing that to understand style as a contemporary phenomena we have to go beyond the excavation of origins to stress their contribution to, and articulation with, the project of modernity.

By placing the desire for style and the uses of clothing in this comparative context the anthropological project of relativizing phenomena is re-established. The critique within this chapter is directed against an ideology which insidiously forces us to regard consumption as superficial and trivial, and which therefore insists that the increasing importances of consumption is symptomatic of a loss of depth in the world. This example of a universalizing attitude to modern mass consumption is clearly expressed in writings on post modernism, which may be viewed as merely the most recent manifestation of aesthetic and philosophical ideologies which lie at the core of 'Western' thought. From the perspective of Trinidad, where many of the supposed characteristics appear with unusual clarity, the deluge of recent writings on the assumed global condition of post modernity or some culture of 'late-capitalism' appear parochial and sterile.

The study of consumption has been viewed as the end of anthropology, a symbol of increasing homogenization and the elimination of cultural difference as the anthropological object of study. The new ethnography of consumption points in the opposite direction, to consumption as pivotal to any future anthropology, since it is increasingly through modes of consumption that differences in culture, even at the level of differences in ontology, are constructed.

ACKNOWLEDGEMENTS

I would like to acknowledge the financial support of: the British Academy, the Central Research fund of the University of London, the Nuffield Foundation, The Wenner-Gren foundation for anthropological research. I would also like to thank the many Trinidadian friends and informants who helped me during the fieldwork. I would also acknowledge the help of Brad Lander who drew my attention to the works of Gates and Mercer used in this chapter, and Mike Rowlands who provided the Dumont and Thompson references.

References

Abrahams, R.

1976   *Talking Black*. Rawley Mass: Newbury House. Austin, D. 1984 *Urban Life in Kingston, Jamaica*. New York: Gordon and Breach.

Barthes, R.

1967   *Systeme de la Mode*. Paris: Editions du Seuil. Bell, Q. 1976. *On Human Finery*. London: The Hogarth Press

Bellah, R. *et. al.*

1985   *Habits of the Heart*. New York: Harper and Row.

Carmichael, A.C.

1969   *Domestic Manners and Social Condition of the White, Coloured, and Negro*
1833   *Population on the West Indies*. New York: Negro University Press.

Carrier, A. and Carrier J.

1991   *Structure and Process in a Melanesian Society*. Reading: Harwood Academic Press.

Dumont, L.

1986   Are cultures beings? German identity in iteraction. *Man* 21: pp. 587–604.

Ewen, S. and Ewen, E.

1982   *Channels of Desire*. New York: McGraw Hill.

Fanon, F.

1986   *Black Skin White Masks*. London: Pluto Press.

Freilich, M.

1960   Cultural diversity among Trinidadian Peasants, unpublished Ph.D. University of Columbia.

Gates, H.

1988   *The Signifying Monkey.* Oxford: Oxford University Press.

Giddens, A.

1991   *Modernity and Self-Identity.* Cambridge: Polity Press.

Harvey, D.

1989   *The Condition of Postmodernity.* Oxford: Basil Blackwell.

Jameson, F.

1991   *Postmodernism or the Cultural Logic of Late Capitalism.* London: Verso.

Langer, S.

1942   *Philosophy in a New Key.* Cambridge, Mass: Harvard University Press.

Littlewood, R.

1985   An Indigenous Conceptualization of Reactive Depression in Trinidad. *Psychological Medicine* **15**: pp. 275–281.

Lovelace, E.

1981   *The Dragon Can't Dance.* London: Longman.

Mandle, J. R. and Mandle, J. D.

1988   *Grass Roots Commitment: Basketball and Society in Trinidad and Tobago.* Pakersburg: Caribbean Books.

Mercer, K.

1987   Black hairstyle politics. *New Formations* **3** pp. 33–54.

Morrison, T.

1987   *Beloved.* New York: Knopf.

Miller, D.

1994   Modernity — An Ethnographic Approach. Oxford: Berg.

Paris is Burning. Documentary shown on *Arena*, BBC television.

Simmel, G.

1957   Fashion. *American Journal of Sociology* **62**: pp. 541–558.

Simmel, G.

   1978   *The Philosophy of Money*. London: Routledge and Kegan Paul Smith, R. 1988. *Kinship and Class in the West Indies*. Cambridge: Cambridge University Press.

Strathern, M.

   1988   *The Gender of the Gift*. Berkeley: University of California Press.

Thompson, R.

   1983   *Flash of the Spirit*. New York: Vintage Books.

Veblen, T.

   1970   *The Theory of the Leisure Class*. London: George Allen and Unwin.

Weiner, A and Schneider, J.(eds)

   1989   *Cloth and Human Experience*. Washington: Smithsonian Institution Press.

Wilson, E.

   1985   *Adorned in Dreams*. London: Virago.

Yelvington, K.

   forth-   Gender and ethnicity at work in a Trinidadian factory. In J. Momsen (ed.)
   coming.   *Caribbean Women*. London: Macmillan.

CHAPTER FOUR

Consumer Goods as Dialogue about Development: Colonial Time and Television Time in Belize

Richard Wilk

The house was new and on this ground floor smelled of concrete and paint. The rooms were not yet fully decorated; the furnishings were sparse. But there were fans everywhere; and the bathroom fittings, from Germany were rare and expensive. 'I am craze for foreign,' Mrs. Mahindra said. 'Just craze for foreign.'

She marveled at our suitcases and at what they contained. She fingered with reverence and delight.

'Craze, just craze for foreign.'

V.S. Naipaul *An Area of Darkness* (1968:85)

Belize is a whole country 'craze for foreign'. The wide variety of imported consumer goods on sale in shops, on display in homes, and worn and eaten by members of every one of the country's nine ethnic groups, is juxtaposed with serious urban and rural poverty. Belize has large areas of unoccupied arable land, yet more than 40 percent of the diet (by value) is imported. Supermarkets stock frozen American vegetables and canned tropical fruit from Hawaii. As in many other Third World countries, some Belizeans are sacrificing their health and their longer-term economic prospects, for goods that are usually considered luxuries (cf. Belk 1988). (Some measures of Belize's dependence on imports, not just for luxuries and consumer goods, but also for basic staples, can be found in addendum 1 to this paper).

My goal here is to make some suggestions about the significance of Belize's imports in the local systems of value, in political consciousness, and in the creation of visions of the future — the traffic in significance that Hannerz calls the 'management of meaning.' (1987:550) This is very much a work in progress, part of an ongoing study of consumption and nationalism in Belize which is by no means complete.[1]

TRADITIONAL AND MODERN; CONSUMERISM IN THE THIRD WORLD

Modernization theory may be out of favor in academia, but in Belize, as in most of the Third World, it is alive and well as popular ideology. The polarities of *traditional* and *modern* have become folk models — in Belize Creole 'bushy' or 'krofi' at one pole, and 'bright' or 'modan' at the other.[2] The terms are used by schoolteachers and politicians to describe aspects of their pupils and constituents, by rural people to describe themselves and their relationship to the city, by tourists, emigrants and expatriates to relate Belize to other countries.

These polarities form a basic part of a discourse of power rooted in notions of time and temporality. When Belizeans use these terms to describe themselves and each other, they are creating pasts and futures. And objects of various kinds play a crucial and active role in the construction and use of time and images of personal and collective futures. They present aspirations, alternative views of how the future should be. Different groups contest with each other for that future, using various kinds of goods to stake their claim, map their route, and convince others of its inevitability. As such these goods are inherently political and programmatic. Just as people use objects to invent tradition, they also use them to invent the future.

A good example with which to focus the discussion comes from Nancy Lundgren's research on child-rearing among poor urban Creoles in Belize City (1986, 1988).[3] At Christmas, the parents she studied often scrimp, save and borrow

---

[1] I would like to thank Russell Belk and the participants in the Copenhagen conference on 'Commodities and Cultural Strategies' for their comments and suggestions on an earlier draft of this paper. The stimulating interactions of the group helped me to clarify my thinking on a number of difficult points. Much appreciation is also due to Orvar Lofgren for both inspiring the original paper, and for his deft editorial hand during revision. Anne Pyburn has helped with every aspect of this research project, from planning through every stage of fieldwork, and I owe her an immeasurable debt. Of course, nobody who has helped should be held in any way accountable for defects in the final product. Research has been supported by a Fulbright Fellowship from the Council for International Educational Exchange, a Grant from the Wenner-Gren Foundation, and a summer faculty fellowship from Indiana University.

[2] Belize Creole, spoken as a native language by about 50 percent of the population and as a second language by most of the rest, is similar to the Creoles of Jamaica and the rest of the British Caribbean. Many archaic English usages are preserved, but there are also a surprising number of African roots; 'krofi' for example, meaning scruffy, rough and primitive, is derived from the Fanti day name 'koffi'. Belize Creole has been seen as both a language of resistance and a tool of repression (Le Page 1975; Hellinger 1973; Young 1973).

[3] Out of a total population of about 200,000, some 40 percent are Creole — meaning the mixed descendants of white settlers and their slaves. Creoles are heavily concentrated in Belize City (pop. ca. 45,000). Other larger minorities include Mestizo/Maya (33%), Guatemalan and

to buy their children presents. A highly valued gift from a mother to a girl child is an imported blue-eyed, blonde haired doll. After one session of play, the doll is kept in its sealed box, on prominent display on a shelf in the parlor. How are we to interpret these dolls, and the choice to sacrifice other necessities and pleasures to give and own them?

Recent anthropological work on the demand for commodities attempts to go beyond a simple dichotomy between stable traditional consumption and dynamic modern life-styles (Orlove and Rutz 1989; also Ferguson 1988). In practice, most anthropologists still see a world in which local cultures and their preferences for local products are being subverted by hegemonic foreign ideologies which provide a myriad of seductive images to promote new needs for consumer goods. These models depend on some combination of coercion, seduction, emulation or the undercutting of local systems of self-sufficient production; in the end local cultures lose their identity and autonomy (and one is led to suspect that they also lose their authenticity). The end result is a 'world culture' like that proposed in a recent study of 'the global teenager' (Baker 1989).

An example of this approach is offered by Philibert (1989), who argues that Third World consumption is inherently acculturation caused by exposure to world consumer culture; through a kind of 'bait-and-switch' the consumer never gets what is offered by the object.

> Acculturated individuals purchase objects in order to attain what their image suggests, but there is never enough behind the image. Their desire is forever renewed but never satisfied. Their quest for social identity requires that they spend more and more, yet the logic of consumption itself cancels the sign-effect of their acquisitions. (Philibert 1989:63, paraphrasing D'Haene 1980:183).

Lundgren herself sees the blue-eyed dolls as an example of Third World people accepting an hegemonic ideology of their own dark-skinned inferiority. The blue-eyed doll is a simple token or symbol of the Belizean's aspirations to be white and powerful, an emulation of the metropole. In this interpretation, spending money on useless dolls, like national spending on show projects like dams and model cities, is a form of wish fulfillment where the symbol replaces reality (1986).

This view of consumption is satisfying on a number of levels. It confirms the power of elites and leaders (even anthropologists). It is popular in the literature on media and television, where the 'new world information order' is said to create and perpetuate dependency, substituting images for substance. The media itself takes credit for this power (a headline in an Indiana newspaper shouts

---

Salvadoran refugees (unknown proportion), Garifuna (Afro-Amerindians, 8%), Mopan Maya (7%), and Kekchi Maya (3%).

'Egyptians Empty Streets for Falcon Crest'), though it denies the same power when the discussion turns to promoting crime and violence. And it is convenient and satisfying to cast the people of the Third World as victims of our own materialism, a materialism our moral ideology often condemns (Belk 1983).

One glaring problem, however, is that this model depends on selective false consciousness. Only a so small elite group (Philibert's 'bureaucratic neo-bourgeoisie') takes an active hand in manipulating symbols; everyone else is too stupid or deluded; they are doomed to emulation, wasting their money on blue-eyed dolls. Thus we ignore a century of market research in the United States that finds people's motivations for buying goods to be complex, deeply symbolic, social, personal and contextual. Now that this research is being extended to the Third World (e.g. Wallendorf and Arnould 1988) we are finding the same degree of depth and complexity of behavior among those whose consumption is 'traditional'.

Caribbean countries like Belize pose a direct challenge to these acculturation models of the growth in demand for commodities in the Third World, and to the assumption that these desires are symptoms of the disruption caused when a traditional society encounters the modern world. As Miller points out (1990), Caribbean societies have been modern in an economic and cultural sense, for longer than the metropoles that created them. Belizeans, like Trinidadians, have built a culture from an international melange of commodities and cultural elements. More than other cultures in the world, their identity is independent of history and was not formed in isolation. Belize has been an enclave of capitalism, a creation of the world economy, for 350 years, and during that time Belizean Creoles have lived in a world of commodities. Creoles have never had the stable traditionally-bound regime of consumption, so beloved of anthropologists, and their present desires cannot be depicted as a disoriented response to the invasion of a new global mode of productions.[4] One wonders to what degree *any* consumption in the Third World can be understood in these terms.

The Caribbean cases show us that we need to go beyond seeing the desire for goods like the blue-eyed dolls as deluded, fetishistic, or dominated, as 'false consciousness'. By condemning Third World consumption as emulation or imitation, we denigrate the creative and expressive capabilities of those people, to take and *use* foreign goods for their own purpose. At the same time it is clear that people are not making completely free choices about goods. They are not merely absorbing foreign goods into their existing modes of consumption, and making

---

[4] The image of people as 'newcomers to the world of goods' is seductive and powerful (Gell 1986). It is so attractive that the moment of change has been discovered repeatedly in European history and around the world (McCracken 1988: 4–30). This may be a kind of 'virginity complex', where what comes before and what comes afterward are assumed to be stable and unproblematic. The dramatic moment is the transitional state, which may be depicted as seduction, capture, rape or marriage.

free strategic choices in the global marketplace. Third World consumers *are* subject to various forms of coercion, both economic and ideological. The freedom to consume should not be confused with the ownership of means of production, marketing and communication — though a good deal of advertising seeks to promote just this confusion, according to Jhally (1990).

The challenge for a theory of consumption in the Third World is not to choose one bias or the other (coercion or autonomy, hegemony or resistance). The task is instead to map out the areas where greater autonomy exists, and those where coercion takes place, and to seek explanations for the variation in these areas, as well as for the way in which coercion and autonomy interact and obscure each other. We need to ask why some consumption responds to advertising while other kinds of consumption do not. We must find out which groups are leaders and which are followers, which kinds of consumption promote conformity and loss of identity and which kinds express creativity and rebellion.

One way to settle these more advanced kinds of questions is to concentrate on process, on the ways that people actively dispute and debate the meaning of different kinds of goods, and on their different strategies of using commodities as tools for constructing personal, gender, ethnic, and political identities. But the dialogue conducted with commodities and goods is a very special one that requires new kinds of analytical tools. This is because in the dialogue of goods, unlike the discussion conducted with verbal language *meaning is always in dispute*. Verbal language only works when we agree on the denotative meanings of words. A dialogue is a difference of opinion communicated with a common code.

The consumption of goods, in contrast, sends a message even when sender and receiver do not agree on what the message means. When a Creole man wears his new hat to church, his message may be that he has been to New York with cash in his pocket; he is a success in the monetary world. His kin receive another message; 'look at the way the arrogant fool spent his money on himself instead of his family'.

The contest is over the meaning of the hat. At the village level, at the national level, at the international level, what looks like the flow of objects and meanings is actually a struggle over the meaning of those objects. The dialogue of goods is a contest where there is no common code. The contest *is* the code. As McCracken says, goods 'seek not only to describe, but also to persuade' (1988: 132). When we treat goods as language we make the touristic error of seeing every place becoming more like our own; we don't see that Kentucky Fried Chicken means something very different in Belize than it does in New York.

We are only beginning to construct a vocabulary for discussing this 'politics of value' (Appadurai 1986: 57). In addendum 2 below I discuss some of the more general ways that dialogues of meaning about goods can be described and classified. Here I would like to concentrate on one particularly important contest of meaning in Belize, that over the temporal meanings of goods.

GOODS AND TIME

As mentioned above, in Belize the dialogue of goods is often couched in terms of tradition and modernity — terms with an explicit reference to the passage of time. The contested meanings of goods are alternative views of the past, the present and the future. Social time is ordered by goods at a number of scales, from personal daily routines to life cycles (Douglas and Isherwood 1979: 65–66).

By their physical nature, goods create temporal continuity, and people use them to create paths of connection from past to present (Miller 1987: 125-126; Linnekin 1983). What gives those connections relevance in the real world is not necessarily the past that the goods refer to or break with, but the directionality they create. Material goods contest possible futures, by creating images, and tinging those images with inevitability. Material objects in the present make a particular future seem concrete. 'When culture appears in objects, it seeks to make itself appear inevitable.' (McCracken 1988: 132)

In Belize's history, goods have played a very specific role as markers of time. The colonial regime constructed something I call *colonial time*, where physical distance, cultural distance, and time were merged and became inseparable. The three were seen as aspects of the same phenomenon (as in modernization theory). Time, distance, and culture became interchangeable justifications for the inequalities between the colony and the metropole. In colonial time the colony is described using metaphors that blend the connotative meanings of time, distance and cultural development. *Primitive, backward, and underdeveloped* are such blending terms, while others draw more directly on temporal, cultural, or spatial meanings (e.g. antiquated, uncultured, isolated, natural, savage, barbaric, degenerate, primordial, wild, marginal peripheral, uncivilized, backwater).

One effect of colonial time was to objectify the concept of tradition, of culture rooted in distant time and remote places. The colony was backward because of *timeless*, isolated and pervasive tradition (in Belize tradition was closely associated with the trackless, remote, ageless primeval forest, from which the wealth of mahogany, logwood and chicle was wrested). The flow of time became the enterprise and province of the colonial administrators, clerics and intelligentsia who represented themselves as agents of 'progress'. Progress is movement in time from the unchanging past to the dynamic future, in space from the isolated hinterland to the bustling city, and in culture from static tradition to fashionable modernity. In colonial culture, time is a blueprint for social and political change, a master metaphor that carries the burden of an entire cultural plan.

If *colonial time* is the heart of colonial cosmology, style and fashion are its outward concrete symbols. The gap in fashionable clothes, furnishings, housing styles, language, and customs between the colony and the metropole is the concrete measure of the lag between them. The flow of consumer goods and information between the metropole and the colony is a form of cultural timekeeping; the objects and ideas are clocks marking off *colonial time*. The units might be called 'years behind'.

In Belize in the 1950s the fashions seen on the street — zoot suits, gold watch chains, high collars and bow ties — lagged up to 20 'years behind' those of New York and London. The irony of colonial time is that while it is premised on the promise of progress, there is really no catching up. The lag can become smaller or larger, but the clock is set in the metropole, and the colonies will always be in another time-zone. The flow of fashion requires the colonies to keep running faster to catch up.[5]

While it may seem an elaborate form of bondage, colonial time serves the social and political interests of the colonial elites as well as the metropolitan powers. It assures demand for metropolitan status goods; even when the colonials are starving, the answer is still progress, and progress is still measured by colonial time and the flow of imported goods. On the global scale colonial time affirms the political dependency of the undeveloped and developing on the developed, and keeps the colonial elite in a subordinate position.

On the local level colonial time reproduces inequality by making the colonial elite into timekeepers. Colonial time run through narrow channels, and the local elite, who can travel to the metropole and come back with new styles and fashions, are the conduit through which time flows. They bring new books, new music, new food and new clothing fashions that keep them 'ahead' in legitimate ways. The timeless stasis of tradition is broken only by those who are in contact with the outside world. Even if local society did not choose to emulate the metropolitan fashion (the latest clothes and foods were often rejected as 'impractical' or 'frivolous') those fashions had an unassailable legitimacy.

TELEVISION TIME

Today in Belize there are nine television stations and an equal number of cable systems that rebroadcast a direct feed from United States satellites (see addendum 1), with very limited local programs and some local advertising. For a good part of the day Belizeans watch *real time* network television. Watching

---

[5] It is this very lag that makes it possible for the metropolitan consumer to savor the archaism of an African mask, an experience that emphasizes the time gap even if the wood of the mask is still green. Sections of this discussion appear in a paper entitled "Colonial Time and TV Time" in a 1994 issue of *Visual Anthropology Review*.

WGN from Chicago, Belizeans have become Chicago Cubs baseball fans, and in 1984 a larger crowd turned out at the airport to greet outfielder Gary Mathews than for the Pope or Queen Elizabeth (see Bolland 1987; Lent 1989; Everitt, 1987; Petch 1987).

Why does direct broadcast transmission make such a difference? Because the programs, especially the sports and news broadcasts, are so *immediate*. There is no lag. The Belizean family in their rickety house in a swamp on the edge of Belize City is not only watching the same programs as all of urban America, but far more importantly, they are watching them at the same *time*.

Satellite television has removed an essential element from the equation of colonial time. Distance between the metropole and the colony can no longer be reckoned in terms of time. The immediacy of contact forces watchers to see that only distance and culture — not time — set Belize apart from the United States. Television time is now a single clock ticking away a single rhythm in every place it reaches, a continuous cycle of news, advertising, entertainment and special events. Television time is alarming and strange at first — it is the direct experience of a flow of events that was once far away, safely filtered, and dimly and indirectly perceived. Things seem to be moving more quickly, almost out of control.

And for the political and cultural elite, television time is out of control, at least temporarily (see Wilk [1993a] for a discussion of how the power of television has been partially recaptured). The colonial conduits of power have been circumvented. Fashion is no longer channeled through the local elite because so much information flows directly from television, as well as through print media and the increasing flow of tourists, and migrants in both directions (see Everitt 1987 and addendum 1).

Ten years ago when someone returned from a trip to New York or Miami they strutted their new clothes around for weeks, tried out their new words at parties, and displayed the latest bit of technology in their home. These displays have now lost a lot of their impact.[6] In the summer of 1989, Batman T-shirts, lunch boxes and belt bags appeared in Belize within three weeks of the release of the film *Batman* in America. The consumption styles of the Belize elite are revealed as frauds — though the elite presumes to sit ahead of everyone else on the time line, they cannot come close to matching what everyone can see on Miami Vice, in the advertisements, on the news. The local elite is no longer the only group to emulate, for it is no longer the sole source of new things, the local agent and representative of the metropole. Local people are also now aware that the culture

---

[6] Today the carriers of new fashions are the Belizean-Americans who descend on Belize each year in September for National day and Independence day festivities. They parade the streets of Belize wearing the latest clothes and accessories from American urban ghetto culture, a culture that rarely appears on television. But they get a very mixed reception, for many Belizeans recognize that even in America, ghetto fashions are ambivalent symbols of economic success.

of the metropole itself is diverse and divided, and has its own contending elites and poor minorities.

Watching live television in Belize City, there is an immediacy of experience, an emotional involvement in the present on an equal basis with viewers in Los Angeles and New York. You are not seeing a game that happened last week, you are in the here and now. An when the game is over, both the stinks and the aromas of Belize City are in the here and now too, there is no escaping it. To steal Conrad's metaphor from *Heart of Darkness*, the journey upriver is no longer a journey back in time. It is just a trip upriver that *takes* some time. The lack of speed is a problem, not a metaphor, and it can be overcome by applying a bit of technology. If things are different upriver it is not because of some kind of time lag. We can't just sit back and expect that problems will be solved when the locals 'catch up'. Between Belize and the United States the time lag is gone, the distance is closing, what remains are cultural, economic, and political problems and contrasts that require new explanations.

The Western construct of linear history that grew along with the world system of colonial expansion turned the rest of the world into 'peoples without history'. How could they have a history, suspended permanently in the past? But television time seems to have the power to unfreeze clocks, by extracting the present from the past and objectifying both. It allows time and events to be separated from each other and ordered into sequences that do not all lead inevitably in the same direction — toward the metropole.[7]

The freedom brought by the collapse of colonial time has opened new arenas of competition, though the economic order of the system has changed very little. While independence in 1981 brought a new measure of meaning to local politics, foreign capital remains dominant, and the government depends on foreign grants and loans to balance the budget. The local elite is divided into expatriates, merchants, small business owners, professionals and bureaucrats. The colonial symbolic order that gave some coherence to this messy hierarchy, divided by age, ethnicity, geography and family loyalties, has been undercut.

Today there is an opening; freed from the burden of carrying temporal messages, many categories of material culture — clothing, food and housing among them — can now acquire new meanings. Local foods that were once tainted with connotations of backwardness and unsophistication can now be rein-terpreted as 'roots' (traditional) food, or ethnic food, or national cuisine. Objects can acquire historical and cultural referents that are truly in the present. Different

---

[7] Given that the colony was never seen as having a history of its own, it is no surprise that there is only one historical monument in the whole country — commemorating the final crushing of Maya resistance by the British in 1872. Most of the history of the country has been written by foreigners, and a Belize historical society was only established, with twenty five members (including myself), in 1990. An express purpose of the society is to identify landmarks and national heros.

interest groups can contend to appropriate them and attach new connotations — both positive and negative. Today in Belize a wide variety of groups are using local arts, music, foods and customs in new ways, not the least of which is their marketing to tourists as items of 'traditional' Belizean culture (even though most Belizean souvenirs are imported from Taiwan and Guatemala) (Wilk 1993b).

CREATING POST-COLONIAL HISTORY

The regime of colonial time in Belize was never monolithic and seamless, and local elites were never united in their interests. By excluding so much of the population from anything but passive participation (virtual observers of the élite), the colonial regime reduced the incentive to participate. When the consumption standards of the working classes were pressed by inflation, disasters, or economic depression, riots and demonstrations were common (see Bolland 1977, 1988). But most resistance took the form of attacks on the existing order, the destruction and looting of the importers' shops, rather than the formulation of an alternate order. Marcus Garvey's Universal Negro Improvement Association (Belize chapter founded in 1920), and the labour union movement of the 1930s saw the genesis of a nationalist and class consciousness of sorts, but they asked for a better deal, rather than a different one.

Only when people obtain and consume objects outside the flow of colonial time, do they challenge and resist the social order of the colonial system. Ghandi's *Swadeshi* home-spun cloth campaign in India was a potent political challenge to the colonial economy, because it undercut the order of time, asserting a different image of India's future, rooted in a popular image of its past (Gell 1986).[8]

In Belize today the diverging interests of different groups lead them to rein- terpret the past as part of their efforts to legitimate their plans for the country's future. The interpretation of the 'Battle of St George's Cay', a minor skirmish in 1797 between the British and Spanish, has been as important in the last two elec- tions as the two parties' differences over the role of foreign investment, economic self-sufficiency, and development strategy. For one political party the Battle was the time when slaves and their owners stood 'shoulder to shoulder' in the com- mon interest. For the other it is an example of British colonial mythmaking, and the slaves were unwilling and exploited participants. In the broader context, this disagreement is a symptom of widening conflict over Belize's cultural future, a disagreement that frustrates the government's attempts to forge a national iden- tity (Judd 1989).

---

[8] As in the Kula, the colonial objects of power are those that have passed through foreigners' hands, not through those of the ancestors. Today in the post-colonial world the creation of indigenous history is confronted with the problem that the foreigners have to some extent become ancestors.

CREATING POST-COLONIAL FUTURES

In talking about consumer goods with Belizeans, I often find it difficult to get people to talk about their tastes and preferences; these are topics that people resist interpreting.[9] But when I have asked people about their personal aspirations and their life goals, and ask them to imagine or fantasize about the future they would like to have, they often construct rich material scenarios. Others have found that young people in the Third World have very rich fantasies that reflect their social and political awareness (Caughey 1984; Rubin and Zavalloni 1969; Lundgren 1988).[10]

One way to interpret the role of consumer goods in Belize may be to see them as furnishings for these imagined futures, as vehicles that people use to create directions and mark their progress. They allow people a semblance of control and link their concrete daily circumstances with more vague lifelong goals and plans.

Without this concrete image of the future, consumption in the present loses its meaning. Goods are the vehicles of our intentionality. The important research question then becomes one of asking where those goals come from; how much influence popular movements, nationalist propaganda, organized religion, and other groups may have in formulating the utopic visions that motivate people.

Utopias — templates of what the future should be, are few and far between in the Third World today (Naipaul 1976). At one time Mao, Fidel, Ras Tafari, and Ghandi provided powerful templates or models for the fashioning of images of the future, as do Muslim fundamentalists in much of Africa and Asia today (Arnould 1989). The American television utopia of personal freedom and consumer goods may have a great appeal, but this does not mean that it signifies the same thing to everyone. A man may see the sexual license of Dallas and capture it for his fantasies, while a woman sitting next to him is taking in the independence of women from their mothers and their ability to spend on themselves instead of their family. In Belize most people are selective in their admiration of the America they see on television; they deplore almost as much as they desire. But they are thrown back on their own imagination

---

[9] I have not yet finished analysis of my data on Belizeans' personal favorite objects, a kind of research pioneered by Wallendorf and Arnould (1988).

[10] Caughey argues that the fantasy worlds people create are inherently *social*, modeled on real human relationships (1984). This theory of imaginary social worlds may make more sense of consumer goods than any linguistic or economic model. There is a growing social relationship between emerging middle classes in the Third World and the first world that contains many elements of fantasy. The tourist has a fantasy relationship with the native, the USAID official has a fantasy relationship with the local government, and the middle class Belizean who goes to Disneyworld (the favourite tourist destination from Belize) is building a fantasy relationship with the United States.

when they create their own personal bricolage, and furnish it with a selection of goods.[11]

ALTERNATE UTOPIAS IN MODERN BELIZE

If consumer goods are a medium through which alternate views of the future contend, what kinds of lives are Belizeans trying to create? Given the ethnic and geographic diversity of the country, here I will only try to define four different strategies of using material culture to define the future.

First is the official state future: development through economic modernization while building a national culture from bits and pieces of nine ethnic cultures. State rhetoric speaks of a uniquely Belizean future, of local foods and local products. The cultural symbols are a hasty collection of Caribbean music, Latin food, Garifuna dance, Mayan ruins, and Mennonite chickens. But these cultural symbols are undercut by the economic reality of American wheat and construction equipment, Canadian sewers, British roads, and Hindu shops full of goods from everywhere but Belize.

Nevertheless, many Belizeans, particularly foreign-eduated professionals and local business people, accept this as a viable goal. Their major contentions are over the degree of Latin or Caribbean dominance in the blend (one political party shades towards the Latin, the other to the Caribbean), and over their attitude towards British and American economic and political influence. Their political rhetoric opposes policies of laissez-faire capitalism (opening the country to foreign capital) against state-led and managed egalitarian development under nationalist control.

The second vision is what I call the internationalist metropolitan future (after Hannerz 1987: 549). Many wealthier Belizeans have lived in the United States, have property and family there and now define themselves with their material culture as *citizens* of the United States, as 'Belizean-Americans'. Their Belizean ethnicity is emblematic — not substantive, like the Italian-Americans whose ethnicity consists of a few Italian words and pasta dinner every week. In Belize these spillovers from the melting pot build replicas — not imitations — of the metropole; in their houses, boats, and clubs, they live *in* the metropole. When they must leave and go to the countryside, they go as tourists, as technical advisers, or even as scientists studying a foreign culture. Their attitude toward the Belizean past, and rural Belize today, is romantic, paternalistic, and preservationist. (They share the foreigner's interest in conserving Belize's forests and wildlife.) Where the colonial élite could get away with blending local and foreign material culture, today's élite can only touch local culture wearing foreign-made gloves.

---

[11]   Weismantel is perhaps closer to the truth when she describes the mixture of 'hatred with desire' that marks Ecuadorian confrontation with North American popular culture. (1989:91).

The third vision is that of an ethnic future, the reaction of rural people whose minority status and poverty allows them only a small part of the official national culture, and no entry into the metropolitan enclave. A number of organizations (including foreign voluntary agencies) appropriate, invent, and promote ethnic goods, ethnic dress and ethnic ritual, as they attempt to construct a viable future. They see their economic base in self-reliance and perhaps in eco-tourism, but their vision of the future is still fragmented, and has no strong central symbols. Each ethnic group pursues its own course, though there are some movements towards a common interest. Their inspiration comes from international organizations like the Carribbean Organization of Indigenous Peoples, and from better organized ethnic communities in other countries; the Maya in Guatemala, the Mestizos in Mexico, and the Garifuna in Los Angeles. They receive support from several donor organizations in Europe and the United States, and even from a television station in New Mexico (which has helped Maya villages videotape their rituals).

Yet the ethnic future is clouded by the divided and contradictory motives of its proponents, and the ambivalent, sometimes hostile attitude of the national government. As long as ethnic revival is limited to music, crafts, dance and the cultivation of custom the government only vaguely tries to appropriate these forms as part of the 'national ethnic mix', inviting 'cultural' groups to perform at public festivities. When the ethnic vision extends to claims on land or the building of an independent economic base, the reaction is harsh and direct (Wilk and Chapin 1988).

And last we come to the urban poor, the buyers of blue-eyed dolls. These people have forged a relatively stable cultural order in the midst of a welter of powerful images, including the Cosby show, Rastafarians, the Crips and Bloods (Los Angeles street gangs), Evangelical preachers, Crack cocaine, and *Ebony* magazine. Creole urban culture is socially fluid, with few enduring institutions except churches, social clubs and sporting associations, but its order emerges from two opposing principles of value, locked together in a stable and long standing dialectic. Common in a number of Caribbean societies, Wilson labels the values 'reputation' and 'respectability' (1973: 227–230). They have their roots in the two responses to colonialism — conformity and rebellion. Miller's work in Trinidad (1990) uses a similar, but not identical, polarity between transcendental and transcendent modes, in his interpretation of consumption.

In Belize, reputation is an overtly egalitarian valuation of the ability to master social skills; talking, singing, mating, procreating and innovating. It is the value of the street and the rum shop. Reputation is personal authority granted by peers. At the same time, in the same community, respectability is a counter-value that emphasizes the achievement of rank in the community through acquiring property, forming a stable family, and participating in education and religion. Reputation is more a value of youth, respectability of age, and they often follow this order during a single life course. Women tend to seek respectability earlier in life than men; today many men die from drugs or violence before they have an opportunity to change their goals.

Below are examples of some of the goods and practices used in gaining reputation and respectability among richer and poorer urban Creole.

	Reputation	Respectability
Rich	Guns, car clothes, boat tennis, travel	House, wedding civic office education, rotary
Poor	Drugs, clothes motorbike, stereo, boxing, jewelry	House, furniture, travel wedding, education, religion, social club

Today the main diversion from this regime of value is the possibility of emigration. The option of leaving 'little Belize' and its limited horizons, pursuing a private and personal future in a land of wealth has lured an increasing number of young Belize Creoles from all social strata. Many predict the death of Belizean Creole culture, as Hispanic refugees from the neighboring countries flood in and a dwindling population of Creole children and old people are left behind by the diaspora.

Yet for many the ultimate goal of emigration is not escape, but return. The ambitions of many high school students I have spoken to are to go to the United States for education, experience and wealth, and then to return to Belize as a professional, a civil servant, a businessperson, or a prosperous retiree. Indications are that only the poorest emigrants go north hoping to become Americans and forget about Belize; and paradoxically they are the least likely to succeed in this goal because of their poor education. Still, they return with an enhanced reputation, often for violence and drug use. In contrast, the middle class emigrates in order to improve their education and experience, and they return with increased respectability and standing in the Belizean community.

SOME FINAL NOTES: THE PYRAMID OR THE PUDDLE

Some have depicted the neocolonial social order as a simple pyramid. In this model, 'Goods and wants...filter down from a model group to those deemed socially inferior...' (Philibert 1989:63). Everyone is trying to climb by emulating the elite, who retail images of the good life from the metropole. Bourdieu's model of twin pyramids of economic and cultural capital (1984) is only slightly less inaccurate for a place like Belize.

Instead, reality better approximates a puddle of different colors of paint, with little vertical order. A whole series of images of the good life compete with each other, but only blend at their margins. Any attempt to rise out of the puddle is met with opposition. The economic hierarchy is not unified in a pyramidal order, and it is not congruent with social, ethnic, or geographic groupings. The result is messy, constantly changing and difficult to describe.

Status competition is clearly only one of many roles for consumer goods in Belize. Goods are used for many kinds of display that crosscut status — while I have mainly discussed temporal uses of goods in this paper, they are also used in creating and maintaining all kinds of social relationships and personal identities, and for expressing egalitarian ideals instead of hierarchical ones. Perhaps the essentially *ambiguous*, multivocal nature of goods is the only thing that makes a modern society like Belize *possible*? How else could people maintain a sense of the possible, and create a secure identity in a world where Belize lies at the bottom of a deep economic and cultural well? Who could actually survive in Veblen's competitive society, expanded to the scale of the whole globe, (or the globally homogenized marketplace of Barnet and Muller [1974]) without succumbing to ennui or despair?

ADDENDUM 1: STATISTICS ON BELIZE'S IMPORTS

The following data on imports come from the Government of Belize's annual Statistical Abstracts, from Annual Customs and Trade Reports, British Honduras Blue Books, Colonial Reports, and unpublished materials in the Belize National Archives. The household consumption data is taken from a 1980 survey (Fairclough n.d.).

Gross Trade: In 1980 customs records showed an average of $452 worth of food imported for each Belizean at a time when Gross Domestic Product per capita was about $2,000 (one Belize dollar = .5 United States dollar). For an average household of 5.6 people, the annual expenditure on imported food was $2,530, out of an average income of about $8,800. A minimum of 29% of the average household budget was spent on imported food, lower in the country and higher in the city. This adds up to a national food import bill, for 1980 of over 65 million dollars. The same year, total imports of all goods amounted to $242 million ($1,669 per capita), while exports were only $164 million (mostly sugar cane, orange juice concentrate and seafood). This trade gap is balanced by millions of dollars from Belizeans working in the United States, by foreign assistance, and by the trade in illegal drugs.

Since 1981 food imports have leveled out somewhat because of the general economic contraction. Gross food imports in l986 amounted to $58.1 million, though a decline in exports led to a widening trade gap. Indications are that with the improvement in exports in the last few years, imports of food have begun to climb steeply. (GOB 1987; US Dept. of Commerce 1989).

Tourism: In 1986 80,000 tourists visited Belize for an average stay of 5.5 days (GOB 1986). There are only about 180,000 Belizeans, so this is a large relative number. By 1988 the number of tourists was over 100,000. These tourists are heavily concentrated in three coastal sites, but there is an increasing tendency towards 'cultural' and 'adventure' tourism, viewing wildlife, archaeological sites, and 'primitive' Mayan communities.

In 1983 and 1984, 5% of Belizean adults reported visiting the United States 'often', 15% 'several times', and 16% 'once'. Therefore, a minimum of 36% of adults have been to the United States (not counting the 'no response' answers). This is in addition to 67% of the Belizean adult population that has visited Mexico at least once (Ergood 1987: 9–10).

Emigration: Accurate figures for emigration from Belize to the United States, England and Canada are not available because so much emigration is undocumented and illegal. Estimates range from 35,000 to 80,000 Belizeans living abroad, with an additional 1,500 leaving each year (Bouvier 1984; Everitt 1987). Therefore as many as 31% of Belizeans are now living outside the country. Most urban Belizeans, and a growing number of rural residents, have at least one relative (and often more) living abroad. There are active Belizean organizations in Los Angeles, Chicago, Michigan, New York, and Miami. The number of Belizean who have lived abroad and have now returned to reside in Belize is unknown, but in some areas is very high (Palacio 1982).

Exposure to Media: In 1980, 10% of households reported owning a television set, 19% a stereo, and 71% a radio (Fairclough n.d.:38). In 1985 the number of televisions had grown to about 15,000, or one for every 10.8 Belizeans, and more than half of all households. At that time, video cassette recorder ownership ranked *fifth* in the hemisphere, at about one in ten households (Petch 1987:12–13). Today these numbers are even higher; well over 5,000 televisions and 1,000 were imported into Belize from the US in 1986 (US Dept of Commerce 1989). There are nine licensed television stations and perhaps as many cable systems, all rebroadcasting American programming with very little local content (Lent 1989; Bolland 1987). In 1992 two local television stations started up, one controlled by the government and the other by a private business; both have between one and two hours a day of local or regional programming, but the bulk of their offerings are still from US owned satellites.

ADDENDUM 2: THE DEFINITION OF MEANING IN CONSUMPTION; A PRELIMINARY TYPOLOGY

The consumption of goods is a crucial activity in both creating and changing systems of meaning. Anthropology, however, has an impoverished vocabulary for describing the ways that meanings of goods are manipulated and transformed in an active way. Here I will elaborate and define some terms which may help in the discussion of consumption as an active and political process (based on Wilk and Arnould n.d. and Arnould and Wilk 1984).

The most general terms are *symmetry* and *asymmetry*. In a symmetrical situation, all members of a society agree on the meaning of goods, both those who consume them and those who do not. In a system in asymmetry, there is disagreement over the meaning of goods, because they are new, because some people are trying to change the meaning of those goods, or because there is no communication between the groups that hold different interpretations. As Miller (1987:107) notes, in some situations two groups may disagree about the meaning of an object without conflict.

Here I speak of public meanings only, ignoring for the moment the 'bivocal' (Cohen 1981) character of symbols, that they have individual and personal meanings as well as impersonal and public ones. The manipulation of symbolic objects in public and private contexts ordinarily exploits their ambiguity and bivocality. Competition and change occurs when this manipulation transgresses the boundary of acceptable manipulation, becoming an attack on the system of rules rather than a use of the rules to attack another player.

In order for symmetry to be maintained in a changing social scene, or for asymmetry to be resolved, the meanings of goods must be transformed. *Competition* is active contestation and dispute over the meaning of goods and over their uses. Unless the system tolerates ambiguity (often through the use of secrecy), allowing asymmetry of meaning to persist without dispute, competition can be managed in a number of ways:

Displacement eliminates a category of goods and replaces it with a new one which has the same meaning. This can be envisioned as an old category being transformed into a new one through substitution. For example, Hudson's Bay blankets displaced hand-woven ones in the Northwest coast; steel tools displaced stone in many places.

Identification involves the linking of categories of meaning together, so that a new object joins the same category as an old one. Airtight efficient wood stoves are accepted in California because they are identified with open fireplaces and fireplace inserts.

Promotion is the lifting of an item by a series of steps in a graded hierarchy of meanings within a larger category. Thus running shoes are promoted from athletic footwear to fashion footwear. Bread as a snack food is promoted to the status of a staple (Weismantel 1989).

Appropriation removes a good from competition by linking its consumption closely to a particular situation or category of person. Until quite recently bright hair coloring in American society was not subject to competition; the practice had been appropriated by older women, especially widows. A small stigmatized minority may be able to appropriate a whole costume.

Escalation sees the widening of a dispute over the meaning of particular goods to include other matters. This may take the form of identification, as the meaning of new objects is linked to the meaning of old ones. When modern towns decide who may or may not consume video games, alcohol, or pornographic literature, they generally compete by escalating the dispute to include the morality of divorce, the education of children, the amount of crime, etc. In extreme cases, a combination of escalation and identification can spread a dispute over the meaning of objects so widely that chaos ensues and the social order is threatened, as with the Yir Yiront in the famous case of the steel axes. This can be contrasted with the introduction of shotguns into New Guinea, where appropriation took place and stability was maintained (Mitchell 1973).

In contrast to these dynamic modes of change in meanings, anthropologists have done a great deal to define the ways that stability and symmetry are maintained (at least in non-Western societies). The literature on spheres of exchange, sumptuary regulation, secret societies, mystery cults, taboos and sacred symbolism can be read as a list of strategies for stabilizing the meanings of objects.

Many anthropologists continue to act as though material goods are frozen and controlled in all 'pre-capitalist' societies, and only become dynamic under capitalism (e.g. Philibert 1989:69–70) Presenting categories of people and categories of objects as naturally congruent and part of long-standing tradition, is a common and effective strategy in the struggle for symmetry (and hegemony). Anthropologists and folklorists have by now played their parts as accomplices, on the side of those in power ('the traditional faction') in innumerable political contests.

References

Appadurai, A. (ed.)

    1986   *The Social Life of Things*. Cambridge: Cambridge University Press.

Arnould, E. J.

    1989   Preference Formation and the Diffusion of Innovations: The Case of Hausa Speaking Niger. *Journal of Consumer Research* **16**(2).

Arnould, E. J. and R. Wilk

   1984   Why do the Indians Wear Adidas? *Advances in Consumer Research* **11**: pp. 748–752.

Baker, W.

   1989   The Global Teenager. *Whole Earth Review* **65**: pp. 2–35.

Barnet, R. and Muller R.

   1974   *Global Reach.* New York: Simon and Schuster.

Belk, R.

   1983   Worldly Possessions: Issues and Criticisms. *Advances in Consumer Research* **10**: pp. 514–519.

   1988   Third World Consumer Culture. *Research in Marketing, Supplement* 4, *Marketing and Development.* pp. 103–127. JAI Press.

Belk, R. and Zhou N.

   1987   Learning to Want Things. *Advances in Consumer Research* **14**: pp. 478–481.

Bolland, N.

   1977   *The Formation of a Colonial Society.* Baltimore: Johns Hopkins University Press.

   1987   United States Cultural Influence on Belize: Television and Education as 'Vehicles of Import'. *Caribbean Quarterly* **33**(3 and 4): pp. 60–74.

   1988   *Colonialism and Resistance in Belize.* Belize Cubola Productions.

Bourdieu, P.

   1984   *Distinction: A Social Critique of the Judgment of Taste.* Cambridge Mass: Harvard University Press.

Bouvier, L.

   1984   *Belize: Yesterday, Today and Tomorrow.* Population Reference Bureau, Occasional Series: The Caribbean. Washington D.C.

Caughey, J.

   1984   *Imaginary Social Worlds.* Lincoln: University of Nebraska Press.

Cohen, A.

   1981   *The Politics of Elite Culture.* Berkeley: University of California Press.

d'Haene, S.

   1980   Essai d'analyse du fonctionnement des modeles de consommation dans les pays sous-developpes. *L'Homme et la Societe* **56–58**: pp. 179–187.

Douglas, M. and Isherwood B.

    1981   *The World of Goods.* New York: Basic Books.

Ergood, B.

    1987   *The Belize National Survey.* Ohio University, mimeograph.

Everitt, J. C.

    1987   The Torch is Passed: Neocolonialism in Belize. *Caribbean Quarterly* **33**(3 and 4): pp. 42–59.

Fairclough, E.A.

    1980 Belize Household Expenditure Survey. Belmopan Central Planning Unit.

Ferguson, J.

    1988   Cultural Exchange: New Developments in the Anthropology of Commodities. *Cultural Anthropology* **3**(4): pp. 488–513.

Gell, A.

    1986   'Newcomers to the World of Goods: Consumption among the Muria Gonds'. In Appadurai, Arjun (ed.) *The Social Life of Things: Commodities in Cultural Perspective.* New York: Cambridge University Press. pp. 110–138.

Government of Belize

    1986   *Belize Abstract of Statistics.* Belmopan Ministry of Economic Development.

Hannerz, U.

    1987   The World in Creolization. *Africa* **57**(4): pp. 546–559.

Hellinger, M.

    1973   Aspects of Belizean Creole. *Folia Linguistica, Tomus* **VI**, Judd, Karen 1989 Cultural Synthesis or Ethnic Struggle? Creolization in Belize. *Cimarron* 1–2: pp. 103–118.

Jhally, S.

    1990   *The Codes of Advertising.* New York: Routledge.

Le Page, R.B.

    1975   Polarizing Factors: Political, Cultural, Economic — Operating on the Individual's Choice of Identity Through Language Use in British Honduras: In Savard, J.G. and R. Vigneault (eds) *Multilingual Political Systems: Problems and Solutions.* Les Presses de l'Universite Laval. pp. 537–551.

Lent, J.

    1989   Country of No Return: Belize Since Television. *Belizean Studies* **17**(1): pp. 14–36.

Linnekin, J.

    1983   Defining Tradition: Variations on the Hawaiian Identity. *American Ethnologist* **10**: pp. 241–252.

Lundgren, N.

    1986   Blond-Haired Dolls and Blue-Eyed Christs: The Impact of Colonialism on the Development of Children's Ethnic Identity in Belize. Paper presented to the American Anthropological Association, Philadelphia.

    1988   When I Grow Up I Want a Trans Am: Children in Belize Talk About Themselves and the Impact of the World Capitalist System. *Dialectical Anthropology* **13**: pp. 269–276.

McCracken, G.

    1988   *Culture and Consumption.* Bloomington: Indiana University Press.

Miller, D.

    1987   *Material Culture and Mass Consumption.* Oxford: Basil Blackwell.

    1990   Fashion and Ontology in Trinidad. *Culture and History* **7**: pp. 49–78.

Mitchell, W.E.

    1973   New Weapons Stir Up Old Ghosts. *Natural History* **82**(6): pp. 75–84.

Murphy, R. and Steward J.

    1956   Tappers and Trappers: Parallel Process in Acculturation. *Economic Development and Social Change* **4**: pp. 335–353.

Naipaul, V.S.

    1968   *An Area of Darkness.* Harmondsworth: Penguin Books.

    1976   Power? reprinted in 'The Overcrowded Baracoon' Aylesbury: Penguin Books.

Orlove, B. and Rutz H.

    1989   Thinking about Consumption: a Social Economy Approach: In Benjamin Orlove and Henry Rutz, (eds) *The Social Economy of Consumption.* pp. 1–57. Lanham: University Press of America.

Palacio, J.

    1982   Food and Social Relations in a Garifuna Village. PhD dissertation, UC Berkeley. University Microfilms.

Petch, T.

    1987   Television and Video Ownership in Belize. *Belizean Studies* **15**(1): pp. 12–14.

Philibert, J.

1989   Consuming Culture: A Study of Simple Commodity Consumption: In Benjamin, Orlove and Henry Rutz (eds) *The Social Economy of Consumption*. Lanham: University Press of America. pp. 59–84.

Rubin, V. and Zavalloni M.

1969   *We Wish to be Looked Upon: A Study of the Aspirations of Youth in a Developing Society*. New York: Teacher's College Press.

U.S. Department of Commerce

n.d.   Official Tables of U.S. Total Exports to Belize. Commercial Library, U.S. Embassy, Belize.

Wallendorf, M. and Arnould E.

1988   My Favorite Things : A Cross Cultural Inquiry into Object Attachment, Possessiveness and Social Linkage. *Journal of Consumer Research* **14**(4): pp. 531–547.

Weismantel, M.

1989   The Children Cry for Bread: Hegemony and the Transformation of Consumption: In Benjamin, Orlove and Henry Rutz (eds) *The Social Economy of Consumption*. Lanham: University Press of America. pp. 85–100.

Wilk, R.

1989   Houses as Consumer Goods: The Kekchi of Belize: In Benjamin, Orlove and Henry Rutz (eds) *The Social Economy of Consumption*. Lanham: University Press of America. pp. 297–323.

1993a   'It's Destroying a Whole Generation'. Television and Moral Discourse in Belize. *Visual Anthropology* **5**: pp. 229–244.

Wilk, R. and Arnould E.

n.d.   Why do the Indians Wear Adidas? Culture Contact and the Relations of Consumption. MS in possession of the authors.

Wilk, R. and Chapin M.

1988   Ethnic Minorities in Belize: Mopan, Kekchi, and Garifuna. Cultural Survival International Working Papers. Cambridge, Mass.

Young, C.

1973   Belize Creole: A Study of Creolized English Spoken in the City of Belize. PhD thesis, University of York.

1993b   "Beauty and the Feast: Official and Visceral Nationalism in Belize." *Ethnos* **58**(3–4): pp. 294–316.

CHAPTER FIVE

Beyond Consumption: Meat, Sociality, Vitality and Hierarchy in Nineteenth Century Chile

Benjamin S. Orlove

This chapter analyzes the relation between consumption and identity through the examination of a single good, meat, in a single setting, nineteenth century Chile. At first glance there would seem to be very little that is unusual or noteworthy about this topic. Few readers are likely to be startled at the mention of certain facts about that country at that time; that there was considerable range in wealth and income, and that the rich ate a good deal more meat than the poor. Class inequality is a familiar feature of Latin American societies, and, as Goody has described, the uneven distribution of prestige food items marks cuisines throughout Europe, Asia and many post-colonial nations (Goody 1982: 97–153). Moreover, the strong desire for meat has been found in many societies. Whether or not one accepts the notion that this desire is a universal human propensity, resting on some biological feature which all members of our species share with one another, meat could seem a less promising topic of inquiry for the study of consumption and identity than, say, kula valuables, Coca-Cola, or automobiles.

The apparent simplicity and universality of meat consumption give this case its interest. To suggest that meat is a food which is used by the rich to mark their difference from the poor is to assimilate eating into the more general category of consumption and to argue that the consumption of goods can demonstrate the identity of particular individuals, groups or social categories. This article claims that a closer examination of the case can confound two presuppositions on which these claims rest: firstly, the notion that the world of persons and the world of things can be sharply separated, and secondly, the notion that these worlds of persons and things can be connected by a small number of simple relations.

The case of meat consumption in nineteenth century Chile shows the difficulty of establishing and maintaining a sharp boundary between humans and things (Orlove and Rutz 1989). It is not that Chileans of that period were unable to distinguish between humans and other objects such as mountains, chairs and pigs (as if they suffered from some neurological disorder similar to the famous case of the man who confused his wife with a hat [Sacks 1985]), but that they did not seem to regard humans and things as comprising two homogenous, distinct and well-bounded domains, since they frequently humanized animals (especially horses, cattle and dogs) and they also animalized humans (day laborers, Indians). More specifically, humans and some objects (particularly animals) shared attributes, so that they could be understood as similar rather than different, as contiguous rather than separate. Moreover, the relations which linked humans with some objects (particularly animals) resembled the relations which linked humans with each other. It is virtually impossible to separate relations which connect humans to one another from other relations which connect humans and animals, terming the former 'social relations' and the latter 'ownership' or 'capture' or 'consumption'. It seems more appropriate to say that culturally-constituted social relations sometimes linked humans, sometimes animals, sometimes both. This association, moreover, rests on a recognition of the affinities between humans and animals — in particular, their possession of the ability to work, eat and reproduce that I term 'vitality', though 'life force' comes closer to the Spanish term *fuerza* which is occasionally used to describe it. Rather than separating humans and objects, and showing how the latter symbolically stand for the former, I argue that humans and objects jointly form a single system, in which the links between humans and objects establish and enact identity, as well as representing already-existing identities — a notion expressed well by Appadurai's phrase 'the social life of things' (1986: 3–63).

This case thus calls into question the firm separation between person and thing, a fundamental element of much of the current study of consumption. It bears noting, therefore, that this separation has a long tradition in Western economic and political discourse. One of the tenets of the abolitionist movement, a central feature of nineteenth century politics in Europe, the United States, and Latin America was the complete separation of the categories of "person" and "property". Other fundamental economic concepts rest on this distinction as well: the separation of labor and capital, of services and goods. One can point out the specificity of the notions of individuality and citizenship on which these other concepts rest without denying their fundamental importance. The nineteenth century Chilean case, with hierarchical and antidemocratic impulses strongly in place, calls into question the universality of some of these notions.

MEAT, CONSUMPTION AND IDENTITY

A number of anthropologists have examined patterns of meat consumption to explore the connections between the use of things and identity. One important point of departure is Sahlins' account of contemporary American views on the consumption of dogs, horses, pigs and cattle (1976: 170–179). Following Levi-Strauss' earlier work on the naming of animals (1966), Sahlins separates the more humanized dogs and horses, who are often given individual names, from the less humanized pigs and cattle, and then shows dogs, who are allowed inside houses, to be the most human of all, while cattle, typically reared further from houses than pigs, are the least. Dog meat is strictly tabooed; horsemeat is considered edible though repellent, while beef is more prestigious than pork, supporting Sahlins' dictum that "edibility is inversely related to humanity" (176). This scale is arbitrary, he suggests, since other cultures separate prohibited and permitted animals, and rank the latter on quite different criteria. Sahlins moves on to analyse other cultural domains, including clothing and traffic lights, to show that all objects are essentially arbitrary signs.

Eric Ross directly challenges this view in a piece entitled "Why we don't eat dogs: a beef with Sahlins" (1980;183–186), which appeared in a book he edited, *Beyond the Myths of Culture*. He ranks animals along a different criterion: the efficiency with which they can produce meat. Cattle are convenient sources of protein, since they convert otherwise unusable grasslands into meat, while dogs are particularly inefficient as a source of meat. Along with the other authors in the volume, Ross seeks to show that other forms of cultural representation, such as ritual, myth and, indeed, traffic lights, reflect underlying material necessities of human life, linked to human diet, reproduction, and the interests of elites. All signs, in this view, are essentially useful objects.

Sahlins insists on the autonomy of meat as a sign whose meanings can be arbitrarily created by specific cultures; Ross argues for the complete subordination of meat to nutritional and ecological requirements. Despite their apparent disagreement, Sahlins and Ross coincide on two points: that the world of objects can be separated from the world of humans, and that these two worlds are linked by a single relationship (signification for Sahlins, satisfaction of needs, desires and wants for Ross). More recent work has tended to present multiple relationships between these worlds, suggesting that the social and cultural patterning of food consumption can reflect both the human need for specific nutrients and the human capacity to attribute meanings to objects. Some work explores a third, more performative kind of relation, constitution, in which objects create identities, rather than marking or affirming them. In addition, some recent writings have suggested that meat is not a wholly arbitrary symbol, as Sahlins claims: there are certain inherent qualities of animals and meat as objects which shape the meanings which cultures attribute to them. By exploring these attributes, such work examines the similarities, as well as the differences, between humans and objects.

Fischler's recent study of human diet, for example, suggests that meat is a key element of all human diets (1990). It is always strongly regulated, he argues. In some cases meat is among the most preferred foods, while in others among the most strictly forbidden and in still others some meats are valued and others rejected. He offers two reasons for this universality. Since animals, like humans, are made of flesh, animal meat reminds us of ourselves, and therefore meat-eating brings into question the boundary between the self and the other — and, by implication, the boundary between humans and non-human things. Secondly, because of the large size of many animals, meat-eating entails sharing, and therefore brings principles of human cooperation into question. By showing how the use of objects can redefine human social activity, Fischler moves towards an analysis of meals as performances or enactments of identities, as occasions in which social relations are constituted rather than reflected. Fischler uses this universal framework to consider broad issues such as sacrifice and cannibalism, as well as the process which he terms the "*désanimalisation*" of meat. In modern societies, industrial production permits a high degree of such disanimalization, but contemporory science, in emphasizing our biological evolution as a species, has reanimalized humans. The resulting crisis accounts in part for the current spread of vegetarianism. Fischler notes other tendencies in modern life which have brought the self/other boundary and the principles of sharing into question: the atomization of industrial society, the loss of control which has followed the medicalization of the human body and the spread of government regulation into many arenas of human life. These tendencies, he argues, have lead to the contemporary self-awareness of weight and the obsession with fatness, further reasons for the contemporary shifts away from the eating of meat.

Fiddes (1991) offers a related, but distinct, view of the significance of meat consumption. The eating of meat is an activity which is highly elaborated in all cultures, he argues, because animals, like humans, are made of muscle and therefore capable of action. Our control over animals — expressed at its fullest when we eat them — demonstrates our control over the natural world. Fiddes agrees with Fischler that a crisis of modernity has led to vegetarianism, though he describes this crisis in different terms. Modern technologies have led to massive problems, particularly economic and social dislocations which have followed industrialization, and environmental problems of excessive use of natural resources. As people begin to doubt the wisdom of our efforts to control nature, they also begin to view industrialized meat production with disfavor, and to reject meat as a food. In other words, humans and things can be seen as jointly constituted, rather than as separate worlds linked by signification or by satisfaction of needs.

Fischler and Fiddes, like Sahlins, suggest that meat consumption has a high degree of cultural elaboration. Unlike Sahlins, they do not assume that the significance of meat is arbitrary. Instead, they find particular attributes of meat as an object which allow it to represent features of the relations of humans with one another or with the natural world. They suggest that the elaboration of these features depends in part on the nature of the technology of meat production.

This chapter suggests the value of carrying these analytical perspectives even further. Fischler and Fiddes have advanced considerably beyond Sahlins' treatment of animals as arbitrary signs or Ross' reduction of them to sources of protein. They insist too quickly, however, on identifying one or another attribute of animals as the specific one which cultures elaborate. This chapter proposes that there are a number of specific attributes of meat which may be developed in different ways in different times and places.

Moreover, Fischler and Fiddes agree with Sahlins that cultures are concerned to maintain a sharp difference between humans and animals. Fiddes moves quickly from noting the similarity between human and animals — our capacity for action — to emphasizing the firmness of the line which separate humans from nature, understood as including animals, plants and many other objects. The Chilean case suggests the value of looking more closely at the cultural elaboration of the commonalities which link humans and animals. By looking at these commonalities, it will be possible to consider more widely the relations of human and animals. More generally, this chapter seeks to examine the ways in which objects become fully part of social life, rather than merely serving as significators of prior social relations and categories, or as the means of satisfying human wants, needs or desires.

NINETEENTH CENTURY CHILE: THE SOCIAL WORLD OF THE ESTATE

The discussion of nineteenth century Chile focuses on the country's core area, the central valley which contained most of the large estates, as well as the capital city of Santiago.[1] The traditional large estates or haciendas, which

---

[1] The economic and political changes that accompanied independence from Spain in 1821 and the subsequent decades in some ways had more profound effects on the peripheral regions of Chile than in this core area. The north, which grew in size after Chile defeated Peru and Bolivia in the War of the Pacific (1879–1883) and incorporated portions of their national territories, was transformed by the growth of copper and nitrate mining, the economic activities which underwrote much of the expansion of the national state and economy. When the rebellious Araucanian Indians were conquered in a series of wars from the 1850s through the 1880s, the Chilean control and settlement of the southern regions also grew, as agricultural colonies and coal mining expanded. The north and south both attracted some populations of European migrants.

In the central valley, change was concentrated in Santiago and its port, Valparaíso, which grew, as the Chilean state and overseas trade occupied increasingly important roles in the national economy, and as some manufacturing began to develop in these cities. Unlike Buenos Aires, the capital of Argentina on the other side of the Andes, whose growth was due to large-scale foreign immigration, Santiago and Valparaíso expanded by drawing on rural populations from rural areas of the country, especially the central valley, which, aside from Santiago itself, remained heavily rural in the nineteenth century (Loveman 1979: 162). The labor movement in Chile developed most strongly in the mines and ports. The major strikes in this period were

date back at least to the early eighteenth century, continued to dominate the countryside of the central valley in the nineteenth and early twentieth centuries, making Chile one of the few exceptions to the pattern, common throughout most of Latin America, in which large estates coexisted with small- and medium-sized towns, autonomous peasant villages, or both. These haciendas are thus the central focus of this chapter.

The organization of land and labor was fairly uniform on these estates. The major productive activities — the preparation of fields, the planting, harvesting and threshing of grain, the annual round-up of the semi-feral cattle that grazed on natural pasture in the valley and on adjacent hills and mountains — were performed by human and animal labor, with very little mechanization. The relations of production that had dominated in the colonial period also maintained their basic configuration. The labor force, recruited and maintained with personal, informal agreements rather than written contracts, was divided into two groups, both of whom were usually under the direct supervision of the *mayordomo* or administrator. The *inquilinos* (service tenants) provided labor for the landowner in exchange for access to fields which they cultivated on their own and some pasture on which they could raise a horse and some cattle; the *peones* (peons or casual laborers) were hired seasonally for specific tasks. An *inquilino* family would reside on an hacienda for many years, perhaps generations. The peon often travelled from one hacienda to another, without permanently settling in any one area.

The specific details varied from hacienda to hacienda, depending on time, place and scale. For example, some *inquilino* families would have *inquilinos* of their own, or hire peóns, while others would rely exclusively on family labor. Some *inquilinos* were quite poor, while others accumulated sizeable herds of cattle. Nonetheless, the basic system of labor relations continued, even though railroads extended throughout the central valley in the nineteenth century and landowners sought to increase production to meet the demands of the growing populations in Santiago and the mining regions outside the central valley. The changes that did take place (the obligations of each *inquilino* family tended to increase, and the size of the lands allotted to them often decreased) did not reshape the basic patterns.

Although a detailed historical demography of hacienda workers remains to be done, a number of sources offer suggestions about domestic organization (a topic of direct relevance to the moral economy of food, and hence to the significance of meat, since most meals were served at home). The frequent references to the casual ease with which peons shifted partners and bore children out of wedlock suggest that marriages among *inquilinos* were more stable than

concentrated outside Santiago, though there was some union activity in Santiago, especially among the railroad workers (DeShazo 1983). There was a virtually total absence of a labor movement in the agricultural zones of the country (Zeitlin and Ratcliff 1988).

Figure 3   *The administrator of a large hacienda*

those among peons (Gilliss 1854: 344). The housing in which they lived also differed; some sources mention the gardens which *inquilinos* planted, and they often refer to their houses as *casas*, using the more pejorative term *rancho* (shack) for the houses of peons (Gilliss 1854: 345).

The use of the word *casa* also appears in the local term for the long-lasting ties which hacendados established with mistresses, recognizing and support- ing their children. Such secondary families were known as *casas chicas* ("small houses") which contrasted with the large principal dwelling or *casa-hacienda*.[2] (The Chilean writer Isabel Allende develops many aspects of this image of the *casa* in her novel *The House of the Spirits* [1985].) A portion of *casa-hacienda*, with its fine columns, appears in the background of Figure 3, (Elliott 1911: 236); this contrasts sharply with the poorer house depicted in Figure 4, (Jara 1973: 96–97).

These patterns suggest a highly patriarchal view of the hacienda. Patron- client relations tied men to hacendados, closely in the case of *inquilinos*, weakly for the peóns. The position of a man in rural Chile could be judged by the number of houses, women, children and livestock that he had.

---

[2] I have not seen the term *casa grande*, used in Brazil to refer to plantation houses, applied to the residences of Chilean hacendados.

Figure 4   *"Ranchito"*

Nineteenth century sources make frequent use of the terms *inquilino* and *peon*, but many of them also apply a second pair of terms, *huaso* and *roto*, to apply to roughly the same sets of individuals. The former terms define social classes, categorizing adult males and their dependents by their economic relations to landlords; the latter denote social types, broader, more diffuse characterizations of individuals, each of which is associated with the use of certain goods, specific activities, and particular demeanors. (More widely-known examples of rural Latin American social types in the nineteenth century include the Argentine *gaucho*, the Mexican *charro* and the Brazilian *caboclo*. Poole [1988] provides a fascinating exploration of a female nineteenth century Latin American social type, the Peruvian *tapada*, an urban case rather than the rural ones discussed here.) Social types are perhaps inevitably more slippery and imprecise than social classes. However, the repeated usage of terms denoting social types in the sources suggests the importance of examining them, despite the lack of consensus over the true nature of the *huaso* and the *roto*. One nineteenth century source includes engravings of both, as well as of other social types (Tornero 1872: 464, 483). In the engraving entitled *'un roto'*, a barefoot man, wearing a torn jacket, appears seated in a hunched posture; his hooked nose, dark skin, thick lips and straight hair all suggest Indian ancestry, in contrast to the European ancestry implied by the mustache and beard of the figure labelled *"el huaso"* (see Figures 5 and 6). This *huaso* wears boots and more elegant clothing, and appears to be somewhat taller, and a good deal fleshier, than the *roto*; he is galloping by on a horse whose bridle is ornamented, most likely with silver. The *huaso* is depicted in relation to specific places — the houses of a peon or *inquilino* on a hillside, the distant *casa-hacienda* down in the alley to which he is returning; he is free to move around the extensive territory of the hacienda. The *roto*, by contrast, appears without work, without a house; as far as one may judge from the trees just behind him and the mountains in the distance, he is in a relatively wild, uncultivated zone.

Figure 5   *"Un roto"*

Figure 6   *"El huaso"*

Apparently he is resting in the middle of a journey, presumably walking barefoot from one hacienda to another. The *huaso*'s rapid motion thus actually implies a spatial and social fixity, much as the resting posture of the *roto* suggests an uprootedness and mobility linked to spatial and social impermanence. The differences in body size, race, wealth, ownership of horses, dress and other goods in these two images appear in many other sources as well. In particular, Echaíz emphasizes that the typical *huaso* is "fleshy, of a ruddy complexion, sturdy" (1955: 57–58), qualities which he attributes to the consumption of great quantities of meat (1955: 59). (On occasion, the word *roto*, perhaps because of its pejorative connotations,[3] is omitted altogether, and the term *huaso* covers all rural people, as in Darwin [1900].) The terms peón and *roto* were used for residents of mining

---

[3] The Chileans who read earlier drafts of this chapter all objected strongly to my analysis of the term *roto*, telling me that it was nothing more than an insult used by snobbish members of the bourgeoisie. A few suggested that it was not *progresista* ("progressive") to honor such reactionary prejudices by including them in a scholarly context. I explained to them that I had decided to include the term because of its centrality to my argument. In our conversations, we discussed the absence of class-related terms in the current American discourse over "hate speech". Even terms such as "Okie" and "cracker" have an overtly racial connotation, and it is hard to imagine terms like "bum" having as much impact as words about our body-centered categories of race, gender, sexual orientation and disability.

camps and even for urban dwellers; *inquilino* and *huaso* refer to rural dwellers. The terms *inquilino* and peón are widely understood throughout Spanish-speaking Latin America; *huaso* is an exclusively Chilean term, as is *roto* in this usage. The etymological origins of the term *huaso* are quite obscure; the word *roto* is the past participle of *romper*, to break, though the word *roto* can also mean "torn" or "worn out".

Chilean society was thus profoundly hierarchical, whether seen in terms of class relations of property and labor, in terms of superior and inferior social types, or in terms of both. Within this hierarchical order, animals — especially horses, cattle and dogs — were constitutive elements. This hegemonic order, with animals located below humans but within society, raises many interesting questions. The dimension of gender is fascinating; the threshing of agricultural crops in the valley was carried out with mares, the round-up of cattle in the hills with stallions. Chileans at the time did not castrate their stallions, so there were no geldings, which might have performed either task. The racial dimension also raises complex issues, since European men who migrated to Chile often married hacendados' daughters, while the hacendados sought to "improve" their cattle, horses and dogs by crossing them with stud animals imported from Europe.

Moreover, one may question why the people at the bottom of the society — the *rotos* and the women — did not oppose this order more directly. Nineteenth century Chile lacks the history of popular rebellion that marked some other Latin American nations at that time. Here, at least, there are various hints of answers. One may note that the relatively small scale of the haciendas gave a personal quality to the domination by the landlord class (significant political opposition emerged in twentieth century Chile in large cities and mining camps). Moreover, individuals had the chance to leave unsatisfactory situations, seeking another hacendado (for the male *rotos*) or another man (for women of different social settings). *Rotos*, both men and women, moved easily in the nineteenth century — to the military frontier against the Indians in the south, to the gold fields of California, and, in the latter part of the century, to mines in the far north and to Santiago. It is also possible that the estate system gave even the poorest persons the opportunity to express their domination over social inferiors, even if these inferiors were only animals.

NINETEENTH CENTURY CHILEAN MEALS

The differences in social class and social type, important to economic and social relations on the large estates, also shaped the meals and the patterning of meat consumption. Nineteenth century sources describe the abundance of food in Chile. There was much poverty, but little real starvation. A number of sources point to the abundance of meat among the wealthy, whether in private homes and clubs in Santiago or in the main hacienda houses. The principal dishes around which meals were organized were invariably based on meat.

An English journalist whose social contacts were primarily restricted to the elite offers an account like many others:

> One soon gets used to Chilian cooking. . . . of specially Chilian dishes, which one meets everywhere and always, may be mentioned *cazuela*, a chicken broth flavoured with many vegetables [and] *puchéro*, boiled beef. (Hervey 1891–2: 330)

An early twentieth century source makes the same point:

> As regards the cooking, it may be said that it is, as a rule, excellent, especially for those who are content with the national dishes of the country, and do not encourage ambitious cooks to aim at British cookery. There are certain familiar and regular *plats* which do not lose their satisfying and agreeable character even after continued iteration. Such is the *cazuela*, a grand soup usually with a large piece of meat in it, and resembling a glorified Scotch broth. (Elliott 1911: 255)

Even breakfasts regularly included meat, whether broiled (Graham 1824: 197) or prepared in stews (Merwin 1863 : 52).

Many sources (Bauer 1975, Merwin 1966, Villalobos 1972, Wright 1904) describe the great hospitality of wealthy Chileans and the abundance of food at their tables, especially on Sundays and on civic, religious and family celebrations, both in Santiago and on the haciendas. The English traveler Maria Graham provides a particularly full description of a dinner in Santiago:

> . . . we met Don Jose Antonio de Cotapos, whose family had kindly invited me to stay in their house while I was at Santiago; and though I had declined it, fancying I should be more at liberty in an English inn, my intentions were overruled, when I was met a few miles farther on by M. Prevost, who told me the ladies would be hurt if I did not go to their house, at any rate in the first instance. . . . After a little rest, and having refreshed myself by dressing, I was called to dinner; where I found all the family assembled, and several other gentlemen, who were invited to meet me, and do honour to the feast of reception. The dinner was larger than would be thought consistent with good taste; but everything was well dressed, though with a good deal of oil and garlic. Fish came among the last things. All the dishes were carved on the table, and it is difficult to resist the pressing invitations of every moment to eat of everything. The greatest kindness is shown by taking things from your own plate and putting it on that of your friend; and no scruple is made of helping any dish before you with the spoon or knife you have been eating with, or even tasting or eating from the general dish without the intervention of a plate. In the intervals between the courses, bread and butter and olives were presented. . . . After dinner we took coffee . . . (Graham 1824: 198–199).

At the other end of the social scale are the rural poor, whose simple diet, centered on grains and beans, lacked meat. One account, from the early nineteenth century, comes from the most widely travelled European to visit Chile, Charles Darwin, who toured throughout the country in 1833:

> Each landowner . . . possesses a certain portion of the hill-country, where his half-wild cattle, in considerable number, manage to find sufficient pasture. . . . Wheat is extensively cultivated, and a good deal of Indian corn: a kind of bean is, however, the staple article of food for the common laborers. (1900: 290)

Other sources corroborate the meatlessness of the diet of the poor in the later decades of the nineteenth century. (Gilliss 1854: 258; Merwin 1863: 68; Smith 1899: 37)

> As to the second and poorer class of the Chilenos, the peónes . . . Born as inferiors and dependents, the highest ambition of the peónes is to serve masters or mistresses of wealth and consequence, addressing them as Patrón, and Patrona. Their necessities are few, and may be summed up in a mud, or adobe hut, a hide in one corner on which to sleep, an iron pot and mate cup, bread and beans for substantial food, with garlic, or onions and fruits for relishes. (Merwin 1863: 88)

Lieutenant James Gilliss, who traveled through Chile in the middle of the nineteenth century as head of an astronomical expedition organized by the United States Navy, also suggests that meat might be a luxury to the poor, even though he could count on being served "the never-failing casuela" (1854: 390) himself. In an account of his visit to "the hacienda of an accomplished and hospitable friend, whither I had gone for relaxation, after a long series of observations on the planet Venus" (1854: 343), he describes the manner in which a peón[4] is paid:

> He receives three rations in meals, and from fifteen to eighteen cents per day, paid weekly, in money. A ration for breakfast consists of a pound of bread; for dinner, a pint of beans, mixed with wheat and grease [beef tallow]; and for supper, a peck of corn or wheat each week. Usually the food for the peóns is cooked at the house, whose mistress, when present, strives to send something extra from her own *dispensa* [stores]. Prepared at the kitchen of the residence, it is served to them at the sound of a bell, each one conveying his allowance to his family, if he has one. Perhaps, too, they are permitted to milk a cow or two, and cultivate a little ground immediately round their ranchos, in onions, beans, and potatoes. But these are favors, not rights of the peon. (1854: 345–346)

The reference to tallow may be significant, since the poor may have felt that it partially compensated for the frequent absence of meat in their diet. Granted

---

[4] The peons whom he describes were somewhat better-off than most (Bauer 1975), but still less self-sufficient than the *inquilinos*.

the frequent references to the careful rendering and storage of tallow when cattle were slaughtered, tallow may have been widely consumed. Other observers may have failed to mention it, perhaps because they would not have noticed its presence in cooked beans, because they considered it to be a seasoning rather than an ingredient, or because they took it for granted, as they must have done with salt.

Only in a few exceptional cases did Lieutenant Gilliss find that some rural poor ate meat. In one small Andean settlement, more prosperous than most because its location allowed its inhabitants to support themselves by wood-cutting for a nearby urban market and by smuggling tobacco across the Argentine border, the local people

> appeared to be very hospitable and polite, and invited me to share their meal; but as it was the first time I had noticed their style of eating, I preferred taking my dinner in camp. Five or six were seated around a very small table, on which was a wooden bowl of beef and potato stew; but there were neither plates nor bread, and each one helped himself from the basin with a wooden or horn spoon. (1855: 5)

Another source describes specific meals among the poor in similar terms:

> On the 14th of August, we went by rail a little distance into the country, to dine with a friend who has a contract for building some of the railroad bridges. We found our friend living in a shanty near a gorge in the coast range of mountains, where the grade is very steep, and where five bridges are required within one mile. A large number of peones were at work here, each of whom the contractor paid five reales a day, and furnished with a sufficiency of bread and beans. They have a brush shanty in which to sleep at night ; a stone oven to bake their bread, and a large iron kettle to cook their beans. The bread was leavened with yeast, pieces of the dough were weighed, made into loaves, and covered with a dirty poncho, and then placed in the sun to rise. At noon, old nail kegs, filled with cooked beans, were placed on the ground; three or four laborers squatted around each keg, and with a piece of bread in one hand, and in the other a stick flattened at the end, or mussel shell, with which to scoop up the beans, they ate their dinner. When their hunger was satisfied, they threw themselves on the ground, and drew their hats over their eyes for a few moments' siesta. (Merwin 1863: 78–79)

Merwin's description goes beyond a simple iteration of the ingredients which were eaten, but indicated on what occasion and in what manner food was served. The peons' meal differs from that of the elites not merely in its concentration on beans and grains and its lack of meat, but in the absence of dignity and sociality. Graham's "pressing invitations of every moment to eat of everything" contrasts with the simple, and presumably abrupt, placement of old nail kegs on the ground, much as the leisurely pace of the meal in the former case differs from the sudden ending in the latter.

Looking towards the middle of the social scale, meals differ not merely in how much meat they contain, but also in the context and the manner in which the food is served. Several travelers describe occasions on which they were invited into comfortable rural homes, not hacienda houses but those of *inquilinos*, and generously fed meals, which invariably included meat. In one particularly detailed example, Maria Graham describes a meal which she and another English woman, more recently arrived in Chile, ate at a house close to Valparaíso. This particular house attracted their attention because it had a flower garden, a fact which suggests that the family was well-off and established on the land for at least a year or two, rather than being poor migratory peons.

> We were so earnestly pressed to come back after our intended walk . . . farther on, and partake of the family dinner, that I, loving to see all things, readily consented; and accordingly returned at two o'clock to the flower-garden house. . . . We found the mother sitting alone on the estrada [veranda], supported by her cushions, with a small low round table before her, on which was spread a cotton cloth, by no means clean. The daughters only served their mother; but ate their own meals in the kitchen by the fire. We were accommodated with seats at the old lady's table. The first dish that appeared was a small platter of melted marrow, into which we were invited to dip the bread that had been presented to each, the old lady setting the example, and even presenting bits thoroughly sopped, with her fingers, to Miss H., who contrived to pass them on to a puppy who sat behind her. I, not being so near, escaped better; besides, as I really did not dislike the marrow, though I wished in vain for the addition of pepper and salt, I dipped my bread most diligently, and ate heartily. The bread in Chile is not good after the first day. The native bakers usually put suet or lard into it, so that it tastes like cake; a few French bakers, however, make excellent bread; but that we had today was of the country, and assimilated well with the melted marrow. After this *apetizer*, as my countrymen would call it, a large dish of charqui-can was placed before us. It consists of fresh beef very much boiled, with pieces of charqui or dried beef, slices of dried tongue, and pumpkin, cabbage, potatoes, and other vegetables, in the same dish. Our hostess immediately began eating from the dish with her fingers, and invited us to do the same; but one of her daughters brought us each a plate and fork, saying that she knew that such was our custom. However, the old lady persisted in putting delicate pieces on our plates with her thumb and finger. The dish was good, and well cooked. It was succeeded by a fowl which was torn to pieces with the hands ; and then came another fowl cut up, and laid on sippets strewed with chopped herbs; and then giblets; and then soup; and, lastly, a bowl of milk, and plate of *Harina de Yalli*, that is, flour made from a small and delicate kind of maize. Each being served with a cup of the milk, we stirred the flour into it; and I thought it excellent from its resemblance to milk brose. Our drink was the wine of the country;

and on going out to the veranda after apples and oranges were offered to us. (1824: 159–160)

The same author also describes another house, further from any town:

. . . we came to the post-house, and rested our horses; while doing so, the hostess obliged us to walk in and sit down at her family dinner. The house is a decent farm-house and not by any means an inn, though the post is stationed there. Our repast was the usual stew, *charquican*, of the country, fresh and dried meat boiled together, with a variety of vegetables, and seasoned with aji or Chile pepper, the whole served up in a huge silver dish; and silver forks were distributed to each person, of whom, with ourselves, there were eight. Milk, with maize flour and brandy, completed the dinner. At length, ourselves and our horse being refreshed, we renewed our journey, our peon and mules having gone on before . . . (Graham 1824: 195)

Notable here is the final point, that this hospitality did not extend to a peon. In this regard, Graham's experience was similar to Darwin's, who commented on a trip of several days which he took with guides whom "[t]he major-domo of the hacienda was good enough to give me" (1900; 290–291)

I was quite surprised to find that my companions did not like to eat at the same time with myself. This feeling of inequality is a necessary consequence of the existence of an aristocracy of wealth. (1900: 293–294)

Although these meals appear to have been served with at most, a few hours' advanced notice, it may still be questioned how representative they were, since the servers may have wished to offer their foreign guests particularly elaborate meals. Some accounts, however, describe another context, presumably less influenced by the presence of foreigners, in which common people ate: large work parties on haciendas.

Several accounts describe the annual *trilla* or threshing, in which dozens, and in some cases hundreds, of mares ran in circles on enormous heaps of wheat laid out on the threshing-floor.

In general, a *trilla* of 100 hectoliters requires three days of work, and the same number for a *fiesta* for those who took part in it. (Tornero 1872: 478)

An American observer provided a particularly detailed account of the labor, which corroborates the lithograph of a *trilla* from around 1830 (see Figure 7 [Gay 1862–65, vol. 1, pl. 19]). This description indicates that the feasting took place not only after the completion of the *trilla*, but on each day that the *trilla* lasted:

Figure 7   *A lithograph of a trilla*

While in Concepción I had an opportunity of witnessing the labors of the wheat threshing, which is an annual event of great importance. As the wheat is cut, it is placed in a pile on an elevated site, until it rises to the height of a considerable hill. The pile I saw was as large as six of our common hayricks, and was inclosed by a high fence of poles and bushes, adjoining a field in which were some forty mares, only used in this country for the purpose of increasing the stock. A portion of the grain was thrown from the pile upon the ground; the mares, with a half dozen guasos to drive them, were turned in, and at a signal from the mayordomo, stationed on the summit of the pile — away they went at full speed, incited by the whips of their drivers, and the yells of a crowd of men and boys outside. After a certain number of rounds, "Vuelta!" [Reverse!] roared the mayordomo, when the mares turned in their tracks and ran in an opposite direction — half obscured in straw and clouds of dust. Now and then one lost her footing and fell, of course bringing all behind her to a full stop, but doing no injury to herself in the mass of straw. When exhausted, the mares are turned into the corral to rest, while the grain was scraped up near the fence, and a new supply of unthreshed ears scattered over the ground. After the grain is threshed, it is winnowed by being tossed into the air, with shovels, when the wind blows away the chaff. On some haciendas, where the crop

of wheat is large, one or two hundred mares are employed in the threshing
. . . A daily feast for the laborers is provided by the patrón as long as the
trilla lasts. (Merwin 1863: 95–96)

Though neither of these courses specify the food that was provided, the
word "feast" suggests that it was abundant, and served with some courtesy; quite
possibly it was like the meat, wine and brandy that was served to the workers at
a threshing-party in 1786 (Pereira Salas 1977: 60).

The extensive cattle herds of the haciendas led to another major work
event, the annual round-up and slaughter. These events, even more dramatic
than the *trilla*, are also more fully described, at least in terms of the food that was
served. Meat was served in abundance:

> In addition to the work everyone took part in the celebrations. The patrón
> was gratified by the yield, the huasos entertained themselves in the evening
> . . . and even the dogs received succulent recompense. (Villalobos 1972: 92)

In his *Notes on a History of Chilean Cuisine*, first published in 1944, Pereira
Salas quotes a description of late nineteenth century round-ups which a friend of
his, the grandson of a wealthy landowner, provided him with. These accounts
(Pereira Salas 1977: 37–40), though based on personal memory, appear dubious
because of their retrospective nature and the class bias reflected in their sentimen-
tal evocation of bucolic life; however, it seems unlikely that the source invented
the dishes served at the round-up. These dishes are notable not only for their
number (there were eleven distinct named dishes) and for the correspondence of
particular recipes to particular muscle and organ meats, but also for the dimensions along which the dishes differ. Some were served on the first day of the fiesta and others on the second, some were eaten in the morning and others in the
afternoon, and some were reserved for the slaughterers (*matanceros*) and others
distributed more widely, all suggesting a complex semiotics of meat more often
associated with ritual sacrifice than with ranch-hands engaged in the production
of commodities.

Graham also describes a round-up and slaughter. She indicates that some
of the meat was reserved for the hacienda and some distributed to the *inquilinos*.
Her account suggests that these events were performances as much as work,
since they provided opportunities to display a fundamental masculine quality:
the mastery over large animals and rugged landscapes.

> Soon after breakfast we all mounted our horses, and rode to the . . . point
> . . . where the cattle of the estate were to be collected in order to be counted.
> This sort of meeting is technically called *rodeo*, and . . . takes place in
> the summer, or rather autumn; when the young animals are sufficiently
> strong to be driven to the *corral*, or place of rendezvous, from the mountains
> and thickets where they were born. All the tenants of an estate assemble
> . . .; and the young girls are not backward to dress themselves gaily, and

appear at the *corral*. When the day of the rodeo is appointed, the men, being all mounted, divide; and each troop has a chief, under whose orders it advances, keeps close, separates, or falls back, according to the nature of the ground, — none is too rough, no hill too bold, no forest too thick to pierce. . . . These men often stay several nights with their dogs on the hills to bring in the cattle; and when collected, all stranger beasts are set apart for their owners, and the estate cattle are marked. A rodeo is a scene of enjoyment: there one sees the Chilenos in their glory; riding, throwing the laça, breaking the young animals, whether horses or mules; and sometimes in their wantonness mounting the lordly bull himself. . . . The head vaccaros, or cowherds, ought, generally speaking, to be born on the estate where their business lies. The haunts of the cattle are so wide apart, and the country so little inhabited, and so little travelled, that tracks and landmarks there are none, and only experience can guide the vaccaro at the different seasons to the different haunts of the beasts. His business is, besides attending at the rodeos, to bring them either to the plain or to the hill, to feed or to browse, according to the season; to portion them so as to secure free access to water; and to be watchful over the young, whether calves, young horses, or mules. A real vaccaro is seldom off his horse . . . Each of these men has a certain number of cattle committed to his charge, for which he is accountable to the land steward. One part of the ceremony of the rodeo is very agreeable to the men concerned. About 12 o'clock to-day, one of the peons was desired to laza a bullock; which was immediately killed and dressed for the public: the skin, however, belongs to the estate, and was instantly cut up into thongs to make lazas, halters, and all manner of useful things. (Graham 1824: 189–190)

Such a rodeo is depicted in Figure 8, a photograph from around 1900, captioned "A Round-up on the Hacienda" (Wright 1904: 235). Within a large enclosure fenced in by boards and brush are fifteen men on horseback, presumably *inquilinos*, with a number of rather thin cattle in front of them. Just behind the fence stands a crowd of seventy or eighty people, presumably peons waiting for the slaughter of cattle and the distribution of meat. Even if this event had been staged, like some of the other scenes of hacienda life which were photographed and included in this volume, the arrangement of the people would suggest how some people believed round-ups ought to look. However, several elements in this photograph suggest spontaneity: the horsemen are lined up unevenly, and some of them are talking to one another, rather than facing the camera. Some people in the crowd also have their backs to the camera.

These sources suggest that the threshing and round-up were not simply occasions on which productive tasks were performed, but also the occasions on which hacendados provided the workers with festive meals. In this sense, these events were marked by consumption as well as production. The accounts suggest that participation in these events was limited to certain categories of men, at times described as *inquilinos,* better-off than the peons and with more stable ties to the

Figure 8   *"A round-up on the Hacienda"*

hacendado, and at other times as *huasos*, more dignified and prosperous than the *rotos*. This involvement followed from the fact that *inquilinos/huasos* usually owned horses, necessary for taking part in the threshing and the round-up, and *peones/rotos* did not. Much as the *inquilinos* had the obligation to participate in these large work parties, they also had the right to participate in the hacienda-sponsored festivities that followed, and, in the case of the round-up, to receive meat as well — a privilege that on occasion extended further down the social hierarchy to include peons and even dogs.

This extension of commensality to non-human animals merits attention. A number of accounts comment on the presence of dogs at meals, at least those served outdoors. Dogs were fed both at hacienda work parties (at the slaughtering of cattle, meat was so abundant that portions not sold, distributed or made into jerked beef were given to the dogs [Gilliss 1854: 362; Villalobos 1972: 92]) and on verandas (the puppy whom Graham describes as waiting just outside the circle of people at the table, to whom her companion Miss H. slipped the pieces of marrow-sopped bread that she did not wish to eat [1824: 159]). These meals, then, linked eaters of different species. Unlike many other cultures, in which it would be unthinkable for animals to be present at meals, Chilean practices allowed for meat to be distributed to dogs as well as to humans. The dogs in many ways seem like the only social inferiors of the peons (other, perhaps, than the Indians, entirely expelled from the central valley much earlier): like peons, they exist on the spatial and social fringes of the hacienda, performing tasks — herding sheep, protecting the homes and property of their masters against thieves — in exchange for the rights to scrounge food. They occasionally have a chance to consume some meat, their favorite food, at moments of particular abundance and festivity or when someone is moved to generosity. And like peons, dogs can be expelled altogether, wandering in search of another place to settle temporarily. Gilliss tells of how he once ate a *cazuela* in a spot in the central valley while

> half-starved dogs . . . prowled round us, eyeing each mouthful askance. These brutes are among the curses of the land. They infest its streets and highways, fill it with fleas and other vermin, render night hideous by their barkings, and are eyesores by day as well as nuisances at night. There being neither taxes on their owners nor laws limiting their numbers even in the large cities, everybody possesses one or more; and as their usual sleeping-places are the sidewalks before the houses, it is difficult to walk without kicking them aside . . . (1854: 342)

Kristeva also explores this image of hungry dogs in *Powers of Horror: an Essay on Abjection*, the book in which she examines the odd combination of fascination and repulsion often elicited by humiliation, servility and abasement. Though her universalizing frameworks (a semiotic analysis of alterity, a psychoanalytic interpretation of the mother-child link) are quite opposed to the historical and cultural specificities which I present here, she does show the forcefulness of the image of hungry dogs in sources as varied as the New Testament (Christ sees as an injustice the fact that someone would feed dogs while letting people go hungry, but finds it acceptable for dogs to eat the crumbs that are left over from a meal [1982: 115]), and the novels of Céline (unconcerned with the way that food is presented to them, dogs are willing to eat entirely without dignity [1982: 143,165]).

In her study of a poor urban neighborhood in Northeastern Brazil, Scheper-Hughes shows how dogs provide a powerful image with which people may describe conditions in their own lives:

> The people of Bom Jesus [the town about which Scheper-Hughes writes] sometimes refer to deaths from dehydration with the very stigmatizing term, "*doença de cão*", literally dog's death. They are referring to rabies which in Portuguese is called *raiva*, or literally rage, fury, madness. The madness of hunger is, indeed, very much like rabies, and a death from hunger is, indeed, a dog's death. (1988: 434)

This use of language is common in Spanish as well as Portuguese: *me da rabia*, which literally means "it gives me rabies", is a frequent way of saying "it infuriates me" or "I can't put up with it". The commonness of this phrase implies a linking of two qualities of dogs, their humility and the danger which they pose to their owners. It is as if rabies were a form of canine rebellion in which dogs finally responded to hunger and abuse by wildly attacking humans, their social superiors, and by infecting them with a fatal disease.[5]

These different sources, then, are all consistent in depicting a single pattern of meat consumption in nineteenth century Chile. The quantity and frequency of meat consumption corresponded closely with an individual's position in the social hierarchy (cf. Douglas 1971); the quantity of meat that was served also corresponded to the scale of the social event, with meat invariably associated with large festive occasions, whether civic or religious holidays or large work parties. The word "distribution" seems appropriate to describe this pattern, since it can denote not only the varying amounts of meat consumed by different individuals but also the specific acts in which some individuals give meat to others. In the first sense, meat is something which individuals have; in the second sense, it is something which they receive. This emphasis on distribution may also be noted in the two most frequently-reported names of dishes, *cazuela* and *puchero*. These words are much like the English term 'casserole' in that they refer both to food prepared for eating in a particular way, and to the container (a large pot which can be carried from the stove to the table) in which the food is prepared and served. (This linkage brings to mind the *marchas de cacerolas vacías*, anti-government demonstrations protesting the scarcity of foodstuffs in 1972 during the Unidad Popular government, in which women marched down major avenues in Santiago, banging empty pots together.) This metonymic association between stewpots and stews is entirely in keeping with the nineteenth century descriptions of Chilean meals: a high-status person (landlord, employer, host, senior woman of the household) brings (or has a servant bring) a potful of food (*cazuela, puchero*, cooked beans) to the spot (table, floor, ground) where a circle of people is gathered. They all may serve themselves, and the host may also give out portions of food. This relatively egalitarian etiquette could exist in so hierarchical a society as Chile because its range was limited. The sources which describe Chilean meals include many instances of exclusions (of peons, of women, of children, of dogs) from the circle of commensality.

These distributions of meat from cooking-pots make also be taken as redistributions from the person of the hacendado to others. On some occasions, the hacendado directly gave meat to the members of his household (or, including the *casas chicas*, to the members of his households); on others, he served guests

---

[5] Similar connections among epidemic illness, anger and social breakdown are explored quite differently by García Márquez in *Love in the Time of Cholera* (1985). The play on words is somewhat different, since the Spanish word *cólera* means anger when used in the female gender, cholera in the male gender. The female *cólera* can also mean bile, suggesting connection among these terms through a humoral theory of disease — a notion also present in the example discussed here, in which rabies is figured as hydrophobia.

or workers. The meat that *inquilino* families served would have come either from meat which the hacendado gave them directly at round-ups or on other occasions, or from the livestock which they raised on the plots which the hacendado had given them. Peon families served meat less often; they, too, would have received smaller amounts of meat at round-ups, or taken meat — or, more likely, rendered tallow — to their *ranchos* as payment for their work.

A RECONSIDERATION OF CONSUMPTION

This discussion of work and meals of nineteenth century Chilean haciendas shows the difficulty of placing the eating of beef into the more general category of consumption for several reasons; the specific problem of separating consumption from redistribution and the more general problem of placing animals into a well-defined and well-bounded category of objects which can be consumed. This second problem in turn raises an additional obstacle: the difficulty of claiming either that meat materially satisfies some human want, need or desire, or that meat semiotically serves as a sign to represent some other quality such as status or selfhood.

The link between consumption and redistribution suggests that meat-eating forms part of a social world. A reviewing of the discussion of nineteenth century haciendas shows that the limits of this social world do not correspond to a boundary separating humans and animals. On the one hand, some humans were excluded from fundamental aspects of sociality in certain contexts (the *rotos* did not live in real houses, for example, and, like Darwin's guides, often did not eat with other people). On the other hand, animals were often included in the social world, as shown by their participation in commensalism, work and reproduction. Rather than being outside the meal (having scraps thrown to them, having leftovers saved for them), dogs received their portion of the food, along with the humans. This sharing of food may have been as recognition for their work; indeed, the dogs in figure 3 seem to be organized in their efforts to protect the administrator from the photographer, much as the dogs worked in the round-up and protected their owners' houses. Horses, too, seem to have been directly involved in work, not simply as tools or implements. Finally, livestock seem essentially tied to the definition of a man's position in society: the number of his children and the size of his herds were two measures of his capacity as an adult man to reproduce.

These social links between humans and animals have two crucial aspects. Firstly, they rested on the location of animals at the bottom of, rather than outside, the social hierarchy, a hierarchy which ranked hacendados at the top, *mayordomos* below them, followed first by the *inquilinos/huasos*, and then by the peóns/*rotos*, and finally by animals. Secondly, this social hierarchy reflected a key quality, vitality: the greater one's capacity to own, to work, to reproduce and to eat, the higher one's position. This hierarchical order appears at times as patriarchy, quite literally the rule of fathers and patrons, at other times as redistribution, at others as mastery. These relations are all relations of domination: a domination of inferiors by superiors which included the domination of animals by humans as well as the domination of the poor and weak by the rich and powerful, a domination which contained as central elements raising animals, killing them and eating their flesh.

The question with which this chapter opened — the reason for the fact that, in nineteenth century Chile, the rich ate more meat than the poor — can now be addressed, not as Sahlins might have (by noting that meat served as a sign of status), or as Ross might have (by pointing out that the powerful seek to limit the access of the poor to necessities), nor even as Fischler and Fiddes would have (by suggesting some universal human tendency to distinguish ourselves from animals). Rather, the consumption of meat was a central part of the hierarchical order; not an indication or a consequence of a social world, but an integral element of the constitution of that world. To repeat Graham's description of the round-up

> there one sees the Chilenos in their glory; riding, . . . breaking the young animals . . . and sometimes in their wantonness mounting the lordly bull himself. (1824: 189)

The notion of "glory" at the round-ups — the occasions at which meat was most abundant and most widely distributed — suggests the centrality of animals to Chilean social life. The round-ups were not merely productive labor, not merely representations of social order, but performances in which a social order was enacted. The ordinary meals, though less dramatic, were similarly not merely semiotic comments on social life or nutritional prerequisites to social life, but social life itself: a life built jointly of humans and objects.

References

Allende, I.

   1985   The House of the Spirits. New York: Knopf.

Appadurai, A.

   1986   The Social Life of Things. Cambridge: Cambridge University Press.

Bauer, A. J.

   1975   Chilean Rural Society from the Spanish Conquest to 1930. Cambridge: Cambridge University Press.

Darwin, C.

1900   *Journal of Researches*. New York: P. F. Collier and Son.

DeShazo, P.

1983   Urban Workers and Labor Unions in Chile 1902–1927. Madison: University of Wisconsin Press.

Douglas, M.

1971   Deciphering a meal: in Clifford Geertz, (ed.) *Myth, symbol and culture*. New York: W. W. Norton, pp. 61–82.

Echaíz, R. L.

1955   Interpretación Histórica del Huaso Chileno. Santiago: Editorial Universitaria.

Elliott, G. F. S.

1911   Chile: its History and Development, Natural Features, Products, Commerce and Present Conditions. London; T. Fisher Unwin.

Fiddes, N.

1991   Meat: a natural symbol. London and New York: Routledge.

Fischler, C.

1991   L'Omnivore: le Goût, la Cuisine, le Corps. Paris: Odile Jacob.

García Márquez, G.

1985   El Amor en los Tiempos de Cólera. Barcelona: Bruguera.

Gilliss, J. M.

1854   The U. S. Naval Expedition to the Southern Hemisphere during the Years 1849 – '50 – '51 – '52. Volume 1. Washington: A. O. P. Nicholson,

Gilliss, J. M.

1855   The U. S. Naval Expedition to the Southern Hemisphere during the Years 1849 –' 50 –' 51 –' 52. Volume 2. Washington: A. O. P. Nicholson.

Goody, J.

1982   Cooking, Cuisine and Class; a Study in Comparative Sociology. Cambridge: Cambridge University Press.

Graham, M.

1824   Journal of a Residence in Chile, during the Year 1822 and a voyage from Chile to Brazil in 1823. London: Longman, Hurst, Rees, Orme, Brown and Green.

Hervey, M. H.

1891–92   Dark Days in Chile: an Account of the Revolution of 1891. London: Edward Arnold.

Kristeva, J.

1982   Powers of Horror: an Essay on Abjection. New York: Columbia University Press.

Loveman, B.

1979   Chile: the Legacy of Hispanic Capitalism. New York: Oxford University Press.

Merwin, Mrs. G. B.

1966 [1863]   Three years in Chile. Carbondale and Edwardsville: Southern Illinois University Press.

Orlove, B. and Rutz, H.

1989   Thinking about Consumption: a Social Economy Approach: in Henry Rutz and Benjamin Orlove (eds). The Social Economy of Consumption. Lanham, MD: University Press of America. pp. 1–57.

Pereira Salas, E.

1977   Apuntes para la Historia de la Cocina Chilena. Santiago: Editorial Universitaria.

Poole, D. A.

1988   A One-Eyed Gaze: Gender in 19th Century Illustrations of Peru. *Dialectical Anthropology* 13: 333–364.

Ross, E. B. (ed.)

1980   Beyond the Myths of Culture: Essays in Cultural Materialism. New York and London: Academic Press.

Sacks, O.

1985   The Man who Mistook his Wife for a Hat. London: Duckworth.

Sahlins, M.

1976   Culture and Practical Reason. Chicago: The University of Chicago Press.

Scheper-Hughes, N.

1988   The Madness of Hunger: Sickness, Delirium, and Human Needs. *Culture, Medicine and Psychiatry* 12: 429–458.

Smith, W. A.

1899   Temperate Chile: a Progressive Spain. London: Adam and Charles Black.

Tornero, R. S.

    1872   Chile Ilustrado: Guía Descriptivo del Territorio de Chile, de las Capitales de Provincia, de los Puertos Principales. Valparaíso: Librerías i Ajencias del Mercurio.

Villalobos, S.

    1972   Imagen de Chile Histórico: el Album de Gay. Santiago: Editorial Universitaria.

Wright, M. R.

    1904   The Republic of Chile; the Growth, Resources, and Industrial Conditions of a Great Nation, Philadelphia: George Barrie and Sons.

Zeitlin, M. and Ratcliff, R.

    1988   Landlords and Capitalists: the Dominant Class of Chile. Princeton: Princeton University Press.

CHAPTER SIX

The Material Culture of Success: Ideals and Life Cycles in Cameroon

Michael Rowlands

INTRODUCTION

T he desire for success is taken as such an unproblematic aspect of most people's lives that it remains surprising that so little detailed research has been carried out on how people evaluate it. Success is assumed to be read off by the possession of status markers, by the capacity to consume or to be wasteful which inevitably becomes both its measure and the imperative for its achievement. But, as Campbell has observed, it is difficult to see why either of these should imply that 'others' had been suitably impressed nor why this alone should be fundamental to the need for people to succeed (Campbell 1993).

Campbell goes on to discuss various ways of formulating criteria for evaluating success, including the subjective meanings of actors, judging the estimated or actual outcomes or consequences of conduct and the qualities or features intrinsic to the conduct itself. For example, the fact that 'the poor want to succeed, not just survive' may be a truism, yet it is an aspiration contextually bound to the modern ideal of achieving a 'better life' for oneself (Jones 1993: 247). Success, evaluated according to such a set of ideals, is motivated by an outcome, in this instance escape from poverty. Jones claims that discussion about the aspirations for success are virtually absent in the literature on poverty even though it may be basic to how the poor see themselves in relationship to the rest of society. A problem with defining success as an index of social mobility is that it can only be evaluated in terms of a tension between effort and failure, usually experienced in puritanical overtones of devotion to 'hard work' and austere life styles. The tendency for people not to know what to do with success once achieved, that 'too much money does not necessarily bring happiness', is consistent with the ideal of escape from a set of conditions rather than a choice of a sense of self to be achieved. Resentment and bitterness as a consequence of success is therefore half expected in most modernist interpretations of the experience.

Another limitation of a view of success that does not wish to take seriously its own achievement, is seen most strikingly in perhaps the most well known sociological doctrine on this subject, that of Veblen's thesis of conspicuous consumption (Campbell 1990). Inspired by anthropological observations on competitive feasting and destructions of wealth, Veblen defined success as a rational, purposive form of action in societies where status considerations predominated. Conspicuous consumption is an activity where the actors have a clear and specific goal in mind: to impress others and thereby gain their esteem or envy. Inequality is simply the inevitable outcome of demonstrating one's own pecuniary strength and the ability to possess what is denied to others. The motives for success are therefore individual and instinctual in the sense that one argues for an innate human disposition to desire the envy of others to maintain self-esteem. What is essentially a psychological argument, was synthesized by Veblen into a general social theory of emulation (invidious comparison with others) whereby success is evaluated through competition with those with whom one is accustomed to class oneself. Bourdieu has developed a more refined argument based on evaluation of taste and judgement as a property of difference assigned through unequal access to symbolic or cultural capital (Bourdieu 1979). The important difference is that for Bourdieu success is not something to be achieved outside of personal strategies devoted to its attainments. Personal practice is directed rather to gaining the position to define and have generally accepted the criteria used to define success.

What is lacking in sociological approaches to status emulation is a sensitivity to what people claim to be their ideals of success and how these are tempered in the way they objectify or represent them. Anthropology should be particularly open to such a perspective since it requires knowledge of how people perceive their own motives and achievements. An anthropological starting point might be Evans-Pritchard's discussion of Azande witchcraft which he interpreted as human action directed towards a pragmatic understanding of the causes of misfortune and failure (Evans-Pritchard 1937). In this schema the contingent event, whether interpreted as good luck or misfortune, is relatively unimportant since it is human intentionality that has to be evaluated. Keesing (1984) in his reinterpretation of the concept of 'mana' in the Pacific, similarly addresses local understandings of two life chances: first, the essential unpredictability of the outcomes of human effort and secondly inequalities among humans as visible evidence of the possession of or by mana. The concept of mana explains the efficacy of an action according to the potency invested in an act or materials by ancestral and other spirits. Keesing argues that personal success was never an abstract quality based on possession of supernatural powers but a quality of actions, words and things that, literally potentiated, would work to free people from illness, make taro grow or give success in warfare. Success was therefore intrinsic to the action as a quality made visible in its results. The same kind of retrospective pragmatism, trying a medicine or a magical spell to see if it works, of attributing mana-ness or its absence on the basis of perceived outcomes is characteristic of Firth's discussion of *manu* in Tikopia and Gilsenan's discussion of *baraka* in North Africa (Firth 1940: 497; Gilsenan 1982: 82). Here good fortune is not a matter of luck or design but attracting support from unseen beings which may or may not take substantivised form as a quality of chiefship or practical achievement. In the sense that here success is attributed to a motivation to behave in a certain manner, the argument can be extended to how others generally perceive the actions of successful people.

But this is still different from how people perceive and represent the nature of their own ideals. In this chapter I will argue that these are often representations of desired future states, willed into being through the possession of material symbols, taken to be indicative in the present of progress towards their achievement in the future. The primary motive for the actors is to remain convinced that present actions and future ideals are in line with each other. Acts of consuming the material symbols of western lifestyles may seem a rather perverse way of investigating these values. It assumes that objects that might be sold or read as statements of emulation of special status in one context will be reconsidered as emblems of local categories of success in another. It suggests that the latter are not fixed since one of the key points about modern success is that it goes beyond what was previously accepted by making claims to be up to date with new criteria and signs known best to those sufficiently familiar with the outside world. With a reliance on material culture as a means of studying how new elites define success, we find another link with Bourdieu, the close relation between educational capital and having style. But just as many reviews of his work have stressed the 'Frenchness' of his interpretation, so the forms that this relation takes may indicate the local form that the objectification of success can take. In Cameroon, this is deeply rooted in the anxiety generated by the desire for modernity as success and the structuring continuities of kinship and kin expectations in tradition. Personal aspirations as ideals which have to be struggled for, are rooted in uncertainties about being on the right path, assuaged through acts of consumption. These punctuation marks in life cycles are both confirmatory and predictive that personal strategies are working, that personalised futures are achievable.

STRATEGIES OF ACHIEVEMENT AND THE EVALUATION OF SUCCESS

In the cases I describe all acts of consumption are considered to be part of strategies for advancing and evaluating personal success. Whatever the 'wish to be' might objectify as a future, is problematically related to a past that, very ambiguously, has to be escaped from. In the cases dealt with in this chapter, this is deeply rooted in what is often glossed as a tension between modernity and tradition, of being 'in town' or 'in the bush'.

In Cameroon, as elsewhere in Africa, a cultural language of development and progress, evaluated in the consumption of western industrially produced goods, has become the touchstone for evaluating personal and group success (cf. Wilks 1990). Moreover the evaluation of development is measured more by the capacity to consume imported western goods than by the capacity to produce local equivalents. In turn, this is related to the time spent abroad, to educational qualifications and generally to the accumulation of symbolic capital as the means of gaining access to the resources of the state rather than wealth producing activities per se. The relation between length of time spent abroad and the acquisition of a western lifestyle as an index of personal and social development is also tinged with cynicism about the reality of the achievement and its endurance.

THE SENIOR CIVIL SERVANT

Joseph Ambah is the head of the delegation for agriculture in Bamenda, the provincial capital of the North West Province of Cameroon. He is forty six, is in the top grade of the civil service and has nine years to retirement unless he leaves his post early and follows a plan to complete a Ph.D in Britain and go into freelance consultancy work. His career exemplifies the typical success of the state functionary in Cameroon based on the pursuit of a long term educational strategy. Born in Bali, a chiefdom twenty miles outside of Bamenda, he gained a scholarship to 'Sacred Heart', a local Roman Catholic school with a reputation for rigorous academic education given by the white fathers. He gained his O levels and then acquired a scholarship to the American University in Cairo where he spent four years from 1963–67 and completed a degree in economics. This was followed by two years in the USA at the University of Massachusetts where he worked for a masters degree in agricultural economics. He returned to Cameroon in 1972 and entered the office of the Delegate for Agriculture in the capital Yaounde, where he held various posts responsible for the national census in agriculture, finally becoming assistant delegate and then provincial delegate for agriculture in the North West Province in 1979.

His monthly salary is set conservatively at 500,000 FCFA (Central African francs/£1,000) whilst his wife, who is a teacher, earns an additional 250,000 FCFA. They both come from a village outside Bamenda where they have farmland and produce a large part of their food, so that except for household expenses and medical expenses, much of their salary goes towards paying interest on loans and making contributions to *njangis* (rotating credit associations). They live in a government rented house at the Station, the old colonial residential area of Bamenda, with a cook and two house boys. The house is furnished with a mixture of government and personally supplied items which at present include a refrigerator, deep freezer, television, telephone, video, radio and stereo, upholstered chairs, dining table and chairs and carpets laid on a ceramic tile floor. Except for the chairs and table, all of these are imported goods. Ambah owns two cars, one a Mercedes, the other a pickup for farm work. He has six children, all in primary and secondary school and he plans to get them all through to 'A level', including the girls. At present, he has another house in Bamenda which he rents, a second in Wum also rented, and he is at present building a "retirement home" in his home village. Up until last year, he would also have enjoyed a free car, petrol allowance and free telephone as well as other allowances such as the paid house staff. Much of his income is therefore set aside for payment of debts to the bank, the Credit Union and the two *njangis* to which he belongs and which together provide the loans for his building and other projects.

The investment in education eventually paid off in gaining the qualifications to enter government service and gain position and privilege within it. He now speaks of being the first Cameroonian to go to the American University in Cairo as having taught him a lot about "the West" and Muslim cultures although as a boy "straight from the village" he admits to great loneliness and wanting to break his studies and return to Cameroon. In part, too much education can be bad thing — staying too long abroad to complete a Ph.D has meant that a number of his classmates entered the civil service at lower levels than himself and have never caught up. He has instead combined the strategies of gaining a sufficiently advanced qualification in a "useful subject" with frequent transfers and nominations in the agricultural and extension fields which is the route for rapid promotion in the Cameroonian state bureaucracy.

Whether due to the recent government austerity campaign or personal inclination, or both, he chose to describe himself and his household in underconsumptionist terms against much other circumstantial evidence. He would use the cheaper household goods in the market, he would buy in bulk from wholesalers to save time and money; he had only three pairs of shoes and chose imports or brought them himself abroad because they would be more durable and practical; he has six suits for formal and daily use and was not concerned with acquiring more.

THE BAMILEKE BUSINESSMAN

Gabriel Nfomyang is a Bamileke businessman resident in Bamenda since before 1950. He owns a petrol station, runs a fleet of three petrol tankers and sixteen Mercedes trucks, which he hires out to Brasseries Cameroon or Guinness Cameroon or to wholesalers in town. In addition, he owns several houses in town which he rents whilst he himself lives in a relatively modest house in the Metta quarter.

By Bamenda standards, Nfomyang is one of the richer businessmen, although this is usually qualified by more educated friends with remarks such as "the man is illiterate" or "he can only speak pidgin". He made the money to buy his first truck by trading in cloth in the markets from Bamenda up to Nkambe (i.e. the northern Grassfields) and back in the 1940s and early 1950s. As he describes it, he would trek with a headload of wrappers (these were calico strips in fathom lengths, worn wrapped round the waist) from Bamenda to markets in Bamessing, Ndop, Ngomeghe, Babessi and Jakiri then on to Kumbo, Kika, Nkosi, Ndu, Binka, finally turning at Nkambe and returning via Tabeken, Lessin, and Mbinon to Nso. He would sell the wrappers in local markets for money, then buy potatoes in Kumbo and return to Bamenda. The markets he sold in were synchronised on the eight day cycle and he could complete the route in one week. From Bamenda, he walked to Calabar with the potatoes and money, where he bought bundles of the white calico cloth (called washgrab) or, if it was too expensive there, he would take the canoe to Onitsha and buy there instead. He returned to Bamenda by "mammy wagon" (twelve ton trucks taking people and goods), selling the bundles here, sold some to other traders and started off to Nkambe again. Bamenda traders follow the same route today with an enormous range of imported goods carried in half-ton pickup trucks.

By 1956, Nfomyang had made enough to buy his first truck which he took down to Calabar and returned with general merchandise for traders in Bamenda old town. He was one of the first to start to break the monopoly of the "trading houses", like R. W. King and United Africa, in Bamenda, and to establish independent wholesale/retailing stores on Commercial Avenue. After the plebiscite in 1961 and the reunification of French East and British West Cameroon, he redirected his activities to Douala where he bought Mercedes trucks on special credit terms, buying another as he paid off the last, and hiring out space in them to wholesalers in Bamenda. He originally came from near Dschang, being part of the Bamileke migration into West Cameroon to escape French administration. It is said that he belongs to one of the Bamileke *tontines* (informal rotating savings associations) whose contributions run into millions of FCFA every month. Nfomyang acquired the agency for Texaco petrol in North West Province based on his control of transport and then diversified into building materials and houses, constructed to be rented by the state for civil servants such as Ambah.

THE MAKER OF IMPORT SUBSTITUTES

In Bamenda, there are three principal producers of household furniture and numerous other smaller artisans making tables and chairs. Joseph Asitah is one of the principal furniture manufacturers and owns a workshop where he produces upholstered chairs, decorated formica cupboards, tables and pelmet boards. He says he would like to expand his range to interior furnishings, having seen the range of styles offered in magazines of matching wallpapers, curtains, floor tiles and furniture. A number of "snack bars" have been opened in Bamenda recently whose owners have adopted these ideals of co-ordinated paints, floor tiles and formica covered furniture.

Asitah was sent to be an apprentice as a carpenter by his father. He trained with a master for two years and worked for him for a further eighteen months in lieu of paying his fees. He then worked for a carpenter for a year before meeting a man from Baffousam who was recruiting carpenters to work in his upholstery business. It is characteristic that he should describe this as "attaching" upholstery to his carpentry business just as — in the future — he wants to attach other businesses, such as trading in building materials in much the same way that a share-owner accumulates portfolios.

He invests with a Credit Union, a mutual aid association, usually with quite substantial sums such as one million FCFA (c.£2,000) so that after one year he will be able to borrow double the original investment. In the present economic situation in Cameroon, where the banks have lost considerable public credibility, the Credit Union has expanded its loan facilities. He also contributes to a business rotating credit and savings association (called a *njangi* in pidgin) and to two smaller ones in his home village of Mankon which are more like social clubs. He plans to use his savings next to buy a machine similar to that owned by one of his rivals who is able to produce more sophisticated shapes of upholstered chair. He says he gets many of his ideas for new furniture design from visiting large hotels in the cities, where the furniture is usually imported, and from magazines and films.

He lives in Mankon village, which is about twelve kilometres outside Bamenda, where he has built a compound next to that of his father. He has two wives and nine children and professes not to want any more because he will not be able to educate them all. He says he married his first wife from Bali, a neighbouring village, out of love, but his family insisted that he should marry again and also have children by a Mankon girl. Including two dependent relatives, there are fourteen in his household and he also sponsors a junior brother, one of his first wife's brothers, in secondary school (i.e. he pays the fees). His house is built in modern materials on a traditional compound pattern with an outer courtyard and his own quarters set behind. Each of his wives have their bedroom and parlour with a separate kitchen where they stay with their children. The public area is covered with ceramic tiles (which at 20,000 FCFA, c.£40, a square metre makes its own statement). He has a television, video, freezer, radio and a telephone in his own quarters and his wives' parlours are furnished with upholstered chairs, a dining table and chairs and a cupboard. He plans to build a new "more modern" house in front of the existing one which will be self-contained, with water and electricity. He expects his older children will eventually use it, although the plan has only been initiated because a water project is about to be completed in the village by the Swedish agency, Scanwater. He plans to educate all his children up to university level since — as he put it — with education they will be "reasonable" people and be able to achieve something for themselves. As for himself, he appears to have few needs. He last bought a suit second-hand in the market. He has two pairs of leather shoes and a pair of trainers and his anticipation of a special event would be the Fon of Mankon's annual dance when he would wear traditional dress. Assuming his upholstery business will be stable, his future plans include diversifying into "importation and exportation" which in Bamenda is a general term for trading in imported goods.

THE MARKET CARRIER

Chi Molibe pushes a handcart in the Bamenda central market, carrying goods for stall holders. He used to have a stall selling household goods, toiletries and cleaning materials but was pushed out of business by taxes. By selling his stock, he raised 60,000 FCFA and bought a handcart which is a box-like metal frame on wheels with a long handle. Other stallholders hire him to carry goods from the lorries to the market or to their warehouses. He usually works with three others and they share the work and proceeds between them. He came to Bamenda about thirty years ago from a village where he still has farmland and a house. He visits the village at least once a month taking gifts of salt, palm oil, soap and bread and returning to Bamenda with farm produce. In Bamenda, he rents a room and a parlour where he lives with his wife, five children and a junior brother.

I never knew his income but judging from the fact that he paid 3,000 FCFA to his njangi every Saturday, he probably earned an average of 8–10,000 FCFA a week. He pays 5,000 FCFA for two rooms in a cement-faced, mud brick house and shares the use of a firewood kitchen and a latrine. Besides building his house in the village, his principal concern has been to pay the fees to take his children through secondary schools with good technical reputations. Otherwise he buys rice, beans, oil and salt for the house, relies on the farm for much of his starchy foods, and keeps what money he can for medical, school and other expenses. His wife sells roasted food like plantain or maize on the side of the road in the evening to get extra money. Besides educating the children, if he had the money, he would like to have a three bedroom house in town, a television, upholstered chairs and a dining table. Whilst he uses savings from his *njangi* to pay school fees, eventually he would hope to save enough to get back into retailing and selling household goods in the small village markets around Bamenda.

THE SEAMSTRESS

Florence Afik is married to Peter Ngwah, has two children and lives with them and her three junior brothers in a six room house on Ndamukong street in Nkwen, a quarter of Bamenda. She rents a shed in the market in Nkwen where she sews clothes but since these are not selling well at present, she also buys beans at local village markets in Santa and rice from the Ndop plain and retails them in her store. The food gives her daily money whilst the sale of clothes pays the rent, school fees for her junior brothers and some of the household expenses.

She was married directly after she left school and her husband paid for her training to be a seamstress and bought her first sewing machine. One of her 'aunts' lent her 10,000 FCFA to buy cloth to build up a stock of dresses. Success in tailoring depends on having a wide supply of imported cloth to run up new models copied from pictures in magazines or seen on television. She shares the shed with three other women sewing clothes who jointly pay the rent of 12,000 FCFA a quarter. They barely manage to do this at present. What was seen a year ago as a trade with a secure income, allowing her to buy new furniture for the house, has suddenly disappeared. Traders now bring what are seen as exotic French imports from Douala and sell at prices little more than those charged by the seamstress. Moreover what Florence produces as cheap copies of expensive "haute couture", cannot easily be reproduced locally on sewing machines. Her work has been reduced to producing children's clothes, making repairs and items of traditional dress.

CONSUMPTION AND STATUS

These resumés of personal biographies suggest certain common themes in the objectification of different levels of success. A certain normative order is endorsed as a means of evaluating the success of others, based on a pervasive dogma of progress and development. Knowing what this achievement is or should be at any particular time is deeply problematic. Consumption in contemporary Cameroon is often a statement of confidence and a confirmation of personal progress which also motivates a general concern with public ceremonies, honours and titles. Consumption is rarely a personal and private act of gratification. Things are acquired and added to households when 'a time to eat' is ordered by the larger strategy of achievement. The eating metaphor (in pidgin English 'to chop' as in *'mi chop yi chop'* meaning the obligation to share) is used to describe a variety of both positive and negative acts of acquisition . To *chop na hus* for example, which is pidgin for sorcery, graphically describes the key fear of the consumption of family members for personal gain. It is at the completion of a degree, gaining promotion, acquiring a budget, that the achievement requires recognition and confirmation. Since success will elicit envy and hence the danger of a sorcery attack, protection comes from display' and demonstrating that one's own 'sorcery/power' is stronger and can be used to destroy enemies. Important men and women are frequently described as having enlisted diviners, marabouts, Indian fakirs or to have bought charms and amulets to protect their interests.

A fear of what causes failure drives a work ethic, particularly in the young, that is future oriented and outward looking. It also emphasises autonomy and an unwillingness to trust others which is often cited as one of the major reasons why businesses fail or why they rarely survive the death of their founders. Lack of trust also results in a rather frantic diversification of income into a wide range of activities to prevent having all one's eggs in one basket. In general it is seen as unwise simply to pursue one career rather than developing a portfolio of diverse interests and sources of income, symbolised in the 'adding on' metaphor. All of this cannot be done alone and depends on kin ties and patrons. The investment in education to achieve positions in the state bureaucracy, which is the only secure source of income in Cameroon, is enormous and a return may only be achieved after ten or fifteen years. Patrons may be on the look-out for a bright boy in the family or from the same village who would be worth investing in for the future. Quite often it is the threat of family anger that prompts a man or woman to diversify resources from their own careers and help junior members make their way. Florence Afik must earn the money not only for the school fees of her own children but for her three junior brothers as well. No household in town is without 'family members' from the village who work in the expectation of being sent to school, of being given their chance. In a sense the whole mass of family human and material capital which has been transmitted since the origin, must be augmented and handed on for future achievement.

In post-colonial Cameroon, the agenda for success has been set by education abroad in prestigious American and European universities. Credentialism is the means of gaining access to state positions and budgets on which personal fortunes can be established and extensive patronage networks developed. In turn it requires mobilising family networks and patrons to provide the funds to support a candidate through the lengthy and expensive educational process . All have to be convinced that success, meaning access to state power and a budget, is a certainty. Certainty of purpose and eventual success in the future, maintained through consuming the products of modernity in the present, is therefore a vital component of such personal and group strategies. Important occasions are celebrations of achievement and even more so, the mutual recognition that the strategy is working and the enterprise is on the right path. Consumption is orchestrated by these needs to assess position at all levels in the hierarchy of success and is recognised in a typically normative order through emulating the lifestyle of figures of greatest success.

THE HOUSE, THE PARLOUR, LUXURY AND SUCCESS

For people living in Bamenda, a provincial urban centre in Cameroon, the parlour (the living room) is where visitors are welcomed and fed, family meetings are held and the formal aspects of social life carried on. It contrast with the back area of the house where the family congregates during the day and early evening. Houses are open at the back. It is where informal interaction between neighbours takes place; where children rush about. By contrast the front of the house will be shaded by bushes, the windows will have curtains and visitors are expected to knock before entry. It is where most money will have been spent on building materials, on painting the walls, on putting grilles on the windows and on having a proper front door. The kitchen at the back will instead be made of sun dried bricks and probably have an earth floor appropriate to cooking on a wood fire. Below this, in the yard, will be set the pit latrines, rubbish pits and working areas.

The parlour may be described as a transitional space. Its purpose is syncretic in the sense that it absorbs and domesticates the outside for private consumption. As part of a strategy of emplacement, the parlour is a synthesis of inside and outside organised according to certain aesthetic categories that balance correctness, defined by the arrangement of furniture and objects according to the expectations of visitors, with style, defined by the capacity to innovate and shock through the display of individualised taste. It is the play between the ideal order of the household, orchestrated as tradition, and the contingency and arbitrariness of individualising freedom that has to be constantly negotiated over and resolved in the furnishing and arrangement of objects in the parlour. No such problem overtly exists for the back area of the house where the pragmatics of doing things is defined as 'women's things'. Yet the unconnected calor gas stove standing in a clean, modern and unused kitchen contrasts starkly with the mud brick, fire kitchen outside in the yard where cooking by wives on a wood fire goes on, where boys find and bring presents to their mothers and where neighbours gossip.

But the parlour is the space which organises family activities in such a way that everyone knows their place. The decoration and furnishing of a parlour may combine a variety of modern imported goods like televisions, videos, clocks and ornaments with local copies of western furniture and traditional stools, bowls and figures. It should ideally be furnished with sets of upholstered chairs, dining table and chairs, a formica room divider which also serves to store the television and the cutlery, glasses and plates, a stereo, a radio, a wall clock and a telephone. To borrow a linguistic term, such creole material cultures combine elements from more than one historical origin into forms that have quite discrete and innovative meanings. What might be experienced as a clash of elements of disparate origin forms a viable synthesis of meanings anchored in the reformulated consciousness of the people.

Renegotiating status at the interpersonal level critically revolves around the association of commensality with the definition of space. The only viable definition of a household in Bamenda is to describe it as the unit that sleeps and eats together at any particular time. For a variety of reasons, the membership of a household fluctuates over short periods of time. Relatives from the country come to stay for any length of time or they will send their children to stay and work in the house so they can go to school or hospital in town. In households of fluctuating composition, the parlour where all meals are eaten and shared, is the space that symbolically incorporates and unifies diversity. Strangers are welcomed in the parlour and if judged sufficiently important, will be fed and entertained there. Commensality extends further than food and drink. Public television for example has only recently been introduced to Cameroon but their use to show videos has been a long standing feature of domestic life for the successful and has rapidly been assimilated into parlour culture. Unlike the decorous English household where to continue to watch television when a guest arrives would be viewed as the height of bad manners, in a Bamenda parlour it would be insulting to deprive a visitor of the chance to view. Televisions are never switched off as long as there is something to see. Due to the fact that most programmes are in French and Bamenda is predominantly anglophone, the sound may be turned down and the local radio turned on to accompany the pictures whilst conversation on disparate subjects will occupy the viewers as they stare at the screen. In other words it is the consumption of images and not communication that is fundamental to television experience. It is a unifying force that draws neighbours and family members together as an intense act of commensality.

Parlours of important houses usually serve as meeting places for wider family meetings and social meetings such as *njangis* (a pidgin term for rotating credit and savings associations). The room is often decorated with tinsel, Christmas style decorations and coloured lights that give a strong feeling of festivity. It is an image of celebration that associates strong, luminous colours with the desire to impress. Religious symbols in the form of crucifixes, pictures of patron saints, and religious calendars often form the focus of such decorations. Photographs of family members receiving awards or being welcomed at prestigious gatherings will be set alongside.

The parlour is the epitome of the level of comfort that the household can afford and the quality of the furnishings is taken as a straightforward indicator of the family fortunes. If there is a carpet in the house it will be found here. In richer houses, the cement floor will be covered in ceramic tiles. The room will often have large numbers of chairs distributed along the walls. Seating arrangements are also structured by status from left inside the door around the room with the seats in the corners being allocated to important members. Set apart from these may be a separate seating area where important visitors will be invited to retire. The analogue to the VIP lounge in international airports extends to superior furnishings and the presence of imported furniture, the drinks cupboard lavishly stocked with imported whiskies and champagnes, luxury carpets, stereo, imported light fittings and wall decorations. Visually the dominant object in the room is the armchair which is usually a large, overstuffed affair covered in brightly coloured cloth. The cloth is imported, can be bought in different thicknesses and most people know its worth. A set of armchairs and accompanying side tables will cost between 250–300 CFCA (c. £500–600), a not inconsiderable sum. Quality is judged by the size of a chair and the thickness of the layers of dunlop foam rubber used and by the weight and thickness of the cloth covering. By contrast, Europeans will generally prefer 'colonial style' hard wood chairs with cushions where the quality of the wooden frame can be assessed. Hence the number of such chairs in a room demonstrating the capacity of the owner to seat, on occasion, a considerable number of guests comfortably is a sure index of his wealth and social position. However the arrangement of chairs in the room is structured by the sequence of stools that men would occupy in a traditional meeting house. The sequence is in turn organised by seniority and title which is the prerogative that allows a man to sit on a stool with either spiders, wild bats or human head carved on it. In other words such modern looking chairs are obeying the logic of traditional hierarchy, albeit in a more fluid and unstable fashion.

Understanding the notion of luxury in Bamenda is inseparable from the conditions of commensality. The ideal of sharing has been extended out of the range of food and drink to consumables in general and in particular those that signify 'the West', modernity and the cultural capital that flows from access to education and state patronage. An important motivation is the idea that achievement is not simply made tangible in 'things' nor does it belong to anyone individually. The resources received from a father have to be transmitted to future generations at least undiminished and preferably enhanced. 'Things' in this sense embody the value of being acquired through the good fortune of a shared ancestral substance which has guided the successful career of a particular person and the supporting kin group. Sharing 'things' is therefore fundamentally about acknowledging what has been held in common since the origin. However the acquisition of wealth is perceived to be deeply ambivalent precisely because the power that an ambitious person wields to achieve it is recognised to be the same as that which can turned against the kin group and become witchcraft. The belief that wealth and success has been gained at someone's expense, usually a close relative, has generated a whole new range of witchcraft accusations in Cameroon (Rowlands and Warnier 1988; Fishy and Geschiere 1993). Hence sharing the products of success is also a sign of innocence and good intention; recognition that wealth should ideally be shared to the benefit of all kin members who recognise a common origin. Affirmation of the continuing significance of kin categories in the accumulation and dispersal of wealth in modernising contexts is scarcely novel but still, the fundamental drive to consume, it means something very different from the selfish individualism usually attached to such acts in the West.

IMAGES OF THE BEAUTIFUL

Success and personal self affirmation in Bamenda are recognised aesthetically through a preference for luminous, bright colours in house decorations and clothing. By contrast with an English middle class muted aesthetic sensibility, colour is used as a strident and self affirmative declaration of achievement in Bamenda. Working in an office, going to church, and invitations to public ceremonies are the settings in which people will be concerned to display their worth through dressing up in western style clothes and shoes.

Imported clothes from France and shoes from Italy are especially sought after, many of which are specially made in Europe for the West African market. Western style clothing is particularly favoured at present as part of an identification with modernity and a politics of national unity. The majority of people however cannot afford the imported clothes and have them made up by tailors in the local market from models circulated in French mail order catalogues or from imported magazines. Any style will be run up using materials supplied by the buyer, although usually market copies will lack the more sophisticated decorations much admired on the imported clothing. Comparing the imagery in the catalogues and magazines to what is locally produced, is illuminating. The catalogues that circulate are predominantly those designed in Europe to provide formal clothes for older women. Models are chosen for their elegance and the absence of explicit sexual exposure. Women in Bamenda rarely wear short skirts or tops that would expose the shoulders and cleavage. Instead high buttoned dresses and skirt lengths around mid-calf or the ankle are preferred for most public occasions. Women who expose too much flesh, wear too much lipstick, heavy eye make-up, pluck the eyebrows and use the more striking nail polishes risk the accusation of being a 'free girl' in Bamenda. For many women the signs of urban liberalism can be quite muted, particularly if the image of the domesticated woman, dressed in a wrapper around the body and with cloth covering the hair, is invoked. One example, often cited as the sign of being not quite respectable, is the use of a toothpaste called Email Laundry which reddens the lips in addition to cleaning the teeth.

The copies of clothes made in the market combine sophisticated pleats and sashes of the restrained styles associated with 'mature women' in the catalogues, with vivid, electric colours, often inserted as panels of cloth, to stand out and give maximum impact. Aesthetically the emphasis is on sheen and luminosity rather than on a particular colour. The sheer volume and obvious expense of the cloth used, particularly if it is imported, also elicits frequent comment. The use of textiles as representations of status and identity has been frequently mentioned in West African ethnography. In Yoruba Ijebu, relatives of a deceased Osugbo member bring cloth to wrap around the corpse. According to Margaret Drewal (1992: 42) "the sheer volume of the wrapped corpse is indicative of the social significance of the deceased". In life, the constant tying and retying of fathoms of cloth wound round the body as wrappers serve as an active metaphor of the success and achievement of the wearer (Drewal 1979: 11). Debora Heath reaches the same conclusion in her analysis of dressing well among urban elites in Senegal. "Dressing well forges a link between having and being, displaying both wealth and social identity" (Heath 1992: 19). Modern clothes are therefore integrated into a longstanding association of expensive cloth and elite identity in West Africa. The combination of expansive covering of the body with expensive cloth and the preference for textures and colours that shine, brings together two aesthetic codes that are usually kept distinct in Western dress. Whereas in the latter bright colours that stand out are often associated with youth and sexuality, in Bamenda the aim is to represent personal achievement through combining the impact of bright colours with a dress style that signifies maturity and reserve.

Images of physical beauty hint at a similar association of brightness and sheen with personal worth. Both men and women rub their bodies with scented oil to protect their skin against cold weather and the wrinkling effects of the dry season. Skin that is dry and flaky is a sign of ill health, of old age and approaching death. Some of the worst diseases associated with witchcraft, such as leprosy, are recognised as skin diseases, causing eruptions and lesions in what should be a smooth and supple surface. Witchcraft in practice is essentially a question of appearance and the sudden and unexplained onset of disease are the first signs of attack. Health and well-being are therefore visible on the skin and an indicator of the moral state of the person. Girls leaving their father's compound at marriage, are stripped of their clothing, rubbed with a mixture of camwood and palm oil by him and sent naked to the husband's house to be dressed. Most men will rub their bodies and scalp with oil whilst women will use a wide range of expensive scented oils such as Mixa or Joanna, imported from France. A good oil is said to stay on the skin and not be absorbed too quickly. Hence the lighter and more expensive oils are not necessarily preferred and coarser, cheap oils, like Glycerine 900, that can be mixed with strong scents are often preferred. Also women will often say the skin should be sweet, which means to the taste (i.e. tangy or salty not sugary), an allusion to the close skin/mouth contact between children and mothers in suckling and carrying and in the preparation and eating of food.

Physical appearance as a sign of personal and group well-being and achievement is therefore a closely monitored and conscious affair. The body as object becomes the highly polished machine whose completeness should never be in doubt. As if in agreement with Merleau-Ponty's discussion of the phantom limb as a conscious refusal to accept loss, repair of the body in Bamenda is an immediate response to a state of social or interpersonal threat or loss (Merleau-Ponty 1962: 80–81). Feeling at ease with one's body is rarely a matter of introspective evaluation of the degree of convergence between the 'dream body' and reality, but rather a form of 'showing off' that will not only convince others but allay one's own anxiety. 'Cry dies', for example, are ritual occasions for remembering named ancestors whose anger will be incurred if not sacrificed to properly, with sufficient food and drink and descendants in attendance. The effects on direct successors will be swelling of the belly and the inability to retain food and liquids. Women who are unable to conceive are believed to have a substance that prevents male semen and female blood joining and mixing to create a foetus. The body is a container of ancestrally derived substances that should ideally be transmitted to future generations. To the extent that all acts of divination are revelatory, treatment of the body is as much a matter of displaying order as merit, confirming that personal and group strategies remain unaffected by the numerous sources of malevolence and destruction that can afflict one. There is a double benefit to dressing up on such occasions as going to church on Sunday, to family celebrations or to public festivals. It not only legitimises, however tenuously, a hold over the equation of aesthetic and moral value but it also asserts that personal attainment is now beyond criticism.

UNCERTAINTY AND FEAR OF FAILURE

The uncertainties in personal lives and the fears engendered by the prospect that what little has been gained may suddenly disappear, widely permeates social relations in Bamenda. The fear of theft legitimises the most horrendous hues and cries if thieves are disturbed breaking into a house or stealing a car. If caught, the accused will be lucky to escape with a public beating and arrest. There have been several recent cases of public lynching and if arrested, and found guilty, an accused is likely to be executed by firing squad. Perversely, a kind of glory is also given to those particularly successful robbers who stay in the swim of achieving something in Cameroon by taking from others. The country now has its 'national team of armed robbers', modelled on the achievements of the national football squad. The members of the 'national team of robbers' are shown on the front page of the national newspaper, *The Cameroon Tribune*, lined up like a football team with gendarmes standing at each end like referees and with all the stolen goods recovered lying at their feet.

Uncertainty and fear of the conditions of personal downfall are pervasive themes in newspapers, church sermons, wall calendars and street graffiti. The dashboards of taxis, for example, are frequently plastered with stickers that reproduce various well known sayings that warn the occupants. One genre exhorts the reader to deny his or her fate and inevitable downfall: "Let my enemy live long and see what I will be in the future" or "Downfall of a man is not the end of his life". Another reflects suspicion about the intentions of others: "I am afraid of my friends even you". Others enlist the need of supernatural aid to help protect against disasters. People frequently use Indian, Chinese and other amulets and charms to protect themselves in public spaces. Photos on the walls and the ubiquitous Christmas style decorations in the parlour will also be protected by religious icons, posters, and crucifixes. Chalked over the doorway into the house, one finds sayings such as: 'Don't give up, your miracle is on the way' or 'Education and beauty without god means hellfire'. Finally there is the unremitting despair of 'Man no di no' or 'Too much desire of money leads to death'.

These expressions of anxiety in public spaces contrast with the fact that they are rarely found inside the house or mentioned in other dimensions of personal space. Clothes, furnishings, and the serving of food and drink can be seen as statements about the nature of success and the impregnable position of the owner. Which of course implies a fatalistic, somewhat externalised, view of fate, as if misfortune is never a result of bad judgement. Lienhardt made much the same point some years ago in his discussion of the absence of a sense of inferiority in Dinka conceptions of the person. "Experiences as intrinsic to the remembering person appear to the Dinka as exteriority acting upon him, as were the sources from which they derive" (Lienhardt 1961: 149).

The idea that misfortune is like a disease that is contagious and catches some people and not others is the sort of meaning given to the concept of *atchul* in Bamenda (Warier 1993: 145–148). It refers to a taint which affects a person and results in an inexplicable loss of, for example, growing crops or damage to property. An *atchul* would be the sort of person who would have 10,000 FCFA and would lose it all in a week without having anything to show for it. It is used particularly to describe people who cannot hold on to wealth or property. *Atchul* is not an inherited disease and anyone can contract it, usually because of a transgression or having come into contact with someone with occult powers. In pidgin English, people who suffer inexplicable bad fortune are called *balok* (from the English bad luck). Instances of this would be a person who constantly loses things or cuts himself with a machete and the wound refuses to heal. This is consistent with the concept of *ndon*, described in detail by Dillon (1990: 67–75) where such acts are usually a sign of having committed an offence against kin solidarity which requires the help of a diviner to rectify. If the bad luck continues then it implies that the person is resistant to any cure and is best avoided since it spreads by association. An *atchul* is therefore someone afflicted with the disease of failure that cannot be accounted for in terms of bad judgement, venality, moral turpitude or other such convenient means of assigning blame to the person. As with sorcery accusations, the best defence of the *atchul* is to profess ignorance. The only solution is to put oneself in the hands of diviners and elders who are able to cleanse the unintended consequences of some act in the past and make libations against sources of anger. The declaration of innocence and the absence of malevolent intention, is the first step in this process since nothing can be done with the intentionally evil.

CONCLUSION

The danger of evoking these traditional themes in African Anthropology is simply to update the account and re-describe the protection of divination and medicines in the language of a cult of modernity. Acts of consumption would then become part of the protective screen that separates the person from an external world of loss, fear and violence. Yet this would not take seriously the rejection of this world as bush, village, etc. by those who aspire to a different future. The modernist fantasy in Bamenda is organised around the house and in particular around the reproduction of the extended family. The emphasis is on children, health, collective well-being, and is lived in the parlour which contains all the signs that project a desired future. The aspirations are outward-looking, particularly among the young, where emulation of Atlantic black culture transcends local loyalties of region or nation. The television and in particular the video are the principal means of keeping up with legitimate questions of style and effect.

The fact that such identities will be complex and polymorphic is only to be expected since they are negotiated within a wider national setting that has already condemned the people of Bamenda as traditional and backward, as incapable of progress. Yet the ontology of failure and defeat has not been individualised to the same extent as a politics of consumption which has led personal aspirations towards the accumulation of symbolic capital. An incohate and somewhat repressed and resentful belief exists, particularly among the young and the educated, that whatever values might be attached to progress, to the acquisition of expensive imports as emblematic of a future, they cannot ultimately protect against inexplicable failure, disease and death. A national newspaper headline, for example, referring to the death of a successful young businessman or politician in the city, will turn an accusing editorial eye on elders in the village who, it will claim, resentful of success, misuse their powers to exert control over the young. Identities that are stretched between a past dominated by the authority of the father and a future predicated on the successful appropriation and domestication of modernity into a suitably localised form, are therefore inevitably complex and contradictory.

References

Bourdieu, P.

1979   *Distinction. A social critique of the judgement of taste* London: Routledge, Kegan Paul.

Campbell, C.

1993   Veblen's theory of conspicuous consumption. In Brewer and Porter (eds) *Consumption and the world of goods* London:

Dillon, R.

1990   *Ranking and Resistance*: Stanford University Press.

Drewal, H.

1979   Pageantry and Power in Yoruba Costuming. In J. Cordwell and R. Schulz (eds) *From the Fabrics of Culture*. The Hague: Mouton.

Drewal, M.

1992   *Yoruba Ritual.* Indiana: Indiana University Press.

Evans Pritchard, E. E.

1937   *Witchcraft, Oracles and Magic among the Azande.* Oxford: Clarendon Press.

Firth, R.

1940   *Primitive Polynesian Economy.* London: Routledge, Kegan Paul.

Fisiy, C. and Geschiere, P.

     Sorcellerie et accumulation, variations regionales. In P. Geschiere and P. Konings *Itinerarires d'accumulation au Cameroun* Paris: Karthala.

Gilsenan, M.

1982   *Recognising Islam.* New York: Pantheon Books.

Heath, D.

1992   Fashion, anti-fashion and heteroglossia in Urban Senegal. *American Ethnologist,* **19**, 1: pp. 19–33.

Jones, D. J.

1993   The culture of achievement among the poor. *Critique of Anthropology,* **13**, 3: pp. 247–267.

Keesing, R.

   1984   Rethinking Mana. *Journal of Anth. Research*, **40**: pp. 137–156.

Lienhardt, G.

   1961   *Divinity and Experience*. Oxford: Clarendon Press.

Merleau-Ponty, M.

   1962   *Phenomenology of Perception*. London: Routledge, Kegan Paul.

Rowlands, M. and Warnier, J-P.

   1988   Sorcery, power and the modern state in Cameroon. *Man NS*, **23**: pp. 118–132.

Warnier, J-P.

   1993   *L'Esprit d'entreprise au Cameroun*. Paris: Karthala.

Wilks, R.

   1990   Consumer goods as dialogue about development. *Culture and History*, **vol 7**: pp. 79–101

CHAPTER SEVEN

The Political Economy of Elegance: An African Cult of Beauty

Jonathan Friedman

THE NEGOTIATION OF SELFHOOD AND THE CONSUMING DESIRES OF MODERNITY

The aim of this discussion is partly to dissolve the category of consumption into the broader strategies of self-definition and self maintenance. Very much of the discussion of consumption is couched in a language that is dependent on the axioms of modernity, the presupposition of an autonomous rational individual inhabiting an empty space in which meaning is constructed externally, via codes, cultural schemes and paradigms, that define the world as a particular kind of stage where a universal individual takes on different roles. Consumption can thus be generated by a system of social values, preferences, utility etc., categories that are imposed from the outside on an initially empty or random set of potential objects. Contemporary cultural models epitomize this recipe book conception of social reality, since they are based in all their essentials on abstractions from social products, whether dress fashions or forms of discourse. As such, they merely reflect the products from which they are abstracted, but they cannot generate those products. Strategies of consumption can only be grasped when we understand the specific way in which desire is constituted. And the latter of course is an essential aspect of the constitution of personhood.

This argument parallels Bourdieu's modelling of the relation between *habitus* and practice, between the "durably installed generative principle of regulated improvisation" (1977: 78) and specific strategies of consumption. Bourdieu's perspective, however, is rationalist and economistic, insofar as it reduces all practice to the accumulation of cultural capital, i.e. of specific forms of power. As such it fails to account for the essentially arational constitution of desire. Thus, while the *habitus* concept might be a way of avoiding cultural determinism, it is severely circumscribed by the imposition of praxeological criteria on its very construction. This is clearly manifested in the straitjacketing of his analysis of consumption into a strategy of social distinction. In a theoretical development of Veblen who is not properly acknowledged, he presses *habitus* into class position, where it serves quite mechanically to produce the cultural definition of social position.

> Each condition is defined, inseparably, by its relational properties which depend in their turn on its position within the system of conditions which in this way is also a *system of differences*, of differential positions, that is by everything that distinguishes it (from that which it is not) and especially that to which it is opposed: Social identity is defined and affirmed in a field of difference (Bourdieu 1979: 191).

I do not pretend to deny the strategy of difference implied in distinctive consumption in capitalism, but the very fact that the class-consumption style correlation lingers consistently in the 50 percent range ought to make us wonder about what the other half is up to. Even if we grant that distinction plays a role in defining selfhood and thus consumption, there are more spectacular aspects of capitalist consumption in general that cannot be grasped in such an approach which assumes that the only identity is class identity which is relatively static. Distinction as such is neither distinctively modern nor capitalist. The entire Veblenesque scheme was inspired largely by material from the anthropologist, Franz Boas, relating to Northwest Coast Indian potlatch and other models of conspicuous consumption and sumptuary-defined ranking and which he generalized to modern industrial society. What he may have misunderstood was the degree to which prestige competition in kin organized societies was not merely a matter of status separable from a person's identity, but a matter of life and death. A form of social existence that permits a Veblenesque discourse is one in which a person's selfhood is not identical to his social status, thus implying a concept a role. It is an experiential domain in which all socially achieved prestige might easily be understood as false and even alienated. The practice of distinctions is bound to be more consistent and absolute in societies where prestige expressed in conspicuous consumption is the totality of social identity, i.e. where the subject is equivalent to his expressed status.

Campbell's recent analysis of the relation between modern individualism, romanticism and consumerism comes to grips with the more general nature of modern consumption in which change of identity via consumption is instrumental. This would appear to be the opposite of Bourdieu's emphasis on the maintenance of difference, and yet it tells us a great deal more about the central characteristic of capitalist consumption, its continuous transformation. Consumption is driven here by a fantasy fuelled drive to establish an identity space, a life-style, the realization of a day dream of the good life, which always ends in deception and a search for yet other styles and goods. This process is rooted in the dissolution of fixed social identities and the formation of a complex of phenomena known as modernity, and which, with respect to consumption, is dependent on the emergence of the modern individualized subject, bereft of a larger cosmology or a fixed self-definition. The peculiarities of this self are its division into a private = natural sphere and a public = cultural or social sphere, creating a fundamental ambivalence between the desire to find an adequate expression of one's self and the realization that all identity is arbitrarily constituted and therefore, never authentic. This realization is fundamental: The principle of the daydream, the Walter Mitty principle, the principle of alterity, of the construction of a social self, are all specific to the modern individual and cannot be universalized.

> The dialectic of conventionalization and romanticization is the personally concrete expression of the dialectic of class and capitalist reproduction in general, a dynamic contradiction between distinction and revolution, between other directed and self directed images, between dandy and bohemian (Friedman 1989: 128).

Acts of consumption represent ways of fulfilling desires that are identified with highly valued life styles. Consumption is a material realization, or attempted realization, of the image of the good life. Bourdieu's consumer defines a cultural identity by constructing a niche in the world of goods. But one may rightly ask whether or not the purpose of consumption is merely to define one's social position. Campbell seems to imply in his critique of Veblen that the goal of consumption is not difference as such, but the achievement of fulfilment by the creation of a life space. If distinction plays a role here it is as part of the strategy of self-fulfilment. Living like a king is not part of a strategy of potlatch, a political statement of relative status, but the enjoyment of the highly valued luxuries associated with such status. In this model, the practice of distinction refers to other directed strategies of social positioning, of the conventionalization of status, which is both opposed to and contained within the more general strategy of self-directed identification with a particular set of commodities that form a life space.

The common ground in these approaches is the explicit connection between self-identification and consumption. The former may be a conscious act, a statement about the relation between self and world, or it may be a taken for granted aspect of everyday life, i.e. of a pre-defined and fully socialized identity. It is from this point of departure that is is possible to envisage consumption as an aspect of a more general strategy or set of strategies for the establishment and maintenance of selfhood. Consumption, then, in the most general sense, is a particular means of creating an identity, one that is realized in a material reorganization of time and space. As such it is an instrument of self-construction which is itself dependent on higher order modes of channeling available objects into a specific relation to a person or persons.

HEALTH, WEALTH AND APPEARANCE:
A SHORT HISTORY OF LIFE
FORCE IN THE CONGO

While *La Distinction* applies only very partially to modern European societies, it is perfectly suited to Central Africa and especially the Congo. Here, clothing is definitive in the practice of social differentiation. One need only visit the church, the cemetery or the hospital morgue where the bodies of the deceased lie waiting to be turned over to their mourning relatives, to be astounded by a degree of elegance of attire and exquisiteness of taste not to be encountered elsewhere. This area of Africa has long history of traffic in both cloth and clothing. And dress seems always to have played an important role.

> In ancient times the king and his courtiers... wore garments made from the palm-tree, which hung from the girdle downwards, and were fastened with belts of the same material, of beautiful workmanship. In front also, they wore as an ornament, and made like an apron, delicate skins of civet cats, martens and sables, and also by way of display, a cape on the shoulders. Next the bare skin was a circular garment somewhat like a rochet, reaching to the knees and made like a net, from the threads of fine palmtree cloths, tassels hanging from the meshes. These rochets which were called Incutto, they threw back on the right shoulder, so as to leave the hand free, and on the same shoulder carried a zebra's tail, fastened to a handle, according to an ancient custom in those parts... (Pigafetta and Lopes 1970: 108).

The early visitors to the area all report the highly stratified situation where only the upper ranks might dedicate themselves to such elegance.

> For the most part the people went barefoot, but the king and some of his nobles wore sandals, after the antique, like those seen in Roman statues, and these were also made from the palm-tree. The poorer sort and common people wore the same kind of garments, from the middle downwards, but of a coarser cloth, the rest of the body being naked (op. cit 109).

And the introduction of European goods immediately led to further distinctions.

> But since this kingdom received the Christian faith, the nobles of the court have begun to dress according to the Portuguese fashion, wearing cloaks, capes, scarlet tabards, and silk robes, every one according to his means. They also wear hoods and capes, velvet and leather flippers, buskins, and rapiers at their sides. Those not rich enough to imitate the Portuguese, retain their former dress (op. cit. 109)

The violent history of the Kongo kingdom, the slave trade and the disintegration of Congolese society and the colonization of the area by the Belgians and French led to further bloody upheavals and radical transformations. Through all of this hell, however, certain fundamental relations were never dissolved. While the polity all but collapsed, the kinship order remained intact even if greatly trans-formed, from a system of hierarchically linked lineages based on generalized ex-change to a clan organization dominated by councils of elders. Throughout the centuries a basic pattern of socialization remained intact, one based on the rein-forcement of individual dependence on the larger group. The pattern combines abrupt weaning with its accompanying anxieties and subsequent education in the power of elder kin and spirits of the dead in which the subject learns to experience himself as composed of elements of "souls" that are organically connected to the kinship-political network through which is channeled the life force upon which his existence depends. This kind of socialization is bound to produce a subject dependent on his social environment in order to maintain a state of well-being. If there is an internal logic to this field of strategies it might be described as follows:

1. All life force (*makindangolo* in kikongo) comes from the outside, chan-nelled into the person via the political and kinship hierarchy whose very existence is but a manifestation of degrees of proximity to its source.

2. This life force is expressed in a degree of well-being associated with one's rank in the larger cosmological hierarchy. Well-being is both wealth and health.

3. Life strategies consist in ensuring the flow of life force. Traditionally this was assured by the social system itself, a prestige goods system in which goods monopolized at the summit were channelled down through the ranks in the form of bridewealth. When this system col-lapsed it caused a crisis, not only politically but for the person as well, since the flow of force had been cut off. The primary solutions to a scarcity of life force are witchcraft and "cannibalism" i.e. the appro-priation of life force from others and the establishment of cult groups whose purpose is to establish a direct link to the source, *nzabi*, the highest god who can channel life force to the individual, not least in order to protect him against witchcraft and sorcery. Christianity is one of the most important cults insofar as it promises to provide indi-vidual access to life force without the mediation of political hierarchy. There is an unexplored ambiguity here, insofar as religious cults seem to be concerned with the **maintenance** of well-being and protection against evil, while success, political or economic is increasingly asso-ciated with precisely such nonlegitimate powers; witchcraft, sorcery, and the use of magic in general.

4. When political hierarchy is re-established in the form of a colonial regime, life force can again be procured via the strategy of clientship. And real hierarchy, just as real wealth, is the manifestation of life force itself, but one, as we have suggested, that is more often than not associated with unusual and even illegitimate magic.

FIT FOR A KING: FOOD FOR THOUGHT

A central feature of the distribution of life force is the implied ambiguity of real wealth, power and authority. We have suggested that manifest rank is potentially the result of illegitimate magical activity. This applies to all relations, whether they be the power of a maternal uncle or that of a minister of state. This may be related to the catastrophic history of political hierarchy in the Congo region. The legitimate authority of the chiefly and royal hierarchy was originally based on the understanding that fertility and general welfare flowed through the rank order. Even in this early period, however, the representation of political power contains the metaphor of consumption. There are reports of royal cannibalism in the earliest material, and one of its remarkable features consists in the self-offering of a vassal to his prince to be eaten.

> It is a remarkable fact in the history of this people, that any who are tired of life, or wish to prove themselves brave and courageous esteem it a great honour to expose themselves to death by an act which shall show their contempt for life. Thus they offer themselves for slaughter and as the faithful vassals of the princes, wishing to do them service, not only give themselves to be eaten, but their slaves also, when fattened, are killed and eaten (Lopez-Pigafetta 1970: 28).

What is more significant in this representation is the act of self-sacrifice on the part of the vassal, the honor of literally becoming part of one's superior. Whether such cannibalism actually occurred in this period, and its mention is indeed rare, except in reference to the behavior of neighboring enemies, the logic of the image is double: powerful princes who regulate the flow of life force to their dependents whom they nevertheless may consume on occasion. The full force of this logic is only realized in wake of the dissolution of Kongo polity (Ekholm 1990).

With the disintegration of the cosmological connections that guaranteed this flow, with the decentralization of wealth accumulation, with the warfare and political anarchy that succeeded the fall of the Kongo kingdom, the ensuing slave trade and colonial intervention, power, in the sense of any form of social superiority, became increasingly associated with the appropriation of life force by violent means more indicative of the world of insecurity and disaster that became the fate of the region. The delegitimation of power could but only take on an ambivalent quality, since force remained force, no matter how obtained. The fact that a powerful person was a witch did not detract from his power, i.e. his ability to destroy his enemies. The fact that the current president is said to eat the hearts of children and to bathe in human blood is a characterization of the source of his power, and it implies a healthy respect for supernatural proficiency. Witches were not ashamed of their power. Quite the contrary! And in the northern regions of the Congo basin, renowned Bangala cannibals confounded the sensibilities of their European guests.

> When the son of the great Bangala chief, Mata Buike, was asked if he had eaten human flesh, he said: 'Ah! I wish I could eat everybody on earth!' (Johnston 1908: 399, cited in Ekholm 1990).

Ekholm (1990) has argued that the violent upheavals of the mid and late nineteenth centuries which featured both rampant witchcraft in the southern Congo and cannibalism in the north can be accounted for by variations of a unitary strategy whose goal is the appropriation of life force in a situation in which the usual channels have broken down. And cannibalism appears to be a satisfying if not perhaps satisfactory means of solving the problem.

> I never saw natives exhibit so much fondling and affection for each other as was shown among these erstwhile cannibals (Weeks 1913: 78).

Eating in the current framework is not consumption, as we know it, of meat, or animal protein, not even of a tasty meal, but the ingestion of the power that animates the living universe, that is the source of health and of well-being and which is constantly in danger of vanishing.

In yet another domain we might similarly argue that the millenaristic movements that opposed the colonial regime during the early and middle decades of this century were not concerned merely with the expulsion of the whites but with the appropriation of their life force. The cargo-like nature of such movements is merely a displacement of the general strategy into a new domain. Such movements have today become a vast array of therapeutic cults whose goal is precisely the transfer of the *force vivante* of god to those in need. This is consumption in the deepest sense of the word.

We have moved briefly between clothing and religious cults, between cargo and cannibalism, arguing that there is a connection among these different forms of consumption, more, perhaps than a mere connection, an identity of demand distributed among different fields but expressing a unitary structure of desire. It is here that one may speak of a continuity with the past, not a continuity of cultural meanings or categories, but of the conditions of constitution of personal experience. If we concentrate on dress in what follows, it is because it represents the generalized form taken by the strategies we have discussed and because, due to its potentially symbolic nature, its capacity to represent something **other** than itself, it has come to play an unexpected political and perhaps transformative role in Congolese society.

CLOTHING AS CARGO

The French colonial regime and the political and economic dominance that has continued into the post-colonial Franc Zone era reinforces the kinds of structures that we have discussed above. While cannibalism, itself a mere historical episode, has disappeared, if not in theory, the system of life force has been elaborated throughout the entire period. Paris as the exemplary center and Brazzaville, its extension in the Congo, are two levels of a concentric and hierarchical model of the world. The Congolese capital is itself a typical colonial space of power, with an old colonial center, *la ville des blancs*, fitted with all the trappings of modernity, surrounded by black bidonvilles, cramped oversized villages. The organization of space is both a product and expression of the social hierarchy and its distribution of life force. And the French did much to cultivate a model of a cultural continuum from Black to White, referring to those more integrated into the modern sector as *évolués*.

The Kongo are the major population that became involved with the commercial and administrative development of the colony and as involved implies evolved, this emergent ethnic group dominated the rank order of the civilizing process.

> While the groups belonging to the Téké have maintained their ancestral style of raphia clothing, based on square patches sown together and worn like a "toga" by men and a "pagne" by women, the Congo very early on abandoned this for imported cloth (Soret 1959: 43).

This dominant expression of status is complemented by an entire range of imported European goods.

> In Bacongo country there is a facade of modernism that is not nearly as evident in most of the other regions of Congo-Gabon (Balandier 1956: 43).

Needless to say this transformation of the Kongo created an ethnic division as well, between the South and the North of the region. The latter zone, more conservative and culturally defensive, referred, not without a certain admiration to the Kongo as *kôgo mindele*, white Congolese. The art of dress, as we have emphasized, was and is the ultimate means of self-definition and the strategies of clothing the body have a generalized effect on all Congolese that was clearly documented as far back as the 1950s.

> The city dweller makes his appearance as a new kind of personnage expressed and clearly marked by his very European clothing; this is the sign recognized by the Whites and acknowledged in none too pejorative terms by the designations evolved (*Evolue*) or detribalized. Still dependent upon exclusivity of appearance, the Central African invests a significant part of his/her income in the latter, on average 20% according to estimates made by M. Soret in 1951. The prominence of imported cotton cloth (ranked second after 'machines and parts' in 1950, ranked first by a large margin in 1938) and the large number of tailors established in urban centers (1 for every 300 inhabitants in Poto-Poto and 1 for every 95 in Bacongo) is a clear indication of the interest in cloth and clothing (Balandier 1955: 22).

The importance of imported cloth which was in the 1950s made into clothing by tailors who represented a significant proportion of the population of the city, had a powerful impact on the trade statistics of the colony. And the density of tailors was also of a distinctive nature, since Poto-Poto, which was inhabited primarily by Northerners and non-Congo had only a third as many tailors per capita as the cultural elite of Bacongo.

One might be tempted to interpret this consumption of modernity as an expression of the colonial complex discussed by Fanon, Manoni and others (Gandoulou 1989: 27–28), but, at least in the Congolese case, it is more a question of complementarity in which a colonial regime maps onto an already existing hierarchical praxis. Thus the specific form of the strategy of consumption is organized in accordance with the racial hierarchy, i.e. an appropriation of all that is associated with white status, but it is not reducible to some form of colonial culture or the inferiority complex of the colonized.

EXISTENTIALISME À LA MODE

In the 1950s there appeared a number of youth clubs whose identity was tied to the French institutions introduced in the colonial capital of Brazzaville. The cinema had been introduced and was frequented by *les évolués* on a regular basis. Images of modern life à la Parisien were diffused via the new media and the cafés, themselves associated with the new life style. The new groups which developed primarily but not exclusively in the quarter of Bacongo came to be known as existentialistes or *existos*. This was not due to any explicit adoption of Sartre's philosophy but to the fact that it was associated with a dominant mood and mode in Paris after the war.

The Congolese clubs adopted the colors black and red, among others, which they imagined to be the colors of their Parisian peers. In fact this was no more than the construction of an image at a distance of what was conceived as the Parisian Existentialiste since here was no correlation between the latter and black and red clothes.

These youth clubs, in which the average age was eighteen, were also mutual aid associations in which members contributed to each other's expenses and to the furthering of the goals of the group. Identification with a Parisian life style was part of a strategy of hierarchical distinctions in which different clubs competed with one another for status expressed entirely in the realm of clothing. Clubs had their own couturiers who were key figures in the fashioning of status.

> Bacongo was both feared and admired for its clothing. There was a kind of reverence for this quarter... (informant in Gandoulou op.cit. 34).

In spite of the lack of interest in existential problems, the *existo*'s entire existence was predicated on such problems and fashion as a project was a self-evident solution to personal survival in a colonized population where selfhood was identical to the appropriation of otherness.

The strategy of dress in the 1950s might also be contextualized in terms of the general transformation of Congolese society. Rapid urbanization, the increase in the wage based sector and the monetarization of the economy, the formation and spread of new forms of sociality — numerous associations for mutual aid, common projects and the maintenance of emergent ethnic identity. All of these transformations did not, however, succeed in dissolving the kinship networks that linked urban and rural areas and which absorbed a large part of the new urban income as well as providing food for hard pressed urban dwellers. The opposition between the developed south dominated by the Congo and the undeveloped north, represented increasingly by the Mbochi, came increasingly to the fore. The concentric hierarchy as represented by the Congo is one in which Paris>Congo>Mbochi>Pygmies>nature. Another group, the Teke, are tricksters in the system, straddling north and south and making alliances with both. The Teke are often considered traitors (also tricksters) insofar as it is they who made the original treaty with De Brazza that surrendered the region to the French. Thus the strategy of dress partakes and even demarcates a set of "tribal" or ethnic distinctions that animate the political history of the Congo.

LA SAPE

If the *existos* were into clothes, they were also family men with jobs, well integrated into the developing urban culture of the country. The decade of the 1950s was one of economic expansion in which salaries rose faster than prices. This decade also led to the independence movement and the establishment of a national state all within the framework of a growing socialist ideology. During the 1960s these clubs declined, along with religious cult activity. Numerous spokesmen for the socialist movements attacked the clothing cults as offensive to African identity and the new social revolution. Instead, political engagement in the future and the simultaneous revival of traditional culture as nationalist spectacle became dominant. The former *existos* disappeared and from 1964–68 there were only a scatter of youth organizations, called *Clubs des Jeunes Premiers* who carried on the tradition of dress which had become a sign of Congo identity in the new multiethnic struggle for political power.

The new Congolese state like other African states had emerged as a class structure where instead of white colonials, local politicians now occupied the same hierarchy, imbued with the same values. In a system where consumption defines identity and where the trappings of modernity not only represent but are the very essence of social power, the social structure tends to take on the attributes of a perfect scalogrom of conspicuous consumption.

> If the Occidental meaning of the adjective "rich" qualifies individuals in terms of their possession of large properties, means of production, or having high paying positions, in the Congo...the idea of wealth is measured in terms of consumption power whose only value comes from the degree to which it is identified with Western consumption (Gandoulou 1984: 41).

In 1968 the Congo were displaced by the Mbochi as the result of a military coup. From the point of view of Congo ideology this represented a barbarian invasion. At the same time the economy began to stagnate in a way that, in spite of the oil boom of the late 1970s and early 1980s left a permanently crippling mark on the prospects of future growth. In this period a second and more intensive wave of fashionable consumption made its appearance, located again primarily among the southern groups from Bacongo who had now been successively deprived of their political and bureaucratic positions as well as their leading ideological role in the country.

La Sape, from the word *se saper*, meaning to dress elegantly, connoting the flâneur of our own society, takes on an especially powerful meaning as it emerges among the youth clubs of Bacongo. As an institution it refers to *La Société des Ambianceurs et Personnes Elégantes*. While the earlier *existos* were employed family heads who had their own group tailors and competed as groups or teams, the *sapeurs* are largely unemployed, unmarried youth who rank local couturiers on the bottom of a scale that progresses upwards from imported ready-to-wears to the ranks of *haute couture*, and who compete individually in their strivings to attain the position of a *grand*. *La Sape* is a network of individuals that form ranked hierarchies by building reputation and clientéles in the larger arena of the urban night spots. Yet the ranked hierarchies that are the clubs themselves are a perfect mirror of clan organization.

> It is not unusual for Sapeurs to use the word "family" when referring to the club, they have a tendency to perceive the other members as real kin (Gandoulou 1989: 90).

Each club generally has a name, a territory, a set of ranked sub-groups, specialized appellations and a division of labor. There are special rules and regulations for how members are to address one another, special linguistic usages and rituals that are symbolic of group identity.

THE PRACTICE OF ELEGANCE AND THE PRODUCTION OF STRUCTURE

The *sape* is a ritual program for the transformation of ordinary unranked youth into great men. It begins and ends in Bacongo, with a "liminal" phase in

Paris. It consists in the continual build up of a wardrobe and ritual display at organized parties and dance bars. In Brazzaville one can begin to accumulate lower ranked clothing, *non-griffés*, copies and ordinary ready-to-wear. The move to Paris, *l'aventure*, is the beginning of the real transformation of the ordinary *sapeur* into a person of higher status. Paris is, as in the liminal phase of many rituals, a time and space of ordeals, where life consists of scrounging, by hook and crook, to obtain the cash and credit needed to accumulate a real *haute couture* wardrobe, called *la gamme*, i.e. the scale of great names in clothing. In one sense, Paris, as the center of *La Sape* is a kind of heaven, but in terms of hardship it is closer to hell. This contradiction is understood as the result of the low rank of blacks in the sacred abode of white power. The rank order of dress greatly elaborates on the earlier home based range of the *existos*. From highest to lowest, clothing is ranked as follows:

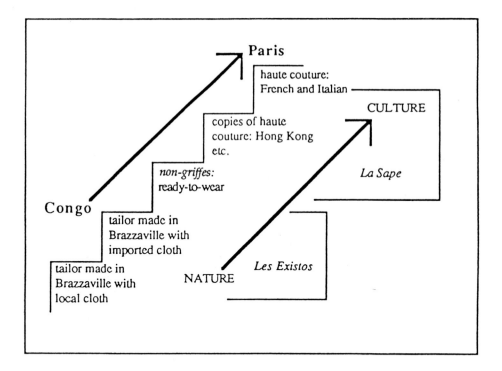

Figure 9   *The hierarchy of La Sape*

The same kind of hierarchy exists in all domains of body ornamentation. Labels play a crucial role. Westin shoes, for example, are ranked among the highest. There are other less well known English and French names and even copies, etc. all the way down to local sandals. Rank is essential and, therefore, no substitution is possible. This is the fundamental principle of *La Sape*. An excellent example of the strength of this constraint is the case of a factory producing imitation Capo Bianco crocodile shoes that in 1984 cost 5,200FF. The copies, quite excellent, cost only 900FF which enticed some *Parisiens* to buy them. When the word got around the reaction was positively deadly.

> *ah non, za fua zé...* you have buy real shoes. Even if the article is high quality, the moment it becomes known to be an imitation all is lost, *affaires zi fuidi*. The cheapest pair of croco(dile)s cost 2,000FF (Gandoulou 1984: 75). *za fua zé* – "that's it, its finished" *affaires zi fuidi* – idem. That won't do, *affaires zi fuidi*. The cheapest pair of crocos cost 2,000FF (Gandoulou 1984: 75).

The accumulation of *la gamme* is not merely about appearance as we understand it. It is not enough to have a certain look, for the look must be authentic and the only sure sign of authenticity is the label. Copies are not inacceptable but they have a lower rank in the system. Elegance is not, then, merely about looking elegant, about appearing in clothes that *look* like haute couture. It is about wearing the real thing and in this sense of being the real thing.

Another domain related to the transformation of the body is the practice of *maquillage à outrance*, the use of a mixture of strong chemicals, including bleach, to lighten the skin. The expression, *se jaunir*, refers to such widespread practices, but also means to become wealthy and powerful, i.e. to become more white. While this is one of the least expensive activities of the adventurer, the products used are variable and also ranked on the scale of elegance, according to their efficiency. The Lari (a Congo dialect) *kilongo* which has a strong connotation of "medicine" is the general term for this "makeup". While we do not have the space to discuss this very elaborate domain, it is noteworthy that its logic is identical to that found in other domains, i.e. the use of "medicine" in the accumulation of life force, expressed in the true beauty of light skin as much as in the elegance of clothing.

The *Parisien* maintains a continual contact with *sapeurs* at home, telling them of his adventures and most importantly of his acquisitions. At some point in this process he makes a *descente*, a return to Brazzaville to display his status rank. *La descente* is usually performed several times, and with constantly renewed ensembles, before the final return and attempted reintegration into Congolese society. This process is the making of a great man or *un grand*, a true *Parisien*, the highest category in the rank order. It is accomplished by means of the ritual gala, an expensive affair in which contributions are made from the entire club for hiring a dance restaurant, a band, food and drink. Invitations are made, and the night of the trial is a veritable potlatch of elegance in which the candidates must, as is said, *se saper à mort*. An official panegyrist introduces the star or hero, carefully listing his qualities and the entire gamut of his ensemble, clothing, shoes and makeup. His girlfriend, also dressed to the teeth, publicly embraces him and offers a gift after which others come forward with similar offerings. This is followed by a signal from the eulogist to the orchestra — several bars of intensively rhythmic music during which the *sapeur* displays himself for the public. The next *sapeur* is introduced, and this pattern continues until all the presentations are made. The function of this phase is the initial *frime* or pretense, here in the sense of ostentation. After the presentation begins the dance itself and the festivities are formally opened. What is referred to as *la danse des griffes* consists in the meticulous display of the entire array of labels on one's person during the dancing. This difficult task must also be accomplished with the utmost refinement. As there are several great *sapeurs* present at any one celebration, there are bound to be status conflicts. These are expressed in the exchange of elaborate gestures of disdain, superiority and studied indifference. A particular act of humiliation has been described by Gandoulou (1989: 115) in which a man steps on the toes of his adversary's Westin shoe, signifying "*ngé za fua zé*" meaning "you (familiar)! That won't do" interpreted as "you've got no place here". A *sapeur* must be very sure of his superiority before engaging in such acts. It is, furthermore, not uncommon that his adversary will slip out, change his clothes and/or shoes and return to defy his opponent (Gandoulou: ibid). Such celebrations of beauty generate an entire mythology of great men and are the intergroup condition of intragroup hierarchy in the clubs.

The structure of relations produced by these activities is one where a set of leaders or great men function as the equivalent of lineage chiefs in a vast network of clientship and exchange. A great man attracts dependents, who are eager to work as his slaves in order to gain access, however temporary, to his prestige goods, the lower orders of which are quite sufficient to build up junior hierarchies. The organization of the clubs becomes a hierarchy of great men, seniors, and juniors. A *sapeur* may often have what is referred to as a *mazarin*, named after the well known minister of Louis XIV, who functions as a personal servant and messenger. A network of clients emerges out of the prestige accumulated through the adventure of the *sape*. Clients, novices with great aspirations, are able to gain access to social connections as well as borrowing the great man's apparel for use in their own exploits. There is also exchange and borrowing of apparel among great men themselves, a veritable circulation of prestige goods reminiscent of traditional Congolese politics.

This structure can only be maintained by the constant circulation of people from Brazzaville to Paris and back, with the continual accumulation of *haute couture* that defines the rank order of elegance. The objective limits of this process are determined by the economic conditions of the Parisian adventure. And the end point of this process reveals the precarious fate of *sapeurs* when they make the final return to Brazzaville. For the ultimate paradox of the entire project is that it begins and ends in consumption, yet generates no steady income. This question is more complicated than it might appear from a simple economic point of view. For insofar as the accumulation of labels gives rise to patron/client networks, there is often a means of converting such networks into income generating operations in the intricate informal sector characterized by long chains combining the sale and rental of just about everything. While many former *sapeurs* fall into oblivion, others manage to transform their elegance into real economic advantage. There are even extreme examples where the refinement of *La Sape* has been recognized internationally, enabling some to ascend the sacred heights of fashion's French Olympus, where they have become true gods of the movement. A recent sacred priest descended to Brazzaville in March, 1990, where he threw a real *bal des sapeurs* at the Hotel Mbamou Palace. The latter is frequented only by the really wealthy elite of the state-class and their European guests. This event, then, marked in no uncertain terms the capacity to convert image into reality. While only the "real" elite could afford to be present, the act itself legitimizes the entire project of prestige accumulation in its modern context.

PERSONHOOD AND THE SOCIAL SELF: ELEGANCE AS POLITICS

We have argued, thus far, for a certain unity in Congolese strategies of selfhood. Clothing is more than property or the expression of one's already existent self, or the fulfillment of an imagined self. It is the constitution of self, a self that is entirely social. There is no "real me" under the surface and no roles are being played that might contrast with an underlying true subject. One of the continuities in the nature of Congolese consumption, whether its be of people, the power of god, or clothing is the effect of fulfilment that it produces in the individual. *Sapeurs* often describe their state as drugged or enchanted. They participate in an all encompassing project that absorbs them completely.

> I am the happiest man in the world. I am driven by a superiority complex. You can walk right in front of me, but I don't see you. I ignore you no matter what your social rank except if you are my kin, of course (Gandoulou 1989: 162).

The experience of the *sapeur* is not equivalent to that of the flâneur, as we suggested at the start of this discussion, for the simple reason that it is entirely authentic. No tricks are played on reality. The strategy is not to fool the audience, to use appearance as a means to status that is not rightfully attained. In a world where appearance tends to fuse with essence rather than merely representing it, dressing up is not a means but an end in itself. And yet there is a certain overlap in the very experience itself. On the one hand, we know from our experience, the way in which consumption can be used to overcome depression, how the visitor to the solarium, may account for his or her activity in terms of the feeling of well-being attained. If white is beautiful for them, tan may be beautiful for us and for some in a way that appears similar on the surface. Some studies of working class youth culture in England have also often stressed what would appear to be the stronger sense of identification with consumed products.

> The mod saw commodities as extensions of himself, rather than things totally independent of their maker or user and shrouded in a set of rules for their use (Herman 1971: 51).

The fact remains that the Western consumer, no matter what his class, seems primarily engaged in the construction of an identity space that is by and large his own product, his own project. But it might be argued that there is a correlation between the weakening of the self, increasing narcissism and the increasing dependence on other directed consumption.

The *sapeur*, in confronting the social reality of state power that considers his very activity a threat to the social order, i.e. a threat to the identity of power and appearance, may begin to realize a difference between himself as a subject and his elegant image. Conversely, the cynical flâneur may become so absorbed in his own image that he loses all contact with the reality of himself as subject. The union of these two spheres, one characterized by the modern individual, the other by the holistic self, occurs in the realm of a more fundamental narcissistic condition. In our discussion of Congolese selfhood we have suggested that a specific kind of socialization in which individual initiative is everywhere thwarted and where the child is imbued with a cosmology in which he is represented as a set of elements connected to a larger kinship structure of life force, tends to generate an experience of self as totally dependent on the larger group. This is a social situation that reinforces the narcissistic state of childhood with a secure cosmological identity that functions in lieu of what in modern capitalist society are designated as ego functions. The modern individual socialized to experience himself as a self-directed organism, controlled by the projects of his own ego, can only regress to a narcissistic state when his ego projects totally fail. But this is not the secure narcissism of an interpreted universe. It is a state of total insecurity, the anguish of non-existence, that can only be solved by capturing the gaze of the other who can affirm one's own being. By contrast it might be said that for the holistic subject, the "gaze of the other" is always upon one, God is always watching.

The Western narcissist who dresses in order desperately to confirm his own being and value through others, is, in such terms, the abnormal extreme of the normally more self-conscious flâneur, who has lost his ego and become dependent on the other. The behavior of the *sapeur*, on the other hand, is an extreme variant of the normal other-directed self-adornment of the Congolese, a behavior that may inadvertently engender a sense of autonomous selfhood even if it begins as an attempt to accumulate the life force embodied in elegance. This tendency, however partial, is present in the self-understanding, even cynicism of the *sapeurs*, as expressed in the texts of their invitations to parties (see text box).

> ...from the moment when, in the field of physical appearance, its esthetic, in other words, in the realm of the "social masque", one attains a perfect adjustment, almost too perfect, an absolute match with the *grand monsieur*, a rupture occurs: exaggeration, excess, "hyperconformism" ends by subverting the very norm that it strives to attain (Gandoulou 1989: 170).

IMAGINARY POWER AND THE SUBVERSION OF THE REAL

The parody of elegance turns the *sapeur* into a delinquent, an intolerable sociopath, a danger to the very foundations of society. The amount of propaganda directed at destroying a group of youth who merely dress elegantly is indicative of the real threat that they pose to the state-class.

INVITATIONS TO PARTIES

The following texts indicate the degree of cynical self-knowledge expressed in *La Sape*:

"Gaul was a Roman province for more than 400 years. The Gauls imitated the Romans — they dressed and lived like them — learned their language, Latin — gradually one could no longer distinguish the Gauls from the Romans, *all the inhabitants of Gaul were known as Gallo-Romans.*"

LES AZURIENS
(people of the Riviera, Rivierians)
In Extasy

P.D.G. Pamphil Yamamoto Mwana Modé na Motété na yé V.P.D.G. Ostinct Yarota P.D.H. Jeff Sayre de Vespucci who sows the *sape* and harvests success

For their first appearance in the booming crackery (a great scintillating party) *the 3 Sicilians of the Riviera invite Mr. or Miss... to the super Boom that they are organizing on the 19th of March at Cottage (Hut) CI modern Bacongo at 14:30.*

Note: Indigenous people shall not be permitted entry, because the Society of ambianceurs and elegant persons (SAPE) detests indigenes. Come and see the beautiful labels of the finest *haute couture (Zibélé)*.

The dangerous success of their project consists in the demonstration that one can reach the "top" without passing through the accepted channels of education and "work". This is the great crime against the identity of prestige and power. But it is by no means easily dealt with by the authorities. They cannot simply ignore this illegitimate elegance any more than they can give it up themselves, on the implicit understanding that clothes, after all, do not make the man. There is, then, an even more deadly logic at work in this subversion of symbolic hierarchy.

One of the most popular singers among Congolese youth is Boundzeki Rapha, known for two songs, the first 'le parisien refoulé' and a year later, "le parisien retenu". The first deals with the failed Parisian adventure of the hero, who ends up in jail and is sent home where he decides to dedicate himself to the ways of his ancestors, i.e. to "work in the fields". This song ends with a clearly religious tone emphasized in the music. The second song takes up the question of the return to the old ways. It begins religiously again with the wise man instructing his child in the proper ways of life. The hero follows his directives

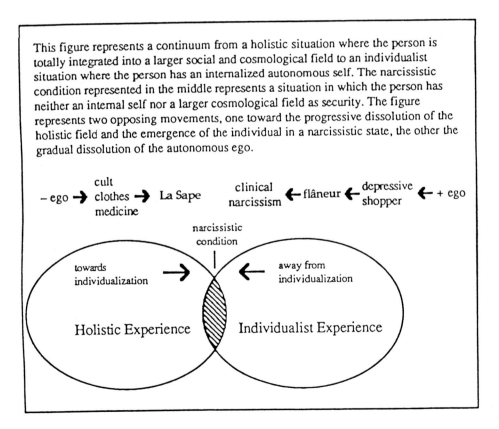

Figure 10   *The convergence of individualist and holistic identity spaces*

but does not believe in them. This is followed by a set of old Lari proverbs...' "you search for your child, but he has been thrown away", "you search for grass (a field that can be sown), but it is gone..." a series of allegories expressing the desperate impossibility of survival. Then suddenly the main chorus bursts forth. "But I am beautiful, and people love me because of it, and if I am beautiful it is because I use *bilongo*" (i.e. I bleach my skin)... Refrain "*kilongo* c'est bon, *kilongo* c'est bon".

The cult of elegance, as cargo cults elsewhere, simultaneously rehabilitates the self and inverts the structure of power. It totally absorbs the subject into the project of the group, yet tends to produce an image of the unbound individual.

Throughout our discussion we have assumed that the practice of *La Sape* was somehow an attempt to capture power via the accumulation of the symbols of power. We did indeed argue that these symbols, *la haute couture*, were not expressions of but definitions of power, of the life force whose form is wealth, health, whiteness and status, all encompassed in an image of beauty. But, in understanding the world in modern terms, we failed to trace the logic through to its conclusion. The very discourse of symbolism legitimizes the materiality of power and wealth. Yet the logic of the political economy of elegance implies the converse, by undermining the significance of such realia. The state-class became great men of elegance by means of political violence and maintain that elegance by means of the theft of the state treasury, and even this can only be ultimately understood in terms of witchcraft and the magic of evil. As the accumulation of life force is the principle of the system, there is no essential difference between *La Sape* and other techniques of accumulation. In this logic, the *sapeur's* reply to the accusation of delinquency is simply, "we are no different than you even if our methods are less violent." Thus, in some deeper sense *La Sape* is all there is.

References

Appadurai, A. (ed.)

1986   Introduction: Commodities and the Politics of Value. In Appadurai (ed.) *The Social Life of Things: Commodities in Cultural Perspective*, Cambridge: Cambridge University Press.

Balandier, G.

1955   *Sociologie des Brazzavilles Noires*, Paris: Colin.

Bourdieu, P.

1977   *Outline of a Theory of Practice*, Cambridge: Cambridge University Press.

Bourdieu, P.

  1979   *La Distinction*, Paris: Minuit.

Campbell, C.

  1987   *The Romantic Ethic and the Spirit of Modern Consumerism*, Oxford: Basil Black-well.

Earl, P.

  1986   *Lifestyle Economics: Consumer Behavior in a Turbulent World*, New York: St. Martins.

Ekholm-Friedman, K.

  1990   *Catastrophe and Creation: The Formation of an African Culture.*

Fanon, F.

  1965   *Les damnés de la terre*, Paris: Maspero.

Friedman, J.

  1989   The Consumption of modernity, *Culture and History*, Copenhagen: 4, Museum Tusculanum Press.

Friedman, M.

  1957   *A Theory of the Consumption Function*, Princeton: Princeton University Press.

Gandoulou, J. D.

  1984   *Entre Paris et Bacongo*: Paris: Centre Georges Pompidou, Collection "Alors".

Gandoulou, J. D.

  1989   *Dandies à Bacongo: Le culte de l'e élégance dans la société congolaise contemporaine*, Paris: L'Harmattan.

Herman, G.

  1971   *The Who*, London: Studio Vista.

Lancaster, K.

  1971   *Consumer Demand: A New Approach*, New York: Columbia.

Manoni, O.

  1950   *Psychologie de la colonisation*, Paris: Seuil.

Miller, D.

  1987   *Material Culture and Mass Consumption*, Oxford: Basil Blackwell.

Pigafetta, F.

1970   *A Report of the Kingdom of Congo and of the Surrounding Countries. Drawn out of the writings and discourses of the Portuguese Duarte Lopez*, London: Cass.

Simmel, G.

1989   *The Philosophy of Money*, London: Routledge.

Soret, M.

1959   *Histoire du Congo: Les Congo Nord-Occidentaux*, Paris: P.U.F.

CHAPTER EIGHT

Strategies of Centredness in Papua New Guinea[1]

Eric Hirsch

INTRODUCTION

In many of the narratives of Melanesian peoples, Europeans are often defined and portrayed by the hold they are seen to have on money and a large array of mass produced goods.[2] A dimension of this discourse, which has features of so-called cargo-cults (see Lindstrom 1993), is that the artefacts and capacities now possessed by Europeans once belonged to Melanesians but were lost (or worse, stolen) in the ancestral past. The capital of Papua New Guinea (PNG), Port Moresby is, for example, the largest metropolitan centre where this European presence is (still) visibly evident and which, in part, lends weight to the continued viability of these discourses. Most regions in PNG are peripheral to this or other smaller metropolitan arenas due to the lack of roads, or roads which have a limited range. Although peripheral, most Papua New Guineans have some experience of Port Moresby by either through periods of labour migration, visits, or the stories recounted from those who have been there. In geographical terms, then, Port Moresby peripheral to lives of most Papua New Guineans. In conceptual terms, however, Port Moresby is of central importance to the way Papua New Guineans imagine their own local lives and how these lives are lived in relation to the (imagined) European. At the same time, the historical emergence of Port Moresby — initially an European enclave — created the conditions for a number of PNG peoples with access to roads and marketable commodities to become involved in the world of money and goods of Port Moresby. This was the situation I encountered in the mid-1980s during my fieldwork among the Fuyuge of the Papuan highlands who had no access to Port Moresy along a road, although their coastal neighbours did; it is a situation that persists into the present-day.

It should be noted, however, the lack of access to money and the world of commodities does not mean that all commodities are equally desired. Rather, as Maclean (1994) has observed, one particular commodity may be treated as a metonym of the world of commodities and money (including the road along which their access becomes possible). In the case to be described here, access to the world of comodities through one metonymic example is also envisioned as gaining access to a realm of lost Fuyuge artefacts and capacities. The link with the former (money creating commodities) is part of a project of regaining that of the latter (ancestrally lost artefacts and capacities). Each, as we shall see, is part of a strategy of sustaining a project of cosmological centredness.[3]

My concern in this chapter is to examine the cultural and historical context through which a single commodity has emerged as emblematic of such a strategy of centredness. The commodity in question is betelnut. In recent decades it has grown in importance to become a pervasive item of consumption in Papua New Guinea. By contrast, the geographical distribution of betelnut consumption in pre-colonial and colonial PNG was confined almost exclusively to coastal and lowland locations. Important changes have occured in the nature of PNG consumption patterns in the intervening decades, of which betelnut is just one example. The Fuyuge interest in betelnut, as part of their more general interest in being connected with the metropolitan milieu, is at the same time, part of a process of recapturing lost ancestral artefacts and capacities.

On one level the Fuyuge perceive themselves, for very good socio-economic reasons, as peripheral to the metropolitan centre. Although they are motivated to participate in its culture, it is only possible to do this from a disadvantaged standpoint. There is a repository of everyday life-styles and status symbols that are needed to have even a marginal place in this metropolitan-based culture, to which they have been connected to by force and history. On another level, though, this peripheral relationship is given a different, inverted form, through the procedures and symbolism contained in their ritual. This is an instance of cargo-cult-like ideas and shares a number of similarities with the cults documented by Worsley (1957). More specifically, the Fuyuge regard themselves not as marginal but as a primordial centre of this metropolitan-based culture. Their ritual attempts to create a supra-local community in which are united elements from the local area, other village based cultures and the metropolitan centre. The ritual gives visible expression of Fuyuge strategies aimed at reversing the processes which have led to a loss of ancestral artefacts and capacities that now leave the Fuyuge as peripheral to the metropolitan centre.[4] Betelnut has emerged as metonymic of this strategy of sustaining centredness (see Hirsch 1994).

Before I proceed to a social and historical contextualisation of betelnut use among the Fuyuge I will provide some background information about Fuyuge society and culture, and highlight some of the changes the Fuyuge have experienced since colonisation of their area earlier this century. I will also provide some information about the forms, effects and distribution of betelnut, and its role in the PNG economy.

THE FUYUGE CONTEXT

The Fuyuge number around 14,000 and inhabit five inter-linked valleys in the Wharton Ranges about 100 km north of Port Moresby. They are bordered in all directions by other mountain peoples and access to their area is only possible by foot, or since the 1970s by light aircraft. The capital and surrounding coastal populations are relatively close as the crow flies, but the Fuyuge are isolated from this environment given their enclosed surroundings. The largest population concentration of 5,200 is in the Udabe Valley, where I conducted research. The valleys are divided into a number of communities, which in turn are separated on the basis of territory and dialect. I refer to these groupings as 'homes'.[5] Homes range in size from 100 to over 1,000 persons. I lived in the home of Visi with a population of 450. Each home is further divided into a number of named sections defined by notions of locality and relatedness. Settlement tends to oscillate between two fairly distinct forms: a dispersed and small-scale pattern of bush hamlets associated with the everyday life of gardening and pig raising, and a concentrated large-scale pattern associated with ritual and ceremonial exchange. This latter form of settlement is referred to by the Fuyuge as a *gab* and is the same name given to the ritual performed within its built environment.

The Fuyuge are swidden horticulturalists and pig husbandry forms a central part of their social and economic life. Small to medium sized sweet potato gardens are cultivated throughout the year among a group of neighbouring bush hamlet residents. Large yam gardens are cultivated before the start of the rainy season which lasts from November to April. Cultivation of yam gardens involves most of a home section, and particularly large gardens are planted before a *gab* ritual. Large herds of pigs are raised in most bush hamlets.

Fuyuge ritual organisation is formed around a number of hereditary chiefs (see Hirsch 1994). Chiefs are indigenously conceptualised as the persons who enable the power of others to become visible. Their role in this respect only emerges during periods of ritual, which are structured around life-cycle transitions of the young and old, and of the deceased. It is around chiefs that other men and women align to organise a *gab* ritual. It is in these contexts that betelnut has emerged today as a central object of display, ritual manipulation, distribution and consumption.

Colonial and mission influence developed in close conjunction among the Fuyuge. Government agents and missionaries entered the area almost simultaneously during the early decades of this century.[6] During the 1950s and 1960s the first group of labour migrants from the area were sent to Port Moresby as part of a scheme to develop the national capital, and to involve members of more remote populations in the monetary economy. At this time, many young men had their first experience of what were hitherto distant or unknown cultures and the associations into which these cultures were categorised (see Strathern M. 1975; Rew

1975). It was also a period when betelnut was first consumed and the ethos associated with its consumption internalised. Since the 1970's, movement to and from the Fuyuge, Port Moresby and its neighbouring coastal areas has become a relatively common and accepted feature of Fuyuge life.[7]

CENTRE, PERIPHERY AND THE CONCEPT OF *TIDIBE*

During my stay in Visi, I was often told a series of narratives which revealed a strong concern with issues of cosmological centredness. The narratives drew on a range of imagery, some of it of a biblical nature transposed on the Fuyuye surroundings. The narratives suggested that Fuyuge men and women were the originators and centre of various artefacts and capacities now associated with Europeans and certain coastal peoples, that these had been lost to Port Moresby and the coast in the ancestral past (see Hirsch 1994).

Similar issues of cosmological centredness have been noted by Biersack writing about the Paiela of the Western highlands. In a manner, analogous to the Fuyuge, Biersack (1991: 231) notes that the Paiela designate themselves, cosmically and historically, "as we who live at the centre." She draws parallel between the Paiela social universe and the 'world system' that is continually impinging upon it: both are open and appropriative. To be on the margins or peripheral is to be in solitude and outside moral involvement. Paiela historicity is emergent within this field of centredness:

> All historical processes unfold in the middle, through the dynamics unleashed by the union of [mind] and body, subject and object, and within the expansive centres such axes generate (Biersack 1990: 79).

The Fuyuge, like the Paiela, do not see the person as a self-centred, autonomous entity, but as centred on his/her relationships with others (Biersack 1990: 69; Strathern 1988: 13). What was clear in the Fuyuge context at least during my field research was that this sense of centredness was more uncertainly achieved. The potential for peripherality was explicit and intrinsic feature of their social process.

It is of note that Williamson discerned a similar tension with those Fuyuge peoples he encountered during his visit to the Mafulu 'home' earlier this century. This emerges in particular around a discussion of the concept of *tidibe* that is found at the end of his book. As he observed at the time:

> [T]here is a general belief among them in a mysterious individual named *Tsidibe*,[8] who may be a man, or a spirit (they appear to be vague as to this), who has immense power, and *who once passed through their country in a direction from east to west...* They believe that it was *Tsidibe* who taught them all their customs, including dancing and manufacture, and

that he ultimately reached and remained in the land of the white man, where he is now living; and that the superior knowledge of the white man in manufacture and especially in the making of clothes, has been acquired from him. The idea of his ultimate association wih the white man can hardly, however, be a very ancient tradition. One of the Fathers was seriously asked by a native whether he had ever seen *Tsidibe*. They seem to think that he is essentially a beneficient being. They regret his having left their country, but they have now doubt as to this... As traces of his passage through their country they will show you extraordinarily shaped rocks and stones, such as fragments which have fallen from above into the valley, and rocks and stones which have lodged in strange positions...(Williamson 1912: 265, emphasis added).

I define *tidibe* in most general terms as life force and more specifically the source of human power, strength and efficacious capacities (*kagava*). The above passage highlights that *tidibe* at once constituted the Fuyuge and then journeyed beyond. There is, then, a precariousness to the Fuyuge sense of their own cosmological positioning; being at once at the centre but also potentially peripheral as disclose through the movement of *tidibe*. The tension between centre and periphery as revealed in Fuyuge cosmological imaginings is also replicated in Fuyuge relations of trade and exchange.

CONTEXTS OF TRADE AND EXCHANGE

Prior to the government and mission presence and for some considerable period after it, the separate valleys of the Fuyuge were invovled in regional systems of trade and exchange. Decorative shells and other valuables were obtained in networks of trade which extended eventually to the coast, stone flints circulated from their points of origin to areas lacking in this all important element of technology. An archeologist who has reconstructed the regional trade system along the Motu coast, which was operative earlier this century, aptly titled his description "Fishing for Wallabies"; that is, fish in exchange for New Guinea kangaroos (Allen, 1977). Trade in the situation he described had elements of an all encompassing symbiosis. Separate cultural groups where able to exploit the much needed physical and/or social resources of neighbours through the trading mechanism. Indigenous conceptions appeared to suggest that none of the cultural groups were at a disadvantage to others participating in the trading system. The object of exchange was not profit but sustenance. I would conjecture that the regional trading system in which the Fuyuge participated, although of a different character, was essentially organised along the same lines of mutual advantage.

Modjeska, by contrast, has argued that similar trading systems which operated in the Sepik and other highlands communities are based upon relations of inequality analogous to those between buyers and sellers in a market. His interpretation rests upon the existence of indigenously constructed notions of 'civilised' and 'uncivilised' cultural groups and their mutual evaluations: "The political and cultural hegemony of large and sophisticated tribes who disdane their 'bush kanaka' neighbours (a widespread and, I believe, pre-colonial phenomenon) would appear to be capable of generating presuppositions of unequal bargaining strength, equivalent in effect to actual conditions of market disequilibrium" (Modjeska 1985: 160).

It is an open question whether Modjeska's interpretation is correct for traditional trading systems. But it is certainly true of the relations that have emerged around formalised markets in the colonial and post-colonial towns and cities. With the advent of a European presence, the introduction of market centres based upon monetary exchange and a myriad of other political and economic changes instituted by European domination, many aspects of the regionally based trade systems fell into abeyance. What has emerged is an orientation of formerly un-utilised or under-utilised resources towards the production of commodities to be sold in the market.[9]

Among the most important items sold in the market are indigenous vegetables and staples (such as taro, sweet potato and yam), fruits, fish, pork, coconuts, handicrafts and betelnut (see Epstein 1982: 29–32). Although some of the traditional trading relationships are still functioning, they are tied more to ceremonial and ritual requirements than to procuring necessary items for daily subsistence. Inter-cultural relations have now been transformed from an alignment to the principle of "Fishing for Wallabies" where all had relative mutual advantage, to one where some groups command control of the markets and gain money wealth, while others only marginally participate or are excluded. The Fuyuge are among the latter. They are perceived by other coastal populations as being among the 'bush kanakas' of the region.

Within this transformed political and regional system the Fuyuge have found themselves caught between the institutions of their mountain homes and a developing metropolitan arena. There is among them an implicit sentiment that, given their relatively isolated position vis-a-vis the metropolitan centre, they have been rather left behind other groups who have more direct access, to a changed life-style and acquired status symbols. In the previous 'fishing for wallabies' regime the differentiation between a supposed progressive, 'high' culture and that of a 'bush kanaka' or 'low' culture might have informed the view of lowland and coastal populations towards their mountain neighbours. It did not, however, preclude the latter from engaging in trade relations with others in the regional trading system. Where this system has now been transformed and specifically focused on money and market relations, betelnut has come to the fore as an index of ability to participate in the wider metropolitan-based culture.

BETELNUT: FORMS, CONTEXT AND THE CULTURE
OF ITS CONSUMPTION

Before considering the relationship between cosmological and trade/-exchange tensions of centre and periphery further let me first turn to the topic of betelnut itself. Betelnut is a psychoactive substance which occurs in a number of regions throughout Papua New Guinea. The distribution of the occurence and/or consumption of betelnut was first documented on the basis of secondary literature by Riesenfeld. In his 1947 paper, "Who are the betel people?" Riesenfeld showed how betelnut consumption was largely confined to coastal and inland areas and virtually absent from vast stretches of the highlands. Although his account pre-dates much of the modern ethnography that emerged from post-war fieldwork in the PNG highlands, it is still true to say that betelnut consumption played little or no role in the pre-colonial life of most highlands peoples. In fact, Epstein (1982:107) has remarked, "in the Highlands [betelnuts] were hardly known until the beginning of the 1960's." Since Riesenfield's paper there have been no subsequent reviews of either the distribution or the changes in betelnut consumption for the entire country. From my own experience and from the personal communications of other ethnographers (D. Gardner, L. Josephides) the distribution and consumption patterns of betelnut have changed dramatically in the post-war period. Epstein (1982: 107) has observed that "the custom of chewing [betelnus] quickly spread among the Highlanders."[10]

There are three essential ingredients to the betelnut mixture: the areca nut, the betel pepper and some form of slaked lime. A psychiatrist, familiar with betelnut from his work in Papua New Guinea, descibes its intrinsic properties and effects in the following terms:

> The active principles are alkaloids of which arecoline and arecaidine are the most important. The former is hydrolised to the latter by calcium hydroxide, that is, by the lime that is chewed with the nut. The chewing of the three ingredients produces [a] bright red saliva by a chemical process... the alkaloids from the nut and an essential oil from the betel pepper are responsible for the euphoric properties of the chew... The net result is .... contracted pupils and increased secretion of tears; sweat and saliva. The suffused appearance, feeling of well-being, good humour *and the undoubtedly increased capacity for activity provide a typical picture* (Burton-Bradley, 1979: 482, my emphasis).

The areca nut grows on a palm in clustered bunches. Soil, altitude and climate are the key factors influencing the quantity, size and quality of nuts grown in any particular area.[11] All three ingredients are necessary for the effect, but it is the size and quality of the areca nut which is perceived to have the most determinate effect on the chew. An informed chewer, like the connoisseur of fine wine in our own culture, has the knowledge and ability to recognise a good product from one of inferior quality and to specify the reasons why.

In broad terms there are two general types of betelnut. A large-fruited variety is actively cultivated in certain coastal and inland areas.[12] It is this large-fruited variety which is consumed and marketed in vast quantities. There is also a small-fuited, wild variety which thrives in many environments, including that of the highlands, but which is not generally consumed. The Fuyuge have a single name for all varieties of betelnut, which they call *kes*. To the large-fruited variety, associated with the coast, they give the name *solon*; the wild variety, which grows on their own lands, they call *inae*. I will have occasion to refer to *solon* and *inae* below.

Betelnut does not appear to have any important nutritional value, but it does have important hunger reducing properties and is often eaten during periods of fasting or when persons are subject to intense food taboos. The manner in which betelnut is consumed, and the techniques associated with its consumption in everyday life, vary slightly across the different cultural groups of the country. Lepowsky, who worked among the Vanatinai, describes the ethos and procedures surrounding the chew. Although the Vanatinai have a relatively long tradition of betelnut consumption, her description fits very closely with my observations among the Fuyuge.[13]

This common core of experience is now regularly reproduced not only in the village contexts described above, but on the streets and less frequently in the shops and offices, throughout the towns and cities. It is also consumed by virtually every section of indigenous society including highly paid civil servants and politicians. The Fuyuge regularly consume *solon* betelnut in this manner — when supplies are available — during gardening, while visiting or socialising within their settlements.

Betelnut is the quintessential PNG commodity. Before the advent of Europeans, though, it could not have been conceived of in these terms. Its rise to prominence is linked to the initial establishment of towns and cities by colonists, along coastal areas where neighbouring populations had relatively easy access. These groups dominated the markets which eventually developed and virtually controlled the supply and sale of betelnut. Given this advantage, determined by both geography and history, it is not suprising that ideas and practices associated with coastal populations have tended to influence the indigenous civilisation of the metropolitan areas.

An excellent example of a coastal population's relation to betelnut are the Mekeo, who were studied by Epeli Hau'ofa during the late 1960s and early 1970s. The Mekeo reside in a fertile low-lying flat land about 120 km northwest from Port Moresby. Betelnut provides the Mekeo today with their main source of cash income. As Hau'ofa (1981: 18) remarked, "[s]ince the 1950s they have largely dominated the lucrative betelnut market in the rapid growing city of Port Moresby." In fact, officials at the nearby local government station in the mid 1970s "estimated conservatively that the Mekeo betelnut trade was worth a million Australian dollars a year" (Halofa 1981: 18).

More fundamentally, however, is the manner in which betelnut is produced and marketed that is significant:

> Unlike other and more approved cash crops such as coconut for copra, cocoa and coffee, all of which are grown on a small scale in Mekeo, the production of betelnut requires little labour. People plant areca trees in the traditional fashion, immediately behind villages and in the gardens. Once they grow above the height of weeds they need little attention; owners simply pick the nuts when ready and take them to Port Moresby for individual sale at Koki Market, on street corners and storefronts throughout the city... The enterprise is so easy and so lucrative that by and large Mekeo have turned a deaf ear to the exhortations by officers of the [Department of Primary Industry] for them to participate in the cultivation of export cash crops (Hau'ofa 1981: 18–19).

Aspects of these production and marketing procedures are certainly well known *b groups* like the Fuyuge. The Fuyuge refer rather ambivalently to the Mekeo as money *u bab*, that is, as the 'fathers', or controllers of money. The Fuyuge themselves want to be money *u bab* and see betelnut as an intrinsic element towards this goal.

SOCIAL AND HISTORICAL CONTEXT OF BETELNUT CONSUMPTION AMONG THE FUYUGE

How, then, have the Fuyuge culturally constructed their relation to betelnut? And what are the implications of the way in which they have done it? I now turn to the Fuyuge material and begin by examining the context in which betelnut makes its most vivid appearance.

One of the central components of present-day Fuyuge ritual is the large-scale display of numerous bunches of *inae* (small-fruited, wild betelnut) and *solon* (large-fruited, coastal betelnut) in the centre of the village plaza at key moments of the ritual process. The display occurs when the chief solemnly hangs betelnut bunches on the branches of a specially placed *hoyan* tree in the plaza centre. Here the betelnut bunches hang until, at a future point in the ritual, several of the *inae* bunches are taken down and used as part of a rite by the chief, while the remainder are then distributed to visiting guests. It is only chiefs, after their formal installation, who can utter the words used in the rite.

Before the *inae* and *solon* betelnut bunches can be displayed, they must first be gathered together from dispersed locations, both within Fuyuge lands, among their neighbours and in particular from the large centre of Port Moresby. Today, Fuyuge ritual is set in motion or comes to a halt in relation to the movements of men who venture from the ritual village to bring back the betelnut bunches. Their movements are the subject of intense speculation on the part of villagers as to whether they will be successful in gathering large quantities of betelnut, how long it will take them, and to which places in particular they will travel in order to complete their journeys. In addition, many of the guests and spectators are brought from these distant locations. The ritual village becomes a focal point of surrounding collective life for the duration of the ritual's enactment.[14]

Although this practice of handling betelnut is pervasive among the Fuyuge, it is of fairly recent origin and until only one to two generations ago was confined to a limited geographical area within the culture. Given the predominance of betelnut today in Fuyuge ritual it is of particular historical interest to consider what objects were placed in the village plaza *before* betelnut became formally used in the way described above. Prior to, and for some period after colonisation of the region, it was very common to find the exposure platform of a dead chief acting as the focal point in the centre of the ritual village plaza.

Upon his death the chief would be placed on the platform, constructed in part from several specially placed *hoyan* trees. His body would be left to rot and decay until only the bones remained. Before commencement of the ritual which followed, only his skull and particularly his jaw, and portions of the arm and leg bones would be left on the platform. Later, at a key moment of the ritual, the platform would be dismantled and the bones taken down. The bones were then manipulated in various ways at specified moments of the ritual (see Williamson 1912).

However, after the Catholic missionaries entered the lands of the Fuyuge earlier this century, one of the first indigenous customs they sought to change was the practice of exposing the dead. As a result of its suppression and the subsequent adoption of burial practices for all of the deceased, what we might call a physical and conceptual 'space' opened up in the ritual system. This space was eventually filled by the use of *inae* betelnut. In recent years, and significantly, the coastal *solon* has been added. Prior to these changes the Fuyuge did not chew betelnut or use it ritually. Today, by contrast, it would be fair to say that they have an obsession for *solon* betelnut and consume it whenever possible.

At the core of Fuyuge ritual is an encompassing cycle of exchange and ancestral power. This exchange cycle is set into motion around the person of the chief. In pre-colonial Fuyuge society (as today) the person of the chief focused upon himself the living sources of ancestral power which includes notions of life-force, strength and vitality – *tidibe* (see above). At death, his bones were used as a means of giving visible expression to the cosmological centredness of the 'home', in the relation to the dispersed and de-centred existence of men and women in their everyday life. At this same event, the life-cycle transitions of others, including other deceased, were enacted. For these persons, as well as for the dead chief, numerous pigs were killed.

The pig served as the important mediating object between the ancestral power embodied in the chief's bones and that of mortal men and women present at the ritual. In order for those men and women witnessing but not experiencing the rites to participate in this process, objects of value, often acquired through trade, were exchanged for portions of pork. In this way everyone present at the ritual became more ancestral, more centred and more *tidibe*-like.

The cycle has been retained up until the present but certain elements have changed. Instead of the bones of the chief, the *inae* and, to an ever-increasing extent, the *solon* betelnut are displayed on the tree. Also, although objects of value acquired through trade are still exchanged in the ritual, their presence has been largely overshadowed by that of money. Among the Fuyuge, money has allowed a greater number of men and women to participate in the exchange of ritual, and hence, in ancestral power. But the prime means of making large amounts of money such as direct access to *solon* betelnut, elude the Fuyuge. The Fuyuge are aware that groups like the Mekeo are able to convert betelnut into money through the market.

This dilemma, I suggest, has created the conditions for some cargo-cult-like beliefs to become crystalised among the Fuyuge. In particular, Fuyuge assert that in the ancestral past all forms of betelnut grew on their lands, but due to certain mythic events the *solon* and other varieties of money-producing betelnut were lost to their lower elevation neighbours. The manner in which these beliefs are physically and verbally represented points to a set of symbolic associations involving *inae* and *solon* betelnut and their attempted re-unifition. *Inae* betelnut is connected with the person of the chief: it is placed in the centre of the ritual plaza where the chief's bones stood in the past. By contrast, *solon* betelnut is associated with everyday social life: it is the form that is generally consumed and associated with trade and commerce. At the same time, by placing it on the tree in the plaza centre with *inae*, there is an attempt to physically and symbolically re-capture it. Let me illustrate these points further:

During the rainy months of 1984, men and women of a home in the Udabe Valley enacted a rite to 'welcome' the *solon* betelnut into their area. The *solon* betelnut which was planted among this group some years previously had just borne fruit. This was an extraordinary achievement in the cool mountain environment. The rite was organised to publicly announce this event and display the betelnut among the hosts and spectators gathered. The rite also formed part of a larger *gab* ritual. In addition to the rite for the betelnut, the home was staging the life-cycle transitions for a number of youths and two old women. It is significant that the rite was staged in this context.

The organisation of the rite for betelnut had a familiar form: One pig was killed in the plaza centre while yams, bananas and smoked pandanus were laid out next to the dead animal. Two men, one a chief and the other a prominent orator, then both entered the plaza centre. Men, women and children around the plaza were silent and looked on. First the orator spoke: in his speech he emphasised how the Fuyuge mythic heroes once had this type of betelnut – *solon* – in the mountains, but that it was lost to peoples near the coast. Now it had come home to its place.

The chief then spoke. He held a mountain variety betelnut bunch in his hands and refered to its large-fruited counterpart:

> We planted this first (i.e. *inae*), got its digging stick and planted the other (i.e. *solon*). So now I am going to get this one (*inae*) and split it for that one (*solon*) and put his foot on the ground (i.e. make him feel at home) so he will stay here.

It is of note that in this rite betelnut is being treated as if it were a person. The rite followed the same form used to enact life-cycle transitions for men, women and children. The metaphors and symbolism in the speech and acts were the same as for the events organised around humans.

This image of the *solon* betelnut having person-like qualities can be further illustrated through the mythical manner in which it was said to have been originally lost by the Fuyuge. The following myth was told to me outside the ritual context to explain how the different varieties of betelnut had come to be distributed in their present-day locations:

> Once those of Lolof (a village name in the Udabe Valley) made a fence of trees (as mentioned above) around their village and killed pigs inside. One day, a woman was sweeping the plaza to remove the branches which had fallen down. While she was sweeping, one of the branches broke off and fell onto her head and she died. As a result, they chased the tree into the big forest. They told him to stay in the bush and if they wanted to make a *gab* and kill pigs, they would come, cut him, plant him around the plaza and then kill the pigs: "You stood here but a branch broke off from you and killed someone, so go to the bush." They broke one branch and brought it down to the Kuni people who live to the southwest, to a village plaza there. One was also planted at Deva-Deva, another village among the Kuni. In this later village, the chief was talking one day in the men's house. At the same time, a woman in the village was having labour pains and making a lot of noise. She was disturbing him and he told her to go away to another place and give birth there; he chased her away. He then kept talking and talking and talking until his jaw fell apart. He then died. When they buried him, the betelnuts called *ivo* and *baumau* came out of his mouth and grew there. The woman gave birth to *solon* betelnut and coconut and put them in the water. The water carried it right down to Mekeo, to a pool there. Here it was turning around in a whirlpool. A Mekeo man took a stick and with it

brought these things out of the water. This is why the Mekeo have plenty
of betelnuts and coconuts.

The Fuyuge perceive the genesis of betelnut in this symbolic manner from
its purported origins in the mountains. This is how they account for the Mekeo's
ability to control a large percentage of all betelnut supplies in Port Moresby, as
described above.

There is also a related issue. Why do the Fuyuge display the betelnut
bunches in the centre of the plaza upon the tree? I suggested this is because of
its connection with the person of the chief. In fact, other objects could have been
placed on the tree and a connection thereby constructed. Why betelnut? Part
of the answer lies in the content of the myth. As we have just seen, the chief's
jaw fell of while he was talking, and out of his mouth grew one type of betelnut.
In pre-colonial Fuyuge culture the jaw bone, particularly of a chief, was a valued
part of the deceased body. Together with the other parts of the skull it was often
kept by close kin and used when needed for power enhancing purposes. Among
many betel-consuming cultures the importance of the jaw bone after death is
often stressed in similar fashion (see Weiner 1976). In the contemporary setting,
the visible connection made between betelnut and the chief in the *gab* ritual is the
moment when Fuyuge men and women reveal to themselves, in the context of
witnessing others, their own centredness (Hirsch 1994).

CONCLUSION

My argument has now come full circle. I began by contrasting the creation
of a metropolitan-based culture with that of Fuyuge village-based culture. I
identified betelnut (*solon*) and is consumption as having a significant role in the
development of the metropolitan-based culture. I also showed how the Fuyuge
identified themselves as standing on the periphery of these processes. At the same
time, though, the Fuyuge assert through their ritual practices that all forms of
betelnut actually originated among them, but were lost in the ancestral past. The
Fuyuge existence on the periphery of the metropolitan milieu is not fortuitous,
but accounted by certain mythic events.

The centrality of betelnut was revealed to me primarily by the Fuyuge's
own keen and almost obsessional interest in obtaining it either for everyday or
ritual use. This must of course be contrasted with the Fuyuge's lack of interest
in betelnut in the past. This raises a complex historical problem and I do not
know whether the materials at present can give us an answer. In principle, it
would have been possible to acquire *solon* through trade in the pre-colonial past,
but this did not happen. In the contemporary setting, however, betelnut and
betelnut consumption has become metonymic for the Fuyuge in two ways: on

the one hand, it is metonymic of Fuyuge exclusion from the world of commodities and money in Port Moresby, unlike that of the Mekeo (to whom it was lost in ancestral past); on the other hand, it is metonymic of Fuyuge connection with this metropolitan centre and the lost artefacts and capacities of *tidibe* (through their attempted re-capture).

It should be remembered that the pre-colonial trading system of the Fuyuge was a mechanism for channelling objects into the ritual village through relations of exchange. The trading system worked in tandem with the display and manipulation of the chiefs bones. Each was part of a process of social and cosmic centredness. The old trading system has been augmented in the present by betel-nut which is involved in the same process of attempted centredness: hence, the placing of *solon* together with *inae* in the centre of the village plaza. The joining of *solon* with *inae* is metonymic of Fuyuge interests in joining their mountain villages with that of the coast and Port Moresby via a road. Each of these processes of joining are part of a strategy of recapturing lost artefacts and capacities of *tidibe* and allowing the Fuyuge to sustain their own image of cosmological centredness.

NOTES

1. Portions of this article appeared as 'From bones to betelnuts: processes of ritual transformation and the development of 'national culture' in Papua New Guinea', *Man*, 25: 18–34, 1990. The present chapter focuses on strategies of cosomological continuity and centredness and less on processes of national culture formation which was the concern of the previous article. Both, however, are closely related issues and their relationship is pursued more fully in Hirsch 1994. I am grateful to the editor of *Man* and to the Royal Anthropological Institute, for permission to reprint portions of the published article here.

2. Writing and literacy are often included in these characteristics.

3. I do not use the notion of centredness to refer to the Fuyuge as a whole. This is because the Fuyuge do not conceptualise themselves as a whole. By centredness, I refer to more locally based units such as the Fuyuge river valleys and more inclusive territorial and linguistic units ('homes'). In other words, centredness is created through relationships with near and more distant others, most often through exchange. The notion of cosmological centredness and related notion of efficacy are discussed more fully in Hirsch 1984 and Hirsch. Forthcoming.

4. The idea that power which is contained in the metropolitan milieu can actively be tapped and channelled into the local context is found throughout

the country (see Strathern, A. 1984) and corresponds to long-held practices. In numerous areas, as Gewertz (1983) and Errington and Gewertz (1985) have recently shown, an active process of cultural "importation" is at work. Depending on the nature of the local institutions and individual perceptions of the wider regional community, certain objects or behaviours will be selected out for this purpose.

5. I have previously called these parishes but now find the notion of home more appropriate (see Hirsch 1987: 3; and the article cited above in footnote 1 on page 22).

6. The missionaries were first to establish relatively permanent stations in three of the five river valleys and have made their presence the most closely felt. By the late 1930's virtually all of the Fuyuge valleys had been brought under effective government control, although so-called 'payback' killings persisted until the 1950's.

7. A number of cattle and coffee development projects have been tried among the Fuyuge, but with little success. These are usually abandoned or improperly cared for because of the time devoted to inter-home and inter-valley *gab* ritual.

8. In the Visi dialect of Fuyuge, the word is pronouced as *tidibe*.

9. By market I mean the geographical or place sense of the term, i.e. open air market (see Epstein 1982: 10n.1); cash-crops such as coffee, tea, rice, rubber, etc, are produced and marketed, but not through the same mode as considered here.

10. In the context of worldwide use and according to some recent estimates betel-nut is regularly consumed by close to 200 million people in areas extending from East Africa across India and Southeast Asia, embracing the Philippines, Indonesia and Melanesia (Conklin 1958; Cawte 1985).

11. Betelnut is the accepted term for the combined mixture which includes the areca nut but it is also commonly used to refer to the areca nut itself. This is because reference to the areca nut normally implies the existence of the other two ingredients.

12. There are numerous sub-varieties that I mention later in the chapter.

13. Lepowsky (1982: 336) writes:

> The betel chew ingredients are essential elements of hospitality offered to whomever is nearby when one wishes to chew... Generally, the areca nut

is cut in halves or quarters and a piece offered to each person nearby. The chewer places the piece of nut in the mouth, moistens... a wooden stick with saliva and dips it into the lime pot, which may be a traditional ornamented gourd [the Fuyuge now carry these as well] or an old tobacco tin [which are common in places like Port Moresby]. The chewer places powdered lime that adheres to the limestick in the mouth and it is absorbed into the betel quid... Then a piece of aromatic bettle pepper fruit or leaf is added to the quid, which may be masticated for about fifteen minutes, stimulating the flow of saliva, which one spits on the ground to the side.... When the quid has lost its flavour it too is expectorated.. [In addition] friends and kinfolk do not hesitate to request one's betel ingredients...

14. Fuyuge ritual has extensive symbolic and temporal complexity which I have described and analysed elsewhere (Hirsch, 1987; 1988). Much of its content revolves around the enactment of life-cycle rites for the young and old, as well as for the deceased.

References

Allen, J.

1977   Fishing for wallabies: trade as a mechanism for social interation, integration and elaboration on the central Papuan coast. In *The evolution of social systems*. M. Rowlands and J. Friedman (eds) London: G. Duckworth.

Biersack, A.

1990   'History in the making: Paiela and historical anthropology', *History and Anthropology*, 5: pp. 63–85.

Biersack, A.

1991   'Prisoners of time: millenarian praxis in a Melanesian valley'. In: *Clio in Oceania: towards a historical antropology*. A. Biersack (ed) Washington, D.C.: Smithsonian Institution Press: pp. 231–295.

Burton-Bradley, B.

1979   Arecadaidnism: betel chewing in transcultural perspectives. *Can. J. Psychiatry*, 24: pp. 481–488.

Cawte, J.

1985   Psychoactive substance of the south seas: betel, kava and pituri. *Aus. and N.Z. J. of Psychiatry*, 19: pp. 83–87.

Conklin, H.

    1958   *Betel-chewing among the Hanunoo.* National Research Council of the Philippines, Quezon City.

Epstein, T.S.

    1982   *Urban food marketing and third world development.* London: Croom Helm.

Errington, F. and D. Gewertz.

    1985   A confluence of powers: entropy and importation among the Chambri. *Oceania,* 57: pp. 99–113.

Gewertz, D.

    1983   *Sepik river societies.* New Haven: Yale University Press.

Hau'ofa, E.

    1981   *Mekeo: inequality and ambivalenee in a village society.* Canberra: Australian National University Press.

Hirsch, E.

    1987   'Dialectics of the bowerbird: an interpretative account of ritual and symbolism in the Udabe Valley, Papua New Guinea', *Mankind,* 17: pp. 1–14.

Hirsch, E.

    1988   *Landscapes of exchange: Fuyuge ritual and society.* Unpublished Ph.D. thesis, London School of Economics and Political Science.

Hirsch, E.

    1994   'Between mission and market: events and images in a Melanesian society'. *Man,* 29: pp. 689–711.

Hirsch, E.

    Forth-   'Efficacy and concentration: analogies in betelnut use among the Fuyuge',
    coming   In: *Peculiar substances: the history and anthropology of additive products.* J. Goodman and P. Lovejoy (eds) London: Routledge (in press).

Lepowsky, M.

    1982   A comparison of alcohol and betelnut use on Vanatinai (Sudest Island). In *Through a glass darkly: beer and modernization in Papua New Guinea.* Boroko: Institute of Applied Social and Economic Research.

Lindstrom, L.

    1993   *Cargo cult: strange stories of desire from Melanesia and beyond.* Honolulu: University of Hawaii Press.

Maclean, N.

1994   'Freedom or autonomy: a modern Melanesian dilemma'. *Man*, 29: pp. 667–688.

Modjeska, N.

1985   Exchange value and Melanesian trade reconsidered. *Mankind*, 15: pp. 145–162.

Rew, A.

1975   *Social images and processes in urban New Guinea*. St. Paul: West Publishing Company.

Riesenfeld, H.

1947   Who are the betel people? *International Archive for Ethnographie*. 45: pp. 157–215.

Strathern, A.

1984   *A line of power*. London: Tavistock Publications

Strathern, M.

1975   *No money on our skins: Hagen migrants in Port Moresby*. New Guinea research bulletin no. 61. Port Moresby and Canberra: Australian National University.

Strathern, M.

1988   *The gender of the gift: problems with women and problems with society in Melanesia*. Berkeley: University of California Press.

Weiner, A.

1976   *Women of value, men of reknown*. Austin: University of Texas Press.

Williamson, R.

1912   *The Mafulu mountain people of British New Guinea*. London: Macmillan.

Worsley, P.

1968   *The trumpet shall sound*. London: Paladin.

CHAPTER NINE

Leisure, Boredom, and Luxury Consumerism: The Lineage Mode of Consumption in a Central African Society

Igor Kopytoff

In 1957, on the way to my first fieldwork, I arrived in Leopoldville, now Kinshasa, in what was then the Belgian Congo and is now Zaire. I sought out anyone who could tell me anything about the Suku, the people I was going to study. I was told that they would be pleasant and easy to live with, but that the men were singularly lethargic and lazy, and spent most of their time doing nothing. To a young anthropologist eager to plunge into an uncharted culture, the picture was not unattractive. As to the claims about Suku laziness, I dismissed them as an example of the sort of colonialist obtuseness that anthropology was meant to overcome.

But after a year or so in the field, my anthropological self-assurance began to fray at the edges. The Suku were indeed easygoing and pleasant to be with, but it was also true that the men were rather lethargic and did spend a lot of time not doing much. I sometimes tried to shift the grounds of interpretation from personal character to cultural character, but without much success. I never came to any convincing theoretical terms with the issue until, several years later, I took part in a conference on labour allocation in Africa and began to look at Suku economy in a macroeconomic perspective (Kopytoff 1967). I should like to explore here the resulting non-characterological approach to the problem of Suku lethargy — a problem that has lived on into the post-colonial era (see for example, Mavita-Kupani 1976).

THE SUKU

The Suku were regarded by the authorities as a problem people in a problem area. Numbering about 80,000 at the mid-century, they lived in the southwestern corner of Zaire, in a region of rolling savanna and poor sandy soil (for ethnographic details, see Kopytoff 1964, 1965; Lamal 1949, 1965). Settlement was sparse, with a population density of some fifteen persons per square mile (ca. five per square km). In pre-colonial times, settlements ranged from hamlets of a dozen or fewer people to villages of fourscore inhabitants, dotting the countryside every few miles. In colonial times the villages had been regrouped into larger agglomerations of a few hundred persons. No mineral wealth had been discovered in the region and no economically feasible cash crops had been found.

The pre-colonial political organization was formally pyramidal, with the king on top and regional chiefs and sub-chiefs below, with sporadic but limited authority. The active socio-political units were the small corporate matrilineal kin groups of some forty or fewer members. These kin groups (I shall refer to them alternately as lineages) were highly autonomous in everyday affairs, and they easily resorted to the use of force in cases of conflict. The colonial administration kept the outlines of the political structure but stripped it of its powers. At the same time, the administratively instituted customary courts preserved the legal status of corporate matrilineages as the basic social units.

The lineage was a corporation of multifarious functions — economic, political, social, and ritual — ruled by the consensus of its middle-aged and older members. It was the legal property-holding entity, controlling all the property of its members; within it, there was a constant flow of goods and money among members. Each matrilineage had a village that served as its central headquarters. A few elders lived in it, but since residence at marriage was patrilocal, most members of the lineage were dispersed — without, however, exhibiting the strains that anthropological theory has often attributed to such matrilineal-patrilocal structures (see Kopytoff 1977). The dispersal, normally limited to an area about a dozen or so miles across, allowed the lineage to conduct effectively its social, political, and ritual affairs but it precluded close cooperation in everyday activities. Indeed, the lineage was a unit of redistribution and consumption, but not of production, which was overwhelmingly individual. Nor was the individual family — which was the residential unit and the stage for everyday activities — a production unit since it was split in its lineage loyalties between the father on the one hand and the mother-children cluster (or clusters, in a polygynous family) on the other.

THE MACROECONOMIC IMPACT OF COLONIAL OCCUPATION

While Suku contacts with Europeans — administrators, traders, and missionaries — began in the very early years of this century, the first serious attempts at missionary activities and colonial administration occurred in the late 1920s.

Over the following decades, the Suku were progressively incorporated into the larger economy and society of the Belgian Congo.

Patterns of regional trade shifted. Where before the Suku were tied into the trading networks of Portuguese Angola, they now turned northward, toward the emerging plantations and administrative and economic centers of the Kwilu river basin. These and eventually the distant capital of the colony, Leopoldville, became magnets for temporary labour service by Suku young men. Taxes were levied, and labour (of some two or three weeks a year) was imposed on adult males to build and maintain roads, resthouses, village schools, and dispensaries. In this disinherited area, no cash crops could be imposed as elsewhere in the colony, but a minimum area of food crop cultivation was demanded to insure against recurrent famines. The lack of natural resources precluded the development of employment-generating local enterprises, and the local demand for wage labour came primarily from the bureaucratic sector. Stints of labour outside of Sukuland were one of the main means by which money flowed into the Suku economy.

From a broad macroeconomic perspective, one may look at Suku society as a self-maintaining system in which various portions of the given labour-pool (which I shall represent here in work-days) were allocated to various tasks. Among these tasks were the production of capital (the "physical plant") and the maintenance of the labour-pool itself (through population reproduction, subsistence activities, and the production of consumer goods). One may ask, then, how was the total pool of available work-days allocated in the pre-colonial and the colonial periods? And what factors made for changes in the allocation, and with what consequences beyond the economic sphere? I shall begin my analysis with patterns of labour allocation to various productive tasks at the mid-century. Since gender was a crucial variable in this, I shall frame my presentation accordingly.

THE WOMEN'S CONTRIBUTION TO PRODUCTION

In general, the Suku female labour force may be said to have been fully employed. Indeed, it had to draw on help from young girls.

The women produced almost all of the food (90 percent of the caloric intake came from manioc alone, Holemans 1959). At the time of my fieldwork, to ward off famines the administration demanded that each adult man cultivate an area of fifty ares (about one and a quarter acres) of manioc, with interplanted subsidiary crops, and ten ares of peanuts. Since Suku men did not engage in subsistence agriculture, the task fell in practice on their wives and female relatives. Government agronomists estimated that the preparation and planting of the sixty ares took 80 to 100 full (six to eight hours) working woman-days a year, usually provided in three to four hour stretches (see Duchene 1931, 1956; Claes and Makabi 1956). To this should be added some twenty days of weeding. Once harvested, the crops had to be processed, and this too was entirely women's work. Manioc roots had to be soaked at the river, brought out, dried, and ground into flour. In addition, women did a little fishing, collected wild food and firewood, carried the water, and trapped small rodents; they also did most of the household chores, prepared all the meals, and minded the children.

The demand for the food that women produced was stable but carried no monetary returns. The slight surplus of food was usable essentially only within the narrow circle of kin — in contrast to pre-colonial days, when this surplus was exchanged by the Suku for palm-oil, palm-wine, and raffia from the more forested areas to the north and east (I shall discuss this trade later). There was one minor source of income for some women — pottery-making in the few areas where clay was available.

MEN'S OCCUPATIONS

In contrast to women, men engaged in quite varied tasks, mainly manufacturing and what an economist would call "services" and "managerial" activities. By contrast, their contribution to subsistence was minor. The men hunted and fished, tapped palm-wine, and kept the larger domestic animals. Within the family, the man was responsible for providing meat, for building and maintaining the huts, for furnishing clothing, and for buying or making all the household utensils. The men were the artisans — blacksmiths, woodcarvers, weavers, basket makers. They were also the professionals: medical and ritual specialists (though a few women were herbalists and ritual healers), diviners, musicians, judges, and holders of political offices. None of these occupations was full-time. Above all, the men managed the society. As they became older, they were ever more deeply enmeshed in lineage affairs, negotiating marriages, organizing rituals, and conducting litigation.

MEN'S CONTRIBUTION TO THE FOOD SUPPLY

Hunting was the activity that was perhaps most valued by Suku men. Given its low returns, it consumed an inordinate amount of time and psychic energy. In June, July, and August, at the height of the dry season, large-scale collective hunts using circular bush-fires each involved from 200 to as many as 500 persons of both sexes and all ages. An adult male might have participated in a half-dozen such hunts a year. On each, he spent at least three or four very exciting full days — preparing, hunting, and recuperating. There were also throughout the year individual hunts and hunts in groups of two or three. In pre-colonial days, collective game drives into nets were organized during the wet season, but this technique had been forbidden by the colonial administration to prevent further game depletion. By the mid-century, the returns from hunting had become quite low. Collective hunts, involving 200 or more people, would yield from none to five antelopes, several dozen of the larger rodents, and scores of field mice dug up by women from nests exposed by the bushfire.

Men's fishing in the larger rivers also yielded poor returns. For example, a six-to-eight-hour fishing effort, using nets and fish drives and involving twenty men and adolescents, was judged successful if it produced thirty pounds of fish. In a year, the village I stayed in had about fifteen such fishing parties. Men and women also trapped fish in weirs in the dry season, on the shallow banks of small streams and swamps. Men also set traps for small rodents — a rather haphazard activity with small returns.

Chickens, ducks, and pigeons were kept by both men and women. Goats and pigs were bred by men. To avoid depredations by them, crops were planted at some distance from the village, and this allowed one to give minimal attention to domestic animals. They were allowed to roam all day and only some men rounded them up for the night into dilapidated huts serving as pens.

The number of pigs and goats varied by region. Following a north-south ecological gradient, the ratio of persons per animal (lumping pigs and goats together) changed from two to five, according to administrative figures. In the village in which I lived, there was a total of fifty to sixty animals in a population of 198 persons, that is three to four persons per animal.

Men also spent some time in random wild-vegetable gathering incidental upon other work, in very sporadic collecting of wild honey, and, more importantly, in tapping palm trees for wine. Wine tapping was a rather specialized activity, usually carried out by younger men (it often requires climbing up a tree). Almost every lineage had its own groves and a least one person tapping them on a more or less regular basis for lineage consumption and occasional local sale.

In Appendix 1, I estimate the labour expended by men on subsistence — on average, sixty work-days a year per adult resident male. Since women supplied about ninety-five percent of the food calories, the men produced (mainly in the form of meat) no more than five percent of the calories consumed — this at the cost of about one-sixth (sixteen percent) of the available male work-days.

MEN'S CONTRIBUTION TO MANUFACTURING AND CAPITAL INVESTMENT

The usual distinction that economists make between capital expenditures and "consumption" is not easy to apply in an economy such as that of the Suku. There is no division here between the home (which is reckoned to take in consumption goods) and the workplace (which takes in capital goods). But a rough distinction may be made, though it is of low analytical power. For our purposes, capital goods would include those relatively durable items without which the production as such cannot go on — tools and utensils that must be manufactured, maintained, and replaced. This would also include food, insuring the continued physical existence of the labour force and the entire apparatus of food processing (including cooking utensils), shelter (houses and furniture), and minimal clothing. Consumption items, then, would be objects of personal adornment, and such "luxury" goods as carved cups, stools, decorative knives and adzes not used in production, ritual carvings, and festive clothing.

The material equipment with which the Suku extracted a living from their environment was simple enough. For women this included, several kinds of hoes, baskets for carrying the harvest and storing food, and calabashes for carrying water. For men there were, the bow and arrows (and for a few, the gun) for hunting, nets and weirs for fishing, traps for snaring small game, and calabashes for collecting palm-wine. The basic food processing equipment consisted of gourds, baskets and sieves, mortars, pots, drying-mats, knives, and more recently, iron and aluminium pots, bottles, and glasses. The most important manufacturing tools were adzes and knives. Of the crafts, only ironsmithing required relatively complex equipment: a special shed, bellows, hammer and anvil; in pre-colonial days, some iron ore was melted.

The capitalization of production was low. And, as we shall see, the investment of labour into maintaining and replacing these means of production was commensurably minor. Some of the labour was provided by the user himself. Most Suku men made their own bows and arrow-shafts, most of the furniture, gourds, simple cups, and traps; and they built their own huts. On the other hand, hoes, arrowheads, adzes, and knife-blades were made by blacksmiths and sold to the consumer. Baskets, weirs, nets, mats, and mortars were made and sold by part-time male specialists; and pots, it will be remembered, were made and sold by women specialists. Thus, a certain portion of what was produced was distributed through the market mechanism, which was monetized both in pre-colonial and colonial times.

THE MARKET AND MONEY

No indigenous market places existed within Sukuland, though there were a few markets at its edges for trading with outsiders. Nor was itinerant trade over distances of more than a score of miles developed to any extent. But there was an internal market — that is, an exchange system based on the market mechanism and operating in shell-money before colonial control and in francs after that. Much of this economic exchange occurred through discrete transactions between the buyer-consumer and the seller-producer rather than through middlemen (let alone chains of middlemen). The volume of goods was not large and their movement was rather sluggish as buyers and sellers had to seek each other out.

Domestic animals were generally sold for money, while food and the cheaper objects (such as baskets) were both sold and bartered. Widely known standard prices provided reference points around which the bargaining and the exchanges took place. These prices, as we shall see, corresponded rather closely to the labour expended in their manufacture.

Shell-money and, later, francs were also the currency of political tribute, fines, legal services, various ritual fees, bridewealth payment, and other transactions involving transfers of rights over people (including "slavery"). And money was lent out at interest (at rates as high as 100 percent a year).

THE RELATIVE CONTRIBUTIONS OF MEN AND WOMEN TO PRODUCTION

I use work-days as units in calculating the labour expenditure by men on subsistence (appendix 1) and on those items of capital equipment that were almost universally made by each man for his own use — houses, furniture, and bows (appendix 2). When it comes to items that were acquired with money (appendix 3), I calculate their yearly cost in work-days by taking the average daily reward of male manufacturers to be twenty-five francs and of female potters to be fifteen francs (appendix 4). My discussion is based on data extrapolated to the overall Suku economic system from the village of Mutangu-Nzenga, where I lived for much of the time. Let me summarize the salient aspects of the data given in the Appendices.

There is, of course, a considerable margin of error in these figures, for it must be remembered that the labour–expenditure figures in my calculations are minimal, representing estimates by the Suku of concentrated and uninterrupted labour in producing a given item. Nevertheless, in rough outline, the pattern is clear. There was scarcely any reserve in the female labour pool; and there was a great deal of reserve in the male labour pool — about two thirds of it. This overall conclusion conforms with my own and others' observations.

Beyond the fact that Suku men were, so to speak, a "leisure class", there is the question of the economic efficiency of the labour that they did supply. The largest category in the allocation of this labour — the sixteen percent allocated to subsistence — yielded, as I have mentioned before, about five percent of the caloric intake, but this contribution was mainly in the form of meat — a precious item in this protein-poor society. But more to the point, perhaps, is the fact that half of this labour — given to hunting — was not merely a subsistence activity. It was also very much of a sporting occupation — a kind of lottery to be enjoyed for its own sake, in which the chances of ending up with meat were very slim for any given individual. There is little question that a greater expenditure of energy in, say, domestic animal breeding would have yielded more protein.

ALLOCATION OF LABOUR BY GENDER IN THE PRODUCTIVE ECONOMY
(as a percentage of available work-days)

	Male (100%)	Female (100%)
Subsistence	16%	50% (est.)
Household work	<1%	50% (est.)
Housing, furniture, bows	10%	
Equipment and tools: locally made and imported	<2%	<1% (pots)
Totals	<30%	100%
TIME/LABOUR "SURPLUS" AVAILABLE	70%	0%

Another striking feature of the statistics is how small a portion of male labour went into producing and maintaining the physical plant of the society: some twelve percent, most of which (ten percent) went into housing and furnishings. The other two percent was sufficient to manufacture and purchase the entire "capital" stock of the economy. Even if we double or triple the labour allocation to capital investment, to allow for a slacker pace of production, raising it to six percent of available labour, the macroeconomic picture remains remarkable. One thinks, by comparison, of complex modern economies in which yearly capital investment can be a fourth of the GNP. Some of the reasons for this low capitalization lay in what might be called the Suku "lineage mode of consumption".

THE LINEAGE MODE OF CONSUMPTION
AND LUXURY CONSUMERISM

The low capitalization of Suku production derived partly from the simplicity of its technology. No increase in production would have resulted from more capital investment by acquiring more hoes, more bows, or more fish-nets. That is, the situation was one that economists would define as extremely efficient plant utilization. But there were also social reasons for this rock-bottom capitalization. These lay in the mode of consumption that characterized the Suku lineage.

Suku production was overwhelmingly an individual matter. Women farmed individually; and men fished, hunted, and pursued crafts and professions as individuals. Even in collective hunting, the rewards went to the individually successful hunters. By contrast, when it came to consumption, the corporateness of the Suku lineage was uncompromising. All goods produced or acquired, and all money earned by individuals were regarded as part of the kin group's corporate estate and therefore easily appropriated by other lineage members.

There was a necessary minimum of equipment that each Suku had to have — for example, at least a couple of hoes for a woman, a machete and a couple of knives for a man. And there was also a maximum beyond which no Suku would go. Thus, a man would resist buying his wife a fourth or fifth hoe nor would he secure for himself a third machete. To acquire more was unnecessary overcapitalization, and the extra capital, moreover, was subject to legitimate appropriation by other lineage members.

The rule of thumb was that when one person had any object that he or she did not actively use or need, other lineage members could legitimately try to lay claim to it. If one visibly possessed too many goods, one was fearful of the jealousy and witchcraft of others and also of being accused of stinginess and witchcraft by others. This resulted in a continuous redistribution of goods and money within the lineage. It also led to a dampening of individual accumulation of capital and consumer goods. However, two factors prevented a completely even distribution of goods within the lineage: the hierarchy within the lineage and the existence of purely personal luxury goods.

In the lineage hierarchy, elders were responsible for the general welfare and success of the lineage and they accumulated the wherewithal to pay for such collective lineage expenses as bridewealth, legal fines, tribute, and taxes. This allowed them to make special claims to goods held by juniors — claims further bolstered by their legitimate power to curse and their suspected power to bewitch. Young men, returning from stints of work outside Sukuland, usually lost their accumulated funds and goods within a matter of a few months, and a disproportionate amount went to the elders. Hence, a Suku who wished to accumulate goods moved away from fluid and toward singularized forms of wealth (on "singularization" see Kopytoff 1986). This meant acquiring personal, relatively unique, and non-utilitarian luxury goods.

The logic of lineage mates' claims to one's goods was utilitarian — they claimed what would otherwise remain an unused part of the lineage estate. Redistribution within the lineage operated most effectively with objects of everyday usefulness, such as tools, household utensils, and ordinary objects of personal use. In this respect, the lineage mode of consumption actively discouraged the accumulation of useful objects. On the other hand, unique luxury goods, such as items of personal adornment and display, could escape the utilitarian rationale for redistribution, since their proper usage lay simply in their being displayed. This encouraged the channeling of savings into luxury consumer goods. The intensity with which such goods were desired allows one to speak of a well-developed luxury-goods consumerism among the Suku — a consumerism that is also easily observed in many other African societies.

In pre-colonial times, such luxury items included decorated raffia cloth, cloth and beads traded over long distances from the Portuguese coast, woven travelling purses, metal bracelets and anklets, necklaces, carved knife-handles, decorative adzes carried over the shoulder by important personages, well wrought long knives, and carved drinking cups. A few of these were produced locally; most were imported from neighboring societies or, ultimately, from Europe.

In colonial times, the variety of luxury goods on which personal claims could be asserted increased dramatically. The 1903 Annuaire de l'Etat Independant du Congo advises traders on the goods that were in great demand in this area of the Congo. Few of the goods are of utilitarian value; the list is dominated by items such as cloth, hats, parasols, decorative nails, and beads (p.105). Later in the century, of course, came kerosene and kerosene lamps, lighters, sunglasses, battery radios, watches, fancy shoes, suitcases, chairs, and so on. Even though some of these had a clear utilitarian value, it was fused with a luxury value (the way the useful value of a Mercedes is). The Suku did not apply to these goods the same calculus of use that they did to productive utensils. For example, they preferred locally produced clay pots to imported metal pots that burned through on the open hearth, and they favored some locally produced knives over the often shoddy imported varieties. But they did favor little used luxury imports such as lamps and watches, even though these goods easily broke down with little chance of repair; and they continued to be displayed even after they were broken.

The desire for luxury goods is one thing. Their affordability is another. Given the limited Suku access to money, these items were extremely expensive. How could the Suku afford to buy them and how did they pay for them?

THE HIGH AND LOW PRICE OF IMPORTS

Within Sukuland, most of the wage employment was provided by the colonial administration and the missions on those islands of the larger colonial society scattered over the countryside: hospitals, dispensaries, schools, mission compounds, chapels, and small and large administrative posts. Here were employed African clerks, male nurses, teachers, catechists, cooks and domestics, mechanics, road-maintenance workers, and policemen. Most came from elsewhere in the colony, but at the mid-century some 200 were Suku. Another 300 or so Suku earned cash while living in their own villages; these were chiefs and customary court judges on administrative salaries, resthouse watchmen, and roadkeepers. In the village of Mutangu-Nzenga, some 10–12,000 francs a year came from such people.

The other sources of employment lay outside the region, in places where the Suku lived as quintessential migrant labourers. In the village of Mutangu-Nzenga, out of its fifty adult males, nine males (three of them married) were away on protracted stints of two to three years' labour, sometimes as far as Leopoldville (now Kinshasa), over 200 miles away. Five other young men remained more or less regular residents of the village, but would periodically absent themselves for weeks at a time by working on the palm-oil plantations in neighboring districts.

One may estimate roughly the net inflow of francs into Mutangu-Nzenga from this migrant labour. After two to three years in Leopoldville or Kikwit, a man came back with savings of 2–4,000 francs — a return somewhat above 1,000 francs a year. The nine full-time migrant labourers may have brought in roughly 10,000 francs a year. Intermittent plantation labour brought in another 8,000 francs.

Thus, the total brought in to Mutangu-Nzenga from outside the Suku economy (that is, from the colonial sector) amounted to some 30,000 francs, about sixty percent of which (18,000 francs) came from migrant and plantation labour. The village spent annually over 13,000 francs on more or less "useful" imported equipment (see appendix 3, substitute and non-substitute imports, and clothing and blankets). It also paid out some 2,500 francs in taxes (about fifty francs a year per male adult). This left it about 15,000 francs a year for other expenditures and for luxury imports.

The labour that brought in this money came out of the large seventy per-cent "surplus" of male work-days mentioned above, and the Suku were quite conscious that it was this labour that largely bought them their luxury imports. What, one may ask, were the "real" wages of this migrant labour and, consequently, the real labour cost of the luxury imports?

When away at work, a migrant faced expenses unknown in the village, such as rent, food, entertainment, transportation, beer, and payments to prostitutes, and he saved little to bring back to his village. A migrant labourer in Leopoldville or Kikwit saved 2–4,000 francs out of wages of 20–30,000 francs over two or three years. In effect, the 18,000 francs a year netted by the village of Mutangu-Nzenga from migrant labour were acquired by pulling out of its male labour force about a fifth of the available male labour force (nine men full-time and five intermittent, for a total of about eleven, out of an adult male population of fifty). The net return to the village per male absentee was about 1,600 francs a year.

To put it another way, the village economy rented out this labour force for a net payment of, very roughly, some six francs a work-day (assuming fifty-two five-day workweeks a year). This is in contrast to the remuneration of local male craft labour of about twenty-five francs a day (see appendix 4).

In this perspective, the returns from the migrant labour portion of the Suku male labour pool were quite poor and the luxury imports they paid for were quite expensive in terms of work-days. But the local wage-labour market was, of course, saturated. There were no more local jobs to be had and there was no need or demand for any more locally-made equipment. Since the local underemployment was so high, the marginal cost of hiring out the surplus labour was very low. One could easily afford to rent out this labour for about a quarter of the local wages. Moreover, one had no choice in the matter, since this labour was one of the principal means for obtaining imported goods.

In effect, the Suku satisfied their luxury consumerism very "dearly" in work-days but with very "cheap" labour. The seeming paradox was conditioned, of course, by their involvement in a classic colonial "dual economy". But only partially so, for a similar situation prevailed within the traditional sector having to do with subsistence production by Suku males. There, as we have seen, sixteen percent of male work-days were spent on producing five percent of total caloric intake — but the luxury (protein) five percent of it. Like luxury imports, meat too was bought "dearly" with "cheap" labour.

LABOUR USE IN THE PRE-COLONIAL PERIOD

In the latter part of the last century, and perhaps before that, the Suku were involved in long-distance trade as middlemen between the ethnic groups in the forested areas to the north and east (Mbala, Kwese, and Pende) and the "BaTsoso". The latter name was used generically for southerners who had trade links with the Portuguese on the Angolan coast.

The most important goods the Suku got from their forest neighbors were palm oil and raw raffia fibre. They wove the raffia into cloth. Some of it was traded to the Yaka in the west; most of it, together with palm oil, was taken by armed expeditions to the south, to be traded to the BaTsoso for salt, European cloth and beads, iron, and shell-money. Of these, the Suku retained some for themselves and the rest they traded to the forested areas, to which they also sold their own produce — manioc, peanuts, and meat (more abundant in the savanna). The trading and, not least, the weaving of raffia cloth obviously consumed considerable time and labour.

In pre-colonial times, women cultivated a little less land but probably put a little more time into it, given the state of general insecurity. The repertoire of crops was narrower, and the harvest was probably smaller. The yearly food surplus was by no means regular, and there were occasional famines. But when there was a manioc surplus, instead of remaining unharvested in the ground, it could be used to fuel the interregional trade.

The labour investment in trade and in weaving raffia for export provided a very tangible return — the Suku had a regional reputation for being wealthy in shell-money. Perhaps they retained so much of it precisely because the outlets for a money surplus were limited in the sluggish regional trade. One result of this wealth appears to have been inflation in the internal Suku economy. The Suku were aware that bridewealth and the prices of goats and pigs (where supply was relatively stable) had crept up continuously in the late nineteenth century and the early twentieth century. But there was no memory of inflation in the prices of manufactured goods (where demand was stable).

With the invasion of the market by imported cloth in colonial times, the weaving of raffia cloth disappeared. It is difficult to estimate how much time went into producing raffia cloth. While clothing was more meager then, it required more rapid replacement than cotton cloth. It took, according to informants, about two full days to put together a raffia wrap-around, and a husband was expected to supply his wife with about two of these every year. If we take two wrap-arounds a year per adult as the norm, the village of Mutangu-Nzenga would have needed some 400 man-days' worth of cloth a year.

Why did the Suku stop weaving raffia cloth? The external demand for it had largely disappeared with the demise of the pre-colonial regional trade, and there was less internal demand for it as well. The imported cotton cloth was softer, easier to wash, and, not least, it was "civilized" personal adornment that appealed to luxury consumerism. At what price was the new cloth obtained? Compared to 400 days spent on weaving raffia cloth for internal consumption, the village of Mutangu-Nzenga now spent 7,400 francs on imported cloth and clothing (see appendix 3). At the local labour price of twenty-five francs a day, the price of clothing had remained about the same 300 work-days. But at the returns from migrant labour of six francs a day, the cost rises to over 1,200 work-days.

Colonial control also eliminated many of the time-consuming activities previously demanded by Suku institutions. Medical services were now supplied by personnel from outside; traditional medicine did not die out, but it shrank in its scope. The new political, administrative, and judicial system — staffed largely by non-Suku — was more efficient in its provision of services. The existence of faster and safer travel had simplified the conduct of much of the business of social life. The management of lineage affairs had also become less time-consuming. In pre-colonial days, conflicts between lineages took a great deal of negotiation, maneuvering, intrigue, and fighting, and the legal mechanisms were complex and indecisive (see Kopytoff 1962). By the mid-century, religious changes had also lessened the time taken up by ritual. The manufacture of ritual objects was lapsing, many rituals had disappeared, and the time given to surviving rituals had diminished. For example, school attendance had reduced the time spent on the circumcision ceremony from about two years of intensive local activity to three months.

To be sure, the colonial economy provided some new employment, especially for the younger men. On balance, however, the total surplus time available after economic production had increased, notably because of the diminution of activities in social management. This raises the question of the role of managerial labour in economies such as that of the Suku.

MANAGERIAL LABOUR

Except for some unregenerate labour theorists of value, most of us accept that production does not derive entirely from the labour of workers but depends very importantly on organizational factors. And we know that much of the increased production in modern economies comes from organizational rather than technological innovations. What then is the role of organizational — that is, managerial — factors in, say, Suku production? And how is this managerial factor to be defined? It may be argued that what is often taken to be non-productive activity in simple economies often serves, in fact, the same functions that good management and morale-boosting personnel practices serve in complex economies. When Malinowski showed the role of magic in organizing production, he was providing a needed corrective to the vulgar nineteenth century thesis about the utter uselessness of superstition. But the corrective can itself become an absurdity when a vulgar relativism takes it to its functionalist extreme: that everything in a social system is necessary to it and therefore ultimately contributes to its production.

How much did the managerial activities of Suku elders contribute to the functioning of the lineage as an economic unit? It is as difficult to evaluate the worth of these activities to the productive process as it is to evaluate the contributions of priests, astrologers, and artists, or of office managers, board members, and university deans. We do know that while we cannot dispense with administrators entirely, some judicious pruning more often helps than hurts. Economists can duck the issue by assuming that, in a monetized market, remuneration itself ultimately reflects the worth of the contribution. But such a circular solution is of no help in the Suku case. At the mid-century, when Suku elders had fewer managerial activities to perform, they performed them more often, more slowly, and more stubbornly. Much back-and-forth social visiting and palavering took place, and much time was spent in taking and retaking old cases to court. Parkinson's law held here as elsewhere: activities expanded with the time available for them. But once again, given the large supply of unused labour, the marginal cost of this managerial inefficiency was low.

FROM MACROECONOMICS TO BOREDOM

Structurally speaking, the traditional Suku economy had many features associated with a developed economy that had stabilized at the depths of a depression — low production, low demand, low consumption, and a large amount of unused labour. In a developed modern economy, this means a large number of the totally unemployed amidst a larger number of the totally employed. But in the relatively unspecialized Suku economy, with no full-time all-or-nothing jobs, such unemployment was spread wide and thin in the guise of general underemployment (of the males, to be sure). The large amount of leisure was distributed more or less evenly throughout the male population. And because the consumption unit was the corporate lineage rather than the individual, what was produced was redistributed rather evenly throughout the population. The point is not that the Suku men did little work, with the corollary (widely held by administrators) that if only they did more, there would somehow be more economic progress, but, rather, that even for a very diligent Suku, it was difficult to find work that could produce goods beyond what was already being produced.

Let me return now to the problem I stated at the outset — that of Suku character as it was widely perceived by outsiders. The large degree of structural underemployment among Suku men was essentially a modern phenomenon and it accounts very well for their striking lack of dynamism and the sense of boredom that pervaded their villages (again, among men). The boredom, though persistent, was a situational matter — like the boredom of the temporarily unemployed in times of deep depression in a modern economy. At the same time, those Suku who could find work did work well and hard in skilled and unskilled occupations, assuring the flow of francs from outside into the internal Suku economy. It is interesting that the glimpses one gets of the Suku character at the threshold of colonial control convey quite a different impression. For example, Torday (who called them Yaka) describes them as a vigorous and somewhat aggressive people (Torday 1913).

One situational factor was the division of labour by gender. Many anthropologists have commented on the considerable amount of surplus time beyond procurement of subsistence found among hunters-gatherers (a point saliently made in several case studies in Lee and DeVore 1968). That a similar situation existed among the agricultural Suku is at least partly explained by a division of labour in which subsistence was overwhelmingly provided by the women. On the one hand, the very low demand for equipment and consumer goods of everyday utility produced a male labour surplus. And on the other hand, Suku ideas about the proper division of labour effectively barred Suku men from directing their labour surplus toward serious agricultural production and relieving the women of some of their burdens.

But there is also in all this, it seems to me, a more central though rather elusive factor — that of cultural pre-adaptation to the increased leisure time brought by colonial control. And this touches on the even more elusive question of cultural creativity. The Suku situation makes the point that one of the functions of culture is to provide standardized ways of meeting the human need for activity and for overcoming the boredom that comes from pure leisure. For if, as Sahlins (1972) has claimed, leisure by itself entails a kind of "affluence", this affluence can in turn entail a certain kind of demoralization. Human beings, no less than laboratory rats, do not behave only in response to external stimuli or utilitarian demands. The human organism actively seeks to express itself in behavior, and the behavior need not always be useful either in a practical or in some sociologically functional sense. There are societies whose cultures have successfully dealt with this problem by cultivating obsessions with carving posts and house doors, or with growing yams in unusable quantities and exhibiting them, or with building mausoleums for ancestors, or with putting down competitors by giving large consumption feasts. When, in the course of economic change, such societies are granted more leisure, they may show an explosion of ever more baroque carving, of ever higher piles of yams, of ever bigger houses for the dead, or of ever larger potlatches.

Whatever the reasons, Suku culture was not pre-adapted in this way to the increase in leisure time brought by the colonial period. It did not provide ready-made grooves for channeling the increased leisure. What it did provide, through the operation of the lineage mode of consumption, was a relatively passive luxury consumerism which avidly seized upon the availability of new luxury goods. These had to be paid for in francs, and francs could be obtained primarily by working outside Sukuland. But local traditions of production were not culturally equipped to satisfy this consumerism, and the men who remained in the villages could only consume leisure time itself; that is, boredom. As Just (1980) points out, in discussing the role of leisure in the elaboration of culture, leisure acquires social value only when it can be a part of the economizing process. In this sense, Suku leisure was indeed valueless.

While Suku boredom can thus be understood situationally, an anthropological approach to boredom cannot stop at a wholly situational perspective. Certain additional questions must be asked. When, for example, is situational boredom so entrenched that it becomes embedded in the institutional arrangements and character of a society? And in what ways do different societies solve the problem of boredom? The solution in modern industrial societies has been through leisure industries, involving hard work by some to provide busy and unbored leisure to others. The cultural repertoire of human societies must contain other solutions. Finally, one may raise an even thornier question: when does boredom affect the actual character of the actors, as it may well have done with some underemployed Suku and as it often seems to do with the non-employed in industrial countries? The question is an old one: that of the role of labour in the self-realization of human beings. It concerned the Puritans and it concerned Marx. But it never found room in the ideology of nineteenth and twentieth century liberalism and in the social sciences so largely shaped by it; these have preferred to see labour not as an existential issue but merely as a curse to be gradually lifted by social and technological progress.

APPENDIX ONE

Annual Male Labour Expenditure in Subsistence Production

ANNUAL MALE LABOUR EXPENDITURE IN SUBSISTENCE PRODUCTION IN WORK-DAY (W-D) UNITS (percentages are rounded out) Village of Mutangu-Nzenga — 1959			
Population 198 Adults (17+ yrs):	50 males, of which 41 in residence and 9 young males absent on 1-to-3-year labour stints.		
Hunting*-Collective	41 men × 5 hunts (3 days each):	615 w-d	
-Individuals	5 men × 50 days	250 w-d	
	36 men × 12 days	432 w-d	1,297 w-d
Fishing-Drives	20 men × 15 days	300 w-d	
-Traps	10 men × 40 half-days	200 w-d	500 w-d
Animal breeding**			450 w-d
Wine tapping***			200 w-d
Total spent by men on subsistence			2,447 w-d

Yearly total resident male work-days available (41 × 365): 14,965 w-d

Average per resident adult male, spent on subsistence: 60 w-d per year

Percentage of available male work-days spent on subsistence: 16%

*   Hunting: Some men were good hunters and many were bad but passionate hunters. For a very passionate hunter, an average of one day (or night) a week would be high. In a village of fifty adult men, such as Mutangu-Nzenga, one could find a maximum of four or five such persistent hunters. For the rest, the variation was great, averaging, I would guess, a day a month.

**   Animal breeding: Of the forty-one resident adult men (seventeen years and older), six of the older men had between four and seven animals each; ten of the middle aged men had between one and three; and the younger men had none or only fractional shares. These counts must of necessity be rough: men were reluctant to reveal the information and in order to hide their wealth they "scattered" their ownership widely by owning not full animals but a great number of shares (halves, quarters, thirds, etc.) in animals kept by other people. Thus, many of the village animals were partly owned by outsiders, just as the villagers had shares in animals outside the village. I estimate, for my village of 198 persons, fifty-five animals. The labour spent on animals can also be roughly estimated. The man with seven animals kept them in a pen and consistently spent a half-hour to an hour every evening rounding them up. He had a reputation as a serious breeder. All the other owners were less consistently involved, lacking his advantage of scale. Thus, ten hours a day of animal care for the entire village is a reasonable estimate. This represents some 450 man-days a year.

*** Wine tapping: Where groves were more ample, the lineage wine-tapper would work up to two or three hours a day every three or four days. A village of around 200 persons would have five or six wine-tappers, working between 1,000 and 2,000 hours per year, or 125 to 250 eight-hour days. In the less favored regions, the figure would be half or even a quarter of this.

APPENDIX TWO

Annual Male Labour Expenditure on Housing, Furniture and Bows

---

ANNUAL MALE LABOUR EXPENDITURE ON HOUSING, FURNITURE, AND BOWS
IN WORK-DAY (W-D) UNITS (percentages are rounded out)
Village of Mutangu-Nzenga — 1959

Population 198

Adults (17+ yrs): 50 males, of which 41 in residence and
9 young males absent on 1-to-3-year labour stints.

Houses*	1,053 w-d
Furniture**	324 w-d
Bows**	70 w-d

Total spent by men on housing, furniture, bows: 1,447 w-d

Yearly total resident male work-days available (41 × 365): 14,965 w-d
Average per resident adult male spent on these tasks: 36 w-d a year
Percentage of available resident male work-days spent on
houses: 7%, furniture: 2%, bows: <1%. Total: 10%

* Houses: Number of houses in all stages of disrepair: eighty-one. Each house required about thirty work-days to build and then lasted about ten years, before totally succumbing to termites. Each thus required three work-days per year to build. Maintenance is estimated at ten work-days a year. Each house, then, took thirteen work-days per year, and eighty-one houses took up 1,053 work-days per year.

** Furniture: Bamboo platform beds, storage shelves, and stools. Estimated time to manufacture these per house; twenty days, plus maintenance and repair: twenty days — for ten years of life. Labour per year: four days. For eighty-one houses: 324 man-days.

*** Bows: Number in village: about fifty. Manufacture takes two days; estimated life five years. Maintenance: approximately one per year. Labour per bow per year: one point four work-days. Total for fifty bows: seventy work-days per year.

APPENDIX THREE

Annual Expenditure on Equipment, Clothing and Blankets

ANNUAL EXPENDITURE ON EQUIPMENT, CLOTHING AND BLANKETS
in 1959 Belgian Congo francs and work-days (w-d).
Village of Mutangu-Nzenga

Most manufactured items were as often bought as they were manufactured by the user. The first group consists of items manufactured locally. The second group is of imports that were interchangeable with locally made items — functionally equivalent to locally made items. The third group involves imported items with no traditional functional equivalents. To arrive at the annual cost of an item, I divide its purchase price by its estimated life. I am costing male labour at an average of twenty-five francs per work-day and female labour at fifteen francs per work-day (see appendix 4)

	Number (est.)	Unit price	Total price	Useful life	Yearly cost
Locally made, by men:					
Arrowheads	200	3–4 frs	700 frs	5 yrs	140 frs
Knives	100	7	700	10	70
Adzes	60	25	1,500	10	150
Mats	350	5	1,750	3	580
Baskets	700	5–15	7,000	5	1,400
Gourds	300	3	900	2	450
Cups (gourds)	250	1–10	1,250	4	310
Hoes	70	40	2,800	3	930
Mortars	120	20–40	3,600	5	720
Fish-weirs	50	10–20	750	3	250
Fishnets	2	35	70	2	35
			Total yearly cost 5,035 frs = 201 w-d		
Pots, by women	400	5–10	3,000	3	1,000
			Total yearly cost 1,000 frs = 67 w-d		

Table Cont'd

	Number (est.)	Unit price	Total price	Useful life	Yearly cost
Substitute imports:					
Knives	20	10	200	10	20
Machetes	50	30	1,500	10	150
Store-bought pots	50	30	1,500	4	375
Bottles	300	5	1,500	10	150
Glasses	50	10	500	10	50
			Total yearly cost 745 frs = 30 w-d		
Non-substitute imports:					
Guns (flintlock)	8	500	4,000	15	270
Kerosene lamps	30	60	1,800	3	600
Iron chests	20	400	8,000	20	400
Suitcases	50	150	7,500	15	500
Bicycles	2	1,000	2,000	5	400
Sewing machines	1	3,000	3,000	10	300
"Modern" furniture*			2,500	10	250
			Total yearly cost 2,720 frs = 109 w-d		
Imported clothing and blankets:					
Clothing**			37,000	5	7,400
Blankets	200	150	30,000	15	2,000
			Total yearly cost 9,400 frs = 376 w-d		
TOTAL WORK-DAYS					783 w-d

*   A very few households also had locally produced 'European' furniture — tables, chairs, and canvas 'deck' chairs — unambiguously 'luxury' goods used almost exclusively for important visitors. For the village: two tables, five chairs, and seven canvas chairs, costing altogether about 2,500 francs. Estimated life: ten years. Yearly cost: 250 francs.

**   The cost of the estimated average clothing per post-adolescent male was 300 francs. (Pre-adolescents wore rags or nothing). Total for males in the village: ca. 15,000 francs. Estimate per post-adolescent female — 400 francs for young and middle-aged, and 150 francs for old. Total for females in the village: 22,000 francs. Total for village: 37,000 francs. Life of clothing: five years. Thus, yearly cost for the village: 7,400 francs, provided entirely by men.

A NOTE ON THE SOURCES OF THE DATA:

The data have been garnered from their random appearance in my field notes to establish average individual holdings by age and sex. These holdings were then projected onto the population of the village of Mutangu-Nzenga (in which I lived for over a year and for over half the period of my fieldwork). The totals are rounded out to avoid spurious precision.

Confidence in the figures is bolstered by the following considerations: a) my calculation from my field notes of goats and pigs in the village conforms to the administrative statistics, based on real counts, for the surrounding regions; b) my figures on the age and sex distribution in the village conform to the overall sex/age pyramid of the Suku population as it appears in the administrative census; c) my extrapolation to the larger village population of sample inventories of equipment is justifiable because the range of individual variation in non-luxury holdings was very narrow. As I point out in the text in my discussion of the "Lineage mode of consumption", the pattern of sharing within the lineage discourages individuals from accumulating productive and basic subsistence goods beyond a certain minimum. There is greater variation in the individual holding of small luxury goods — such as beads, sunglasses, Sunday attire, radios, pencils, etc. — goods that usually had no pre-colonial counterparts and which I am not counting here.

APPENDIX FOUR

Price of Labour

PRICE OF WOMEN'S LABOUR

It is possible to quantify the price of women's agricultural labour as follows. In the later 1950's, 100 kilograms of manioc roots gave about 25 frs (equal to 50 cents US) worth of *kipati* (*chikwange* in KiKongo) balls when sold on the local market. Since processing manioc took at least as much time as planting and harvesting it, a woman's average production of 5 tons of roots a year, requiring a total labour investment of some 100 to 150 days, was worth about 1,250 frs. Thus, a day of what was regarded as unskilled woman's work produced 8–12, 50 francs (between 16 and 25 cents US). By contrast, pottery production — requiring skilled labour — yielded the nearly double figure of 15 to 20 francs (30 to 40 cents US) a day, since 5 pots, requiring a day and a half of labour, could be sold for 25–30 francs.

PRICE OF MEN'S LABOUR

Producers gave the following estimate of time spent on manufacturing:

Object	Days to manufacture	Price	"Pay" man-day
Fishnet	2	35 frs	17 frs
Large basket	1/2–1	10–15	15–30
Mat	1/3–1/2	5	10–15
Mortar	2	50	25
Adze blade (2 men)	1/4	20	40
Hoe (2 men)	1/2	40	40
Machine-Sewn pants	1/2	20	40

Thus, the reward for a full day of male labour fluctuated between 10 and 40 francs. This reflected a gradient of skill. Mats, fishnets, and baskets, it was said, could be made "by anyone", with least skill required for mats, and somewhat more for fishnets. Higher returns come from the skilled work. Mortars, adze blades, and hoes were made by blacksmiths, an occupation requiring some capital investment in equipment and a period of apprenticeship, for which one paid. Similar considerations apply to sewing. Note that pot-making — by skilled women — was rewarded like medium-skill labour by men.

It is interesting that these rates of "pay" in the crafts conform rather well with regional rates for hired labour — suggesting that they all belong to the same market. Unskilled labourers received about 350 francs per month (of $5\frac{1}{2}$ day weeks) — which is about 15 francs per day. Servants and cooks — both skilled occupations — received anything between 500 and 1,000 francs per month, for about 25 days' work; this is between 20 and 40 francs per day, which is approximately what a blacksmith could make.

In my calculations in the text, I convert costs of items in francs into work-days of labour by taking 25 francs per day as the average rate for males and fifteen francs per day for females.

References

Claes, J. P. and Makabi, A.

    1956   Calendrier Agricole. Kimbau, Congo Belge (mimeographed).

Duchene, B. M.

    1931   Rendement possible de la main d'oeuvre agricole indigène. In *Rapport annuel sur la situation de l'agriculture*. Kwango, Congo Belge (mimeographed).

Ducheyne, H.

    1956   *Petit Manuel agricole à l'usage du personnel territorial à Feshi*. Feshi, Kwango, Congo Belge. (mimeographed).

Etat Independant du Congo

    1903   Annuaire. 1e année.

Holemans, K.

    1959   Etudes sur l'alimentation en milieu coutumier du Kwango. *Annales de la Société Belge de Medecine Tropicale*.

Just, P.

    1980   Time and Leisure in the Elaboration of Culture. *Journal of Anthropological Research* **36**: 105–115.

Lamal, F.

    1949   *Essai d'étude démographique d'une population du Kwango: Les Basuku du territoire de Feshi*. Mem., Institut Royal Colonial Belge, Section des Sciences Morales et Politiques. **15**, No.4.

Lamal, F.

    1965   *Basuku et Bayaka des districts Kwango et Kwilu*. Annales Sciences Humaines 56, xii. Tervuren: Musée de l'Afrique Centrale.

Lee, R. B. and DeVore I. (eds)

    1968   *Man the Hunter*. Chicago: Aldine.

Kopytoff, I.

    1962   Extension of Conflict as a Method of Conflict Resolution among the Suku of the Congo. *Journal of Conflict Resolution* **5**: 61–69.

Kopytoff, I.

    1964   Family and Lineage among the Suku of the Congo. In Robert F. Gray and Philip H. Gulliver (eds), *The Family Estate in Africa*. London: Routledge and Kegan Paul. pp. 83–116.

Kopytoff, I.

   1965   The Suku of Southwestern Congo. In James L. Gibbs, Jr. (ed.), *Peoples of Africa*. New York. pp. 441–478.

Kopytoff, I.

   1967   Labour Allocation among the Suku. Paper presented at the Social Science Research Council Conference: Competing Demands for the Time of Labour in Traditional African Societies. Holy Knoll, Va. (MS).

Kopytoff, I.

   1977   Matrilineality, Residence, and Residential Zones. *American Ethnologist* **4**: 539–558.

Kopytoff, I.

   1986   The Cultural Biography of Things: Commoditizatian as Process. In A. Appadurai (ed.), *The Social Life of Things: Commodities in Cultural Perspective.* New York: Cambridge University Press. pp. 64–91.

Mavita-Kupani, N.

   1976   *La conception du travail chez les Basuku du Kwango-Kwilu (Bandundu): Evaluation de quelques facteurs motivationnels.* Kisangani (Université Nationale du Zaire, Memoire de licence en psychologie).

Sahlins, M.

   1972   The Original Affluent Society. In *Stone Age Economics*, New York, pp. 1–39.

Torday, E.

   1913   *Camp and Tramp in African Wilds*. Philadelphia: Lippincott Co.

Index